Marketing to and Through Kids

Selina S. Guber
President, Children's Market Research, Inc.
Publisher, *KIDTRENDS* Newsletter

Jon Berry
Senior Writer, *BrandWeek* Magazine

McGraw-Hill, Inc.

New York   San Francisco   Washington, D.C.   Auckland   Bogotá
Caracas   Lisbon   London   Madrid   Mexico City   Milan
Montreal   New Delhi   San Juan   Singapore
Sydney   Tokyo   Toronto

Library of Congress Cataloging-in-Publication Data

Guber, Selina S.
    Marketing to and through kids / Selina S. Guber and Jon Berry.
        p.   cm.
    Includes index.
    ISBN 0-07-025111-8 (alk. paper)
    1. Children as consumers. 2. Advertising and children.
  3. Marketing research.   I. Berry, Jon. II. Title.
    HF5415.32.G83   1993
    658.8'348—dc20   92-40749
                                            CIP

   3 4 5 6 7 8 9 0 DOC/DOC 9 9 8 7 6 5 4

ISBN   0-07-025111-8

*The sponsoring editor for this book was Karen Hansen, the editing supervisor
was Kimberly A. Goff, and the production supervisor was Donald F. Schmidt.
This book was set in Palatino by McGraw-Hill's Professional Book Group
composition unit.*

Printed and bound by R. R. Donnelley & Sons Company.

*This book is printed on recycled, acid-free paper containing a
minimum of 50% recycled de-inked fiber.*

This book is dedicated with love to Al and Lily, my parents, whose constant encouragement has provided the spark to GO FOR IT in life.

And to my son, Dave, who has kept me a kid at heart.

Selina S. Guber

To my parents. To my wife, Robin, for her love, patience, and encouragement. And to my kids, Joel and Flynn, who let me play with their toys.

Jon Berry

Contents

Foreword   xv
Preface   xviii
Acknowledgements   xix

1. Children of the 1990s   1

Pop Quiz   1
"Mom, You've Gahhht to See This!"   2
The New Baby Boom   3
And a Boom in New Products   4
The Numbers Behind the Boom   6
A Changed Society   9
The Rainbow Generation   10
Today's Parent: Involved with Their Kids   11
But Parents Just Want to Have Fun, Too   12
And Sometimes They're Softies   12
Kids Are Independent   13
Kids Are Worldly   14
Kids Are Family-Centered   15
Kids Are Responsible   16
How Kids View Nutrition   16
Where Marketers Come In   17
Summing Up   18

2. Influence   19

Pop Quiz   19
The Baseball Kid   19

Influence in Action   20
Making Choices Is Important   22
Max and Baseball   23
Peer Pressure   25
NIKE's Full-Court Press   26
Outside Influences   28
How Do They Do It?   29
Influence on the Toy Shelf   31
Influence in the Supermarket   32
And Beyond...   32
Polaroid's "Snap" Thinking   33
Parent-Led Purchases   35
The *Bible* Goes Video   35
Grandparents   36
Summing Up   37

3. Talking to the Market: Focus Groups 38

Pop Quiz   38
And the Children Shall Lead   38
The Birth of a Blue Jeans Ad   39
Starting Out   40
The Ground Rules   44
The Suburbs Are the Middle Ground   45
Setting Up   45
The Work Environment   46
The Warm-Up   47
Drawing Pictures   48
Play Acting   48
The Discussion Guide   49
The Process   50
Analyzing the Results   51
The Management Report   51
A Word of Caution   52
One-on-Ones   52
Anthropological Alternatives   53
Summing Up   54

4. Surveying the Landscape 56

Pop Quiz   56
Why Do Quantitative Research?   56
What Quantitative Research Can Tell You   57

Custom Research   58
Syndicated Research   59
Custom Research: Starting Out   59
Mall Interviewing   60
One Frog or Two? Making It Fun   61
How One Company Did It   62
Phone Surveys   63
Tabulating the Results   63
Summing Up   64

5. Boys and Girls   **65**

Pop Quiz   65
It's a Modern World ...   66
...With Traditional Values   66
Blue for Boys, Pink for Girls   67
The Enduring Barbie   68
Boy Products, Girl Products   71
Nature and Nurture   73
What the Numbers Say   74
The Movement to Control Toy Guns   75
The Fitness Movement   76
Fashion-Conscious Fellows   77
Makeup   79
Going Out on the Town   79
Supermarket Surprise   80
Household Experts on Food   81
Equal Opportunity Walkmans   81
Summing Up   82

6. Bottling Magic   **83**

Pop Quiz   83
The Big Idea   83
Your Goal: To Fill a Need   85
The Basics   86
How Do You Define Success?   88
Children's Toothpaste: A Study in Flexibility   88
"Kidsizing" Grown-up Stuff   89
Research, Research, Research   90
"Straddle" Products   91
Old Product, New Technology   92
Educational Products   93

Updating the Classics   95
Licensing   95
Miniaturizing   96
Topical Products   97
Summing Up   98

7. Getting the Look, Finding the Name   **100**

Pop Quiz   100
What's in a Name?   100
Why Names and Packages Are Important   101
Testing the Name   102
Where Do Names Come From?   103
The Process of Generating a Name   104
The Two Kinds of Names   105
Familiarity Breeds Security   107
A French Catalog   108
Packaging: Make It Eyecatching, Keep It Simple   109
Colors and Design   109
How Much Should a Package Say?   111
Summing Up   112

8. How Kids Shop   **114**

Fast Facts   114
The New American Family   114
Children as Primary Consumers   115
Kids as Shoppers   115
Starting Out: Convenience Stores   115
Grocery Shopping with Mom   117
Toy Stores: The Kid Mecca   119
In-Store Displays and Promotions   119
Sampling: A Small Taste   120
Arranging the Goods   120
Advanced Shopping: Mall Mania   121
How One Store Does It: The Gap   123
Music and Electronics   123
Cards 'n Things   124
Summing Up   124

9. Tuning in TV Advertising   **126**

Pop Quiz   126
What Was Your Favorite?   127

The Hula Hoop Factor   127
Should You Advertise?   128
Beware of the Giants   129
But Don't Be Intimidated   129
The Numbers Tell the Story   130
Club Med, Too?   131
Television: The Traditional Choice   132
Results Now   133
Who Do You Want to Reach?   134
A Note About Ad Agencies   134
This Can Be Fun   135
The Formula: Tell a Story   136
Keep It Simple   136
Limit Your Arguments   137
Know Your Target's Age   137
Use Older Models   138
Make It Fun, Make It Bright, Make It Rock   138
Learn What Kids Care About   139
Not Cynics   140
New Is Cool   140
Tony the Tiger and Co.   140
Media Buying   141
Competition from Video Games   142
What About Mom and Dad?   143
The Rules   143
Product Presentations and Claims, Sales Pressure, Endorsements   144
Disclosures and Disclaimers, Comparative Claims   144
Safety   145
The Good News   145
Summing Up   146

10. The Printed Word   147

Pop Quiz   147
Kids Are Readers, Too   147
The Magazine Explosion   148
Benefits of Print   151
What Magazines Attract Kids   152
Print Advertising: Be Interactive   153
Kids' Ads Are Different   154
Kids Are Curious: Make the Most of It   155
Be Sensitive to How Kids Think   156
Fox Creates *Totally Kids*   157

Direct Mail and Kids   159
Building a List   159
What Do You Say in Direct Mail?   160
Making It Cost-Efficient   161
Cooperative Mailings   162
Custom Magazines   162
Summing Up   163

11. Extending the Excitement   **164**

Pop Quiz   164
Stickers on My Sneakers?!   164
What Premiums, Events, and Promotions Do   165
McDonald's Happy Meal   166
Kids are Joiners   169
Make the Promotion an Extension of Your Product   170
Make It Fun   171
Find What's Hot   173
Plan, Plan, Plan   174
The Barbie World Summit   174
Kool-Aid Summer Fun   176
Make It Educational   176
Keebler Promotes Self-Esteem   178
Make It Collectible   179
Inside One Club   180
Pros and Cons of Clubs   181
The Opportunity in Stores   182
Make It Accountable   182
Summing Up   183

12. Nintendo Case Study   **184**

Pop Quiz   184
Zapping Koopas!   185
What Nintendo Accomplished   186
What Marketers Can Learn from Nintendo   187
The Marketer Behind the Brand   188
Fighting Against History   190
Defining Your Company and Product   191
Controlling the Pipeline   191
The Retail Influence   192
The Chip Controversy   193
The Entertainment Influence   193

The Packaged-Goods Influence   194
Keeping Up with the Consumer   194
The Game Is the Game   195
New Product Challenges   196
Summing Up   197

13. Nabisco Case Study   **198**

The Problem with Graham Crackers   198
The Solution: The Teddy Graham   199
Why Teddy Grahams Were a Clever Idea   200
The Woman Behind the Bear   201
The Competitive Context   202
Why a Bear?   203
The Demographic Match   204
The Parental Compromise   204
What Makes a Good New-Product Person?   205
Getting the Right Design   206
Production Challenges   206
The Launch Program   207
Keeping the Edge   208
The World's Smallest Sandwich Cookie   209
Bearwiches Come to Market   210
Incorporating the Knowledge   211
Summing Up   212

14. KidTrends   **213**

Previous Predictions   213
What's Happening with Kids Today?   214
Trend 1: Save Planet Earth   215
Trend 2: Education—A Means to an End   217
Trend 3: Family Life Is Alive and Well, but Different   218
Trend 4: Health and Nutrition   219
Trend 5: Looking Good   220
Trend 6: Sports—Let the Games Begin   221
Trend 7: Money, Brands, and Possessions   222
Trend 8: AIDS and Sex Education   223
Fast Forward   224
The New American Family   224
The Technology of Tomorrow: Home Life   225
Education: A Means to an End   225
Food and Eating Habits   226

Fitness and Looking Good   227
Environmental Concerns   227
Money and Money Management   227
Know Your KidTrends   228

Index   229

Foreword

If you are interested in one of the hottest marketing trends of the nineties, read this book.

Dr. Selina Guber and Jon Berry will convince you with hard research and solid arguments based on years of marketing experience that footloose, fancy-free young adults, aging baby boomers, and over-50 seniors aren't the only groups with purchasing power in our economy. In fact, most members of the consumer group Selina and Jon are interested in haven't even reached puberty. These are children between the ages of six and fourteen.

Why should you as a marketer be interested in these kids? Because they spend a lot of money. Consider these startling facts about them. They spend at least $7 billion annually in pocket money from their family allowances and part-time jobs and influence much more in family purchases.

The most exciting marketing trend buried in these facts is that the purchasing power of these kids is likely to grow in the nineties. Parents, for several reasons, are involving their children in family decision making more than in previous generations; and many parents are simply giving children more money to spend on their own purchases.

This could represent a major opportunity for marketers. But how can one profit from this market? How does one market to and *through* kids to their parents? And isn't marketing to children supposed to be difficult? Well, for those who are not sure where to begin, have no fear because Selina and Jon have many solid suggestions.

   Both Selina and Jon speak with authority on children's marketing. Selina brings more than 20 years' research on children's markets to bear on the subjects. Jon, a business journalist, has studied and interviewed many of the leading producers of children's products.

   They take the mystery out of marketing to kids. Through incisive case studies they show you what works and what doesn't with children. And, with a persistent emphasis on meeting kids' needs, they take you through all of the marketing steps: Identifying and understanding target groups, including the differences and similarities in marketing to boys and girls; developing the right products and packaging; selecting marketing channels and sales outlets; and creating advertising—TV, magazines, and direct mail—and promotions.

   Selina and Jon also use their expert knowledge to give you some informed futurology about the nineties; predictions that marketers serious about selling to kids ignore at their peril.

   Invaluable insights into children's marketing abound in their book. Although applying conventional marketing techniques and brand-building practices to children's marketing is still considered by many to be uncharted territory, your best guide through it is *Marketing to and Through Kids*.

LARRY CHIAGOURIS
Executive Vice President
Backer Spielvogel Bates Advertising
Former President
American Marketing Association

Preface

One of the most charming moments in the past 20 years in cinema comes midway through the movie *Big*, when the 13-year-old boy, magically transformed into a man played by Tom Hanks, jumps onto the giant-sized piano keyboard at F.A.O. Schwarz in New York City and dances out the tune to "Chopsticks" with the head of a toy company. In one instant, the walls of adult pretension come tumbling down, and we see what it's like to be a kid again. It is to that spirit that we dedicate this book.

We live in an era when people look for easy, sound-bite solutions to complex problems. In that process, *marketing* has become a bad word—a catchall for everything that is wrong with political campaigns, our society, the way we eat, the way we think, and the toys that our children play with. Marketing has become synonymous with exploitation. To some people, marketing to children, the business of creating products and services for children, has come to mean taking advantage of children.

It is, we think, an overly simplistic notion. First, it ignores the changes that have taken place in our society. Children are assuming greater responsibilities. Understanding how they choose and buy products is important for the simple reason that they themselves are choosing and buying a growing number of products and services for themselves and for their families. The second reason we think this negative view of marketing is not in sync with reality is that the growth in the number of children, combined with continually changing conditions in households and the world at large, has created a demand for new products to answer problems, provide solutions, and add benefits for the lives of today's kids.

 We have based this book on the classic definition of marketing—that is, that marketing is the process of supplying a product that fills a need.

It's a process that has given us a multitude of products and services that we ourselves would have enjoyed as kids—LEGO building blocks, Disney videos, Rollerblades, new versions of Barbie dolls, and Fisher-Price infant toys. There are dozens of educational toys that open up the windows of imagination. Today's hotels round off the sharp edges of tables and have peanut-butter-and-jelly sandwiches on the room-service menu to accommodate families. Vacation getaways set up activities for children to draw Mom and Dad's business.

What's fascinating about writing about this market, at this stage in time, is that it is evolving so quickly. We are only beginning to understand how children think. The traditional, brand-building practices of packaged-goods marketing have taken hold in children's marketing only since the 1980s.

Moreover, the demographic burst of baby boomers reaching parenthood has focused so much attention on children and family that marketers both of traditional children's products and service categories and of those from other fields are studying the market more closely than has ever been done before.

We don't intend this book to be a be-all and end-all for marketers. Instead, we hope it will encourage you to think, set your creative energy in motion—and have some fun in the process. We hope it will help spark some ideas. We have tried to write this book in an informal style, with pop quizzes, analysis, surprising statistics, insights from our own personal experiences, and case studies of two of the leading companies in the field. As much as possible, we have relied on our own first-hand experience—Selina's in market research for many of the leading companies and with more than 20 years of experience interviewing children, teens, and parents; and Jon's as a business journalist.

This book is focused on 6- to 14-year-olds. It is between those ages that children learn to integrate information from the world around them and make independent choices.

Many, many products for this age group have been brought to market in recent years, but we think there are still many opportunities. We would like to see more products that encourage creativity, independent thinking, and positive values.

Children are society's greatest asset. We encourage you, as a marketer, to be mindful of this fact. We hope you treat this audience with the respect and appreciation you would show your own children. Children are amazing people—full of insights, surprises, and fun. Most people we know love to work with them. How else, after all, can you spend your work days playing?

Selina S. Guber
Jon Berry

Acknowledgments

Over the years, in meetings with business executives; in interviews with television, newspaper, and magazine reporters; and at industry conferences, the same question has kept coming up: How do you market to children? Marketing executives instinctively know it is different from marketing to 18- to 34-year-olds, or 24- to 45-year-olds, the audiences marketers are most familiar with. But how it is different—what children want in products and services, what they respond to in advertisements and promotions, what the ethical and legal responsibilities are in marketing to children—continues to be a mystery to many business executives.

With the population of children growing substantially in recent years and with their roles in households having changed as well, more companies have become interested in learning about them. The timing seemed right for a book that attempts to answer those questions. For more than 20 years, as president and founder of Children's Market Research, Inc. (CMR), Selina Guber has been answering corporate executives' basic questions about attitudes and behaviors of children to help marketers create, name, and package new products and to develop advertising and promotions for children. Jon Berry, meanwhile, has interviewed many of the leading companies in the field as a business journalist.

In this book we attempt to combine our respective experiences—Selina as president of CMR and Jon as a journalist. Every company that has been a client of CMR or a subscriber to the *KIDTRENDS* newsletter and every executive and demographer whom Jon has interviewed for a story, then, deserves acknowledgment. Unfortunately, we cannot name everyone who deserves credit in developing this book. We would like to name several persons, however, whose contributions have been particularly important. Together, we would like to thank Karen Hansen, our editor at McGraw-Hill, for her feedback and ideas in shaping this book. We also would like to thank our agent, Jeffrey Herman.

We would like to thank The Marketing Institute of New York City, whose Consumer Kids conferences have brought together many of the leaders in this field to share their ideas and experiences. We cite these conference presentations numerous times in this book. We also want to thank the Simmons Market Research Bureau of New York City for use of the information from the Kids Study, which provided the data for two *Children's Market Reports*: *KIDTRENDS* and *SNACKS and PRE-PARED FOODS*.

Jon would like to thank the *AdWeek* Magazines LP. Many of the case studies that he developed for this book had their origins as articles for *AdWeek* and its sister magazine *Adweek's Marketing Week* (today published as *BrandWeek* magazine).

Selina also would like to thank Noel Winberry, research director at Children's Market Research, Inc., for his insights and support, both as a colleague and friend. To Jennifer Berrent for her contributions to the final editing of several chapters, many thanks. Selina would like to pay special thanks to her son, Dave, who opened up the world of childhood to her and was her number one subject in many research studies. Now, as a teenager and young man, his support and keen awareness of what's happening with today's kids has been invaluable.

1
Children of the 1990s

A Primer

Pop Quiz

1. How big is kids' annual spending power in the United States?
   (*a*) $50 million, (*b*) $120 million, (*c*) $5 billion. (*d*) $120 billion-plus.

2. Between allowances and the money they get from their parents as needed, how much do kids aged 6 to 14 get on average a week?
   (*a*) $3, (*b*) $6, (*c*) $10, (*d*) $20.

3. How many kids aged 6 to 14 cook food for themselves at least once during the week?
   (*a*) one-tenth, (*b*) one-fifth, (*c*) one-half, (*d*) two-thirds.

4. What percentage of kids call the shots on what brand of sneakers they wear?
   (*a*) 12%, (*b*) 25%, (*c*) 50%, (*d*) 81%.

5. What percentage of parents say they communicate better with their kids than their parents did with them?
   (*a*) one-fourth, (*b*) one-third, (*c*) one-half, (*d*) two-thirds.

Answers: 1. *d*; 2. *c*; 3. *d*; 4. *d*; 5. *d*.

"Mom, You've Gahhht to See This!"

In a focus-group room in a shopping center in suburban Woodbridge, New Jersey, Christie, aged 13, is demonstrating to nine 12- to 14-year-old girls a survival skill that has been passed down from generation to generation since the Stone Age: the art of begging from your mom.

"Mom, you've *gahhht* to see this jacket I saw," Christie implores convincingly. "It's soooo nice! I want it soooo bad! Can I *pleeeasssse* get it? Ah, come on, mom! I'll pay for it, I swear! If you buy it for me, I'll pay you back!"

The girls, recognizing their own techniques—and one or two new ones—are convulsed in laughter. "My mom," says Linda, aged 12, "like, she'll say no a few times. Then she'll say maybe, probably to have me stop bugging her. Then I'll bug her again anyway."

"And if she *still* says no?" the moderator asks.

"Then I say *everyone* in school has one. It's really nice. Mom, you don't understand."

"And if she still says no?

"Then I go ask my dad," says Linda. "Maybe I'll bug him for $100 and tell him I *swear* I'll pay it back."

"And does he give in?"

"Yeah, usually. Moms are tough. They don't care. Dads are easy." "They say, 'You're still my little girl.'"

"So you get the money?"

"Yeah, usually," says Karen, aged 13. "Most of the time."

"And do you pay it back?"

"Sometimes," says Linda. "They eventually forget."

"They want you to stop bugging them," says Christie. "It's like, 'Stop bothering me. Take the money and *go.*'"

"How do you girls get so good at this?" the moderator asks.

"Practice!" the girls chime back at once.

Of course, parents don't need to be told that. It's a scene that is acted out every day in breakfast nooks, on back porches, around dinner tables, and in front of television sets across the country. And many of America's corporate chieftains know it. They work long, painstaking hours in new-product centers, research laboratories, advertising think tanks, and television production studios to put their products at the center of those debates.

Dress-up dolls. Video games. Candy bars. Cereals. Basketball sneakers. Blue jeans. Catsup. Even cars, carpets, and vacation destinations.

Marketing to and Through Kids is a book for marketers who want to understand children's growing economic importance. In the following pages, we tell you about the often complex consumer attitudes and behaviors that today's youngsters possess. We give you practical marketing advice on how to find out what children want; how to create products for them; and how to create advertising, direct mail, and promotions for them. And we provide lots of anecdotes from marketers who are behind many of the classic children's toys and the rising hot products.

In between, we give you nuggets of information from surveys of children conducted by Children's Market Research, Inc. (CMR). In addition, we offer insights from the foremost authorities on marketing to children—kids themselves, whom Children's Market Research has interviewed in focus groups across the United States.

The New Baby Boom

Never before in human history has a society spent so much time catering to the whims, desires, and needs of its children than America in the 1990s. This year, Americans will spend more than $120 billion on their kids, according to estimates from Children's Market Research. Those affections will take the form of everything from organic baby food, to color-coded boys and girls disposable diapers, McDonald Corp.'s Happy Meals, Barbie dolls, Reebok Int'l.'s Pump sneakers, Hanna Andersson Swedish-inspired clothing, and LEGO building-block sets to family trips to Disney World and the Air and Space Museum of the Smithsonian Institute in Washington, D.C.

There's good reason for companies to be interested in kids. According to estimates by Children's Market Research, America's kids spend $7 billion a year from their own pocket. Much of that comes from an allowance that averages $3 per week per child. In addition, mothers report giving children close to $7 more per week as needed.

Moreover, children influence purchases far beyond what they spend money on themselves. According to the CMR KIDTRENDS REPORT, close to 2 out of 3 kids aged 6 to 14 influenced major family purchases in the past year. They included such high-ticket investments as stereos, computers, vacations, even cars. Kids swayed the selection of where families ate dinners out, what videos and movies they put their entertainment dollars toward, and what foods they purchased in the supermarket—not to mention toys, sporting goods, clothes, and sneakers. Including the influence on purchases, the total economic spending of kids in the United States is $150 billion.

> *I get money from my parents. They give me $5 to $10 a
> week. When I want clothes, I ask for money. My
> grandmother gives me money for no reason. I spend
> it all.*
>
>   Darla, aged 14

Open a kitchen cabinet in a home with a child, and it's hard to find products whose purchase has not been influenced by the child. As one harried mother we know shrugs, "Why should I buy food that my kids won't eat? I don't have time to make a whole, separate dinner!"

Kids, in turn, have become surprisingly sophisticated. They seem to be more attuned to the ways of the world than past generations, from the birds and the bees, to finding their way around a shopping mall, to negotiating the 60 channels of the television dial. Moreover, they have become extremely astute consumers.

Children know brand names and advertising slogans. They know the "points of difference" between the number one brand and the also-rans. They've become students of fashion and entertainment. And they exercise their knowledge. A startling 78 percent of kids 6 to 14 years old exert "some" to "a lot" of influence over the choice of breakfast cereal their family buys, according to CMR KIDTRENDS REPORT, based on the Simmons Kids Study, a survey of 2500 children.

> *I know kids who wear bike shorts even if they don't
> bike. They like the look.*
>
>   Girl, aged 12

And a Boom in New Products

The result of kids' product awareness has been a steady stream of new products—toys, educational products, foods, drinks, video games. Whoever heard of fruit snacks, now a $420-million market, before the 1970s? Fruit snacks have become a major profit stream for Betty Crocker, which controls 50 percent of the market, with its Fruit Roll-Ups, Fruit Corners, and Garfield brands.

And new ideas are far from exhausted. Interest in nutrition, which started among grown-ups concerned about heart risks and other problems, has begun to migrate down to children. In turn, the interest on the part of marketers in providing options for cutting back on cholesterol, fat, and sodium and increasing consumption of fruits and vegetables has begun to move down to children as well. One good way to avoid problems later in life, many parents have concluded, is to start out with good dietary habits.

Kids have been the last holdout of fatty foods, says Bonnie Liebman, director of nutrition for the Center for Science in the Public Interest. "People say kids aren't going to have a heart attack if they have a hot dog or a bowl of ice cream. It's baloney. The diet you eat in the first two decades of life lays the groundwork."

New federal guidelines extend adult dietary standards for fat, cholesterol, and sodium to kids. The National Cholesterol Education Program recommends limiting saturated fat to no more than 30 percent of caloric intake. Sodium is to be limited to 2400 milligrams a day, and cholesterol to 300 milligrams a day.

As parents' concerns have grown, entrepreneurs and some large companies have turned more attention to creating products that will combine the desire for healthier eating with the necessity of convenience in products that will satisfy kids' tastes in food.

ConAgra Frozen Foods, Inc., which set the tone for adults with Healthy Choice, has reformulated its Kid Cuisine line of children's frozen entrées and its Mega Meals line of larger portions for older kids to accommodate the new federal guidelines. ConAgra, which won an Edison Award from the American Marketing Association for new product innovation with its original introduction of Kid Cuisine in 1990, called the move a response to parental concerns over their kids' diet. The reformulated meals reduced average fat levels from 14 grams per meal to 11 grams (a drop from 34 percent of the meals' calories to 28 percent). Sodium was reduced from 710 milligrams to 578 milligrams, and cholesterol from 34 milligrams to 30 milligrams.

In a statement, ConAgra chairman and CEO Charles M. "Mike" Harper, whose own well-publicized heart problems led to the development of Healthy Choice, described the reformulation as a logical evolution of the company's commitment to healthier eating. "Kids deserve to have a more nutritious option, too, and we've produced it by reformulating our products to fit within dietary guidelines."

ConAgra rolled out the reformulation with a hands-on, in-store nutrition educational program for kids 5 to 10 years old, called Nutrition U. The program distributed information to help moms lead their families through the Food and Drug Administration's product labels, the U.S. Department of Agriculture's dietary guidelines, and the American Heart Association's recommendations for limiting fat intake. Booklets broke down the subject into chapters covering specific topics, with charts on fat, calories, sodium, and cholesterol tailored to kids' diets.

"The more kids know about what they're eating, the better able they are to make smart food choices," ConAgra nutritionist Beth Penner said in a statement. "Good eating habits developed now and kept throughout life will help them be healthy and active adults."

Some marketers are slipping nutrition into their advertising as well. For example, Quaker Oats Co. already has ads advising teenagers to eat oatmeal because "it's the right thing to do."

Nutrition probably won't ever supplant taste as the number one thing kids look for in food. Part of ConAgra's motivation with its educational program was to show kids "they can balance food choices to include many of the foods they love, without sacrificing nutrition," Penner said. But it can be expected that more parents will look for products that combine the benefits of lower fat, cholesterol, and sodium with good taste in the 1990s as Americans become more aware that starting life with healthy eating habits helps ensure a healthier life when kids reach adulthood.

The Numbers Behind
the Boom

The economic influence of America's children will only increase over the next decade. Since the mid-1980s, birthrates have exploded as the baby-boom generation has reached its childbearing years. Live births rose gradually from their post-baby-boom nadir of 3.136 million in 1973 to 3.333 million in 1978, 3.639 million in 1983, and 3.910 million in 1988, according to the National Center for Health Statistics in Hyattsville, Maryland. In 1990, 4.179 million children were born—the most since 1961! (See Figure 1.)

Census Bureau experts expect the number of live births to stay well above 3.9 million throughout the 1990s, which is well above the levels of the 1970s and 1980s. As the population bulge of the baby boom exits the childbearing years, the total number of live births will dip slightly in mid-decade. However, the influx of immigrants to the United States will push the number of births right back up in the last years of the decade.

For marketers of baby products, then, there will be a large, stable market through the rest of this decade. And the number of children aged 6 to 14 will *increase*. In 1980 there were about 31 million kids aged 6 to 14. By 1990 there were still about 31 million kids in that age bracket, and a total of 53 million kids under the age of 14. By 1995 the number will

U.S government statistics show that births began a gradual decline from the end of the baby boom in 1964—when 4.027 million babies were born—through 1973 (3.136 million). Then began a gradual upswing through the 1970s and 1980s, reaching 4.179 million in 1990. The National Center for Health Statistics' and the Census Bureau's admittedly low projections (see note below) call for birth levels to stay close to the 1960s baby-boom levels through the 1990s.

1961	4.268	1971	3.557	1981	3.629	1991	4.111
1962	4.167	1972	3.258	1982	3.681	1992	3.962
1963	4.098	1973	3.136	1983	3.639	1993	3.932
1964	4.027	1974	3.160	1984	3.669	1994	3.940
1965	3.760	1975	3.144	1985	3.761	1995	3.932
1966	3.606	1976	3.168	1986	3.756	1996	3.929
1967	3.621	1977	3.327	1987	3.809	1997	3.930
1968	3.502	1978	3.333	1988	3.909	1998	3.938
1969	3.600	1979	3.494	1989	4.041	1999	3.952
1970	3.731	1980	3.612	1990	4.179	2000	3.971

Note: The years 1992 through 2000 are U.S. Census Bureau high series projections made in 1989. Since then, the bureau has admitted it severely underestimated its projections. From 1989 to 1991, the undercount averaged 121,000 births per year. If that pattern continues, 121,000 births should be added for each of the years from 1992 to 2000.

Figure 1. U.S. live births (in millions).

grow to 33.7 million, and by the year 2000—even using the Census Bureau's self-acknowledged conservative projections—there will be 35.5 million children aged 6 to 14.

All along, the media has downplayed the significance of the rising birth levels by focusing on birth rates—the percentage of births per the total childbearing population—rather than the actual number of births. The echo baby boom, the popular term for this focus on birth rates, diminished an awareness of the real increase in the numbers of children. In fact, *there has been very significant growth in the numbers of children.* To marketers—whose concern is not birth rates but the actual numbers of children out there for their car seats, baby strollers, bicycles, and baseball mitts—the bottom line is that there will continue to be a large and significant market for their products through the end of this decade.

And, for marketers of products for 6- to 19-year-olds, there will be significant growth.

There are some other interesting phenomena as well. After having put off having kids until well into their 30s, many of the new parents are creating larger families than they were expected to. The two-decade-long slide in family size has bottomed out and is beginning to show signs of going back up again. According to the 1990 Census, there were 12.3 million households with two kids—only slightly less than the 13.5 million households with one child.

Three-kid families have made a slight comeback as well. According to the National Center for Health Statistics, the rate for third births has risen to 11 births per 1000, its highest level since the early 1970s. Fourth births, which are running about 4 per 1000, are at their highest level since the early 1970s as well. In all, 6.5 million households have three or more kids.

Women in the subsequent baby-bust generation may find it easier than the baby boomers did to drop out to have children and then reenter the job market. Because there are fewer baby busters, the labor market may not be as tight; employers, in turn, may be more willing to strike compromises, such as working part-time or working at home, so they can keep their already-trained employees.

Moreover, after having lived through the roller coaster of the recession in the early 1990s and the wringer of trying to work full-time, then come home to the "second shift" of taking care of their kids, husband, and households in the evening, many women have become more realistic about their prospects of "having it all." In some households, that realization is forcing men to pick up the slack of housework—the things that men should have done all along. In other households, women are making the decision to cut back on their commitment to their jobs while they raise their children. Some are leaving the office at the official end of the workday instead of working into the night. Some are downshifting to half-time jobs or job-sharing positions with other mothers. Some, those who can afford it, are leaving the work force. For the first time in decades, the number of women in the work force hit the skids in the early 1990s—and surveys showed many women expressing an interest in working fewer hours.

Social forecasters see two possible courses for the smaller baby-bust generation that is following the baby-boom generation. Women could follow the boomers' lead by delaying marriage and childbirth while putting their career in order and enjoying the single life. Since many of them were children of divorced parents—coming of age in the 1970s when U.S. divorce rates skyrocketed—this seems like the probable course. But for some baby busters, the divorce experience could have the opposite effect—leading to an increased focus on family. To make sure their children don't suffer from the mistakes their parents made, some women may start their families earlier and give them more attention than their parents or the boomers did.

A Changed Society

For better or worse, today's children and teens are wise beyond their years. They are more savvy and aware of their environment, social issues, and problems confronting their families. The days of complete innocence are gone. In their place, we are seeing children growing up with a keen awareness of drugs, racial problems, environmental concerns, and more. We are seeing a population of young people who are more aware, independent, and conscious of the world than previous generations.

The American family has changed. The roles of parents and children no longer follow traditional patterns. The metamorphosis of the home-centered mother into the working mother has had a dramatic impact. Dual-income households are the norm. Today, 70 percent of American mothers work full-time or part-time, compared with approximately 30 percent in 1980. One-fourth of America's young are growing up in single-parent households.

Upheavals in the workplace and at home have vested America's 47 million youngsters 12-years-old and younger with responsibilities and power earlier generations could not have fathomed. Millions of children have taken on chores from buying groceries for dinner to cleaning the house, to cooking themselves after-school snacks, to even getting dinner started for their working parents.

According to survey's conducted by Children's Market Research, two-thirds of kids aged 6 to 14 cook food for themselves 1 to 5 times a week. Even when mom does not work, kids are assuming a bigger role in the kitchen. They are more independent than previous generations.

Parents are more educated than ever before. Overall, only 1 in 5 Americans have some college education. In contrast, almost one-half of all baby boomers have been to college—46 percent to be exact—and one-fourth have graduated. The boomers are the best educated generation in the United States. And it's paid off in their careers. Fully 30 percent of all boomers fall into professional/managerial occupations. Some 78 percent of the total population works full-time, and 84 percent of those between the ages of 25 and 44 work full-time. The bottom line? Parents today are more vested in providing the best for their kids, and they have the financial wherewithal to do it.

Being brought into the marketplace at an early age has made this generation of children relatively sophisticated shoppers—that is, relative to kids 20 years ago. They know brand attributes advertised in commercials. Being inveterate television watchers—averaging 3-plus hours a day of televiewing—they can quickly pick up on the visual cues in commercials, coupons, and packaging.

And they often get what they want. According to the CMR KIDTRENDS REPORT, based on the Simmons Kids Study, 78 percent of children aged 6 to 14 say they influence the brand of cold cereal their families buy. The same percentage hold sway over the kind of blue jeans their parents buy for them, and an astonishing 81 percent call the shots on the sneakers they wear.

My little brother begged my dad to get a sports car. He got it.

Girl, aged 10

The Rainbow Generation

The other inescapable fact of the generation growing up today is that it is the most ethnically diverse group America has ever seen. Some 38.6 percent of kids under age 5 in 1990 were nonwhite, according to the Census. That is substantially higher than the total U.S. population, of which 28.4 percent were nonwhite. And—since the numbers skew higher as you go younger—it is far higher than the composition of the parents and grandparents of today's children.

Blacks account for the largest nonwhite population. According to the 1990 Census, some 15 percent of 0- to 14-year-olds were African Americans, compared with 12 percent of the entire population. Hispanics are the second-largest nonwhite population among kids; in 1990 they accounted for 13 percent of kids, compared with 8.9 percent in the total population. "Other" comes next, with 6 percent of kids, compared with 3.9 percent in the total population; followed by Asian Americans and Pacific Islanders, with 3 percent of the population, compared with 2.9 percent in the total population; and Native Americans, Inuits, and Aleuts, with 1.1 percent of the population, compared with 0.7 percent in the total population.

Marketers of children's products and services, in turn, are going to be the first wave of companies to face issues that all companies will have to confront in the years ahead, as the mainstream of American life changes to reflect changing demographics. It's hard to believe, for example, that blond hair and blue eyes can remain the standard for beauty. Ethnically diverse dolls and action figures are beginning to emerge. We fully expect to see more ethnically diverse products as well as more ethnically diverse commercials for all products. What civil rights and affirmative action laws put forth as the moral thing to do will be the economically prudent thing to do in the 1990s.

Today's Parents: Involved with Their Kids

Today's parents have gotten a bad rap. They've been stereotyped as self-involved, career-obsessed narcissists who ignore their kids. But research by *Parents* magazine—the bible of childrearing in many households—shows that parents in the 1990s, in fact, are more involved with their kids than their parents were with them.

Close to half of the parents surveyed by *Parents* said that they spend more time with their kids than their parents spent with them. Two-thirds of them said that they communicate better with their kids than their parents did with them. "These parents are not ignoring their children," says Charlene Trentham, director of research for *Parents*. "They're very concerned about their families."

They also show a surprisingly strong streak of traditionalism. Almost three-quarters say it's "essential" to be there when their child wakes up. Two-thirds say it's "essential" to be home when their child comes home from school. The overwhelming majority say they sit down with their family to eat dinner together every night.

> *When my mom works late, dad makes dinner.*
>
> Girl, aged 7

In the *Parents* survey when asked to rate 16 sources of stress, parents put being able to provide their kids with "all they want" dead last. Only 7.4 percent worried about it. What do they worry about, then? A total of 38.4 percent worry about giving their kids "the necessities of life," and 38.1 percent worry about giving kids "a good education." Teaching values, instilling respect for others, and giving them a religious upbringing all finished well ahead of gratifying kids' material desires.

But Parents Just Want to Have Fun, Too

Still, mom and dad are capable of clowning around. Americans' fabled extended adolescence—that little kid, that Peter Pan inside grown-ups—is alive and well. One of our favorite ad campaigns in recent years, for the toy retailer Toys R Us, showed grown-ups fully involved in clowning around. "And we're telling them that's all right," says Marty Rose, account director at J. Walter Thompson. "It's all right to have fun and be a kid."

"We had people telling me, "Yeah, that's me, that's me. I'm a Toys R Us kid," Rose says. "And it would be a 50-year-old woman."

In many cases, parents are egging on their charges. As the most educated generation of parents in the nation's history, they bring excruciatingly high standards to child rearing—be it angling to get their children into the best teacher's classroom, digging deep into their pockets to send their kids to private school and summer camp, choosing organic baby food over traditional brands, or fashioning boom markets for children's fashions and storybooks.

To some parents, the purchases are building blocks for continuing the upward mobility that is the dream of all Americans. To others, the goods are a material expression of a love that cannot be made evident every hour of the day since today's dual-income parents are away at work. And, for some mothers and fathers, the lavishness is a way of proving to the world they have made it.

Historically, parents weren't so involved with kids. Partly, we're seeing the end product of the advances in medicine, which have reduced child mortality rates. In part, it reflects a growing realization that children have special needs and deserve special attention. It has only been in the past 30 years that the great mass of parents have lavished attention on their children—and had the time and money to do so.

Even in hard times, when people may feel self-conscious splurging on a splashy sports car or an expensive dinner out, it's still acceptable to spend on kids, notes Jane Fitzgibbon, director of TrendSights, the social-forecasting group of the advertising agency Ogilvy & Mather. "Who can criticize you for buying wonderful things for your little children? You're just expressing your love in a politically correct way." Parents will cut back last on kids. Despite recession, kids are still getting their $3 weekly allowances.

And Sometimes They're Softies

Since mom and dad with their busy lives need and welcome assistance, many willingly share part of the power of the purse with their children.

Being sensitive to the developmental needs of their little ones—and guilty over being absent from the home much of the week—today's parents also just have a hard time saying no. Wittingly or not, some of them are perfect targets for kids. "I don't ask my parents for something when they're together," one 11-year-old told Children's Market Research in a focus group, "because if one says no, they'll both say no. I ask my dad first. If he says yes, then he helps me convince my mother."

Parents apparently know they're being manipulated. In a study of 1000 children aged 6 to 14 and of 502 mothers, 92 percent of mothers told Children's Market Research that they feel most parents are "too soft" on their kids, that they "give in" too easily, and that they "give their kids too much money."

There is a constant tug at parents between whether they should put their careers first or their home and family first. The conflict between what parents—and mothers in particular—want for themselves and the social pressures they feel often results in feelings of guilt.

Parents play a role in purchases for kids. But it's different from that of past generations. They encourage kids to be in step, but they also feel a great deal of guilt because they are less available to their kids.

It's been played out, so to speak, in video games. Parents invested hundreds of dollars in hardware and software in the first generation of Nintendo video games. But when Nintendo and Sega came out with advanced, 16-bit video game systems, parents went and bought them, too—in such numbers that they became the biggest selling toys in the nation.

> *I like Gatorade. It tastes good and makes you feel good.*
>
> Boy, aged eight

Kids Are Independent

Kids are growing up with more control over their lives. Many have extended curfews. They exercise a great deal of control over what they eat. Many come home 2 to 3 hours before mom and dad arrive from work. A lot of them get themselves up, too. Many have their own alarm clocks. They run errands. They go to town on their own and buy things for themselves. And they go to the mall. Every 1 in 4 children are growing up in a single-parent household.

Forty-nine percent of children either buy their own food or participate in food shopping and brand selection (CMR's Snacks and Prepared
Food Report). Even children who do not go to the supermarket often
request specific products and brands.

Today, 81 percent of children prepare food for themselves at least 2 to
3 times a week. Snacks are the most often prepared food. By far, kids'
favorite frozen food is pizza, followed by macaroni and cheese, TV dinners and snacks, and microwaveable cakes.

> *The mall's my favorite hangout. You really don't have
> to have money to go. You can hang out and talk to
> boys. You can play video games. There are lots of
> restaurants.*
>
> Jennifer, aged 12

Kids Are Worldly

Talk to a child, and you find a person who's acutely aware of social
problems. They see it in the media and, many times, in their own neighborhoods and schools. "School's not safe," a 10-year-old boy told
Children's Market Research. "There's too many fights." "Japan will be
the richest, most powerful country in the world," an 11-year-old boy
said. "They make all the VCRs and cars."

Kids also know about the birds and the bees earlier than their parents
did. "You have to know about it before it happens," one 12-year-old girl
said. "Girls think about it," a boy said. "It's their hormones."

The biggest worry young people have today is how they will make it
in the world. A significant percentage say "school and career" are very
important to them. They feel a great deal of pressure to do well in school
and are very goal-oriented. As early as middle school, kids talk about
careers or future work. Education is seen as a means to an end, necessary to get a good job and make money. Getting good grades means you
will get into the right school.

Children are also concerned about the environment and pollution.
Many are taking positive steps. A lot are leading parents. They sort bottles and cans at school lunch rooms for recycling. They talk about it in
class. In response to surveys, kids say they feel they have a personal
investment at stake. They are being educated even at preschool levels.

They know about drinking and drugs, even though they may not use
them. Many of them know there are pushers in their schools. Alcohol is
used by many teens.

> *Most of the kids in my class drink. If you don't drink,*
> *people think there's something wrong with you.*
>
> Scott, aged 14
>
> *I don't like beer commercials because I don't want to*
> *drink beer. It shows people having fun and beer being*
> *part of it. It's not needed.*
>
> Girl, aged 9
>
> *Beer commercials are gross. People get killed from*
> *drinking. I don't think it's right to drink beer. It's*
> *promoting drinking.*
>
> Boy, aged 11

Kids Are Family-Centered

It's true that kids know more about drugs, sex, crime, and pollution than they ever did before. Still, family values run deep. Asked what is the most important thing in their lives, the overwhelming majority of kids say, "Family." Money and career are also-rans.

In focus groups, kids tell us at Children's Market Research that they have a keen interest in watching family shows on television. The "Cosby Show," "Growing Pains," "Home Improvement," "The Brady Bunch," and other family sitcoms have remained popular with kids for years, even as reruns. Kids will watch their favorite episodes again and again until they know them by heart. They like to watch shows with their parents. Many parents, glad to spend time with their kids, let kids set the viewing agenda. One dad of a 4-, 6-, and 13-year-old said he never watches his favorite show, "60 Minutes," anymore so he can spend time with his kids.

Despite the troubles in the world around them, kids are optimistic about life. They always have been—and probably always will be. To the untrained eye, today's generation of children looks like a jumble of contradictions. In the same room, you can find AC/DC posters all over the wall and a bunch of teddy bears on the bed.

We have found children generally are very supportive of their mothers in keeping the household functioning. Today's working mothers depend heavily upon kids for helping with family chores.

> *I like "Roseanne." It's a typical family because they*
> *argue over bills.*
>
> Girl, aged 10

Kids Are Responsible

The children of the 1990s not only are seen and heard but also they pitch in. Forty-nine percent of kids buy food for their family or participate in grocery shopping, according to the findings of Children's Market Research. The contribution goes beyond the kitchen. Most kids help their moms in household chores and caring for younger children. Both boys and girls pitch in to clean up the house, wash dishes, and do the laundry.

Many say they don't feel burdened. They see their help as necessary for the smooth functioning of the family. It's also a way of spending more time with family members. Here's what kids have told Children's Market Research: "I set the table," says a 7-year-old girl. "After dinner my brother and I wash the dishes." "Sometimes when I help my mommy clean the house, she pays me two quarters," says a 5-year-old girl. "If I clean up my room, I get a lot of money. I get $2," says a 7-year-old boy. "I vacuum the upstairs and sometimes the downstairs and feed my doggie," says a 6-year-old girl.

It's become a way of life. Only 2 percent of mothers express guilt about letting their kids cook for themselves."All my children do chores," one mother told Children's Market Research during a series of focus groups in Denver, St. Louis, and Metro Park, New Jersey, for Ore-Ida Foods. "I wouldn't be able to work if they didn't."

Mom tells me to be good and bring out the trash, and I'll get quarters for the videos.

Boy, aged 5

How Kids View Nutrition

Let's return to the subject of nutrition. How do kids feel about it? Mom and dad control a great deal of their kids' diet before age 5, but then conflicts appear. Kids are surprisingly aware of what's good for them. But they also know what they think tastes good. According to the Gallup Poll, pizza is by far kids' favorite food, preferred by 82 percent. It's followed by Chicken McNuggets, hot dogs, cheeseburgers, macaroni and cheese, hamburgers, spaghetti, fried chicken, tacos, and grilled cheese. In other words, there has not been a great deal of change in recent years.

We don't think their preferences will change. It is hard for kids to relate to claims that a product will make them healthy 20, 30, or 40 years from now. If marketers want to interest kids in healthy eating, it is better to appeal to what kids are interested in right now. Kids are interested in being athletic. Girls want to be slim and fit. Boys want to be macho and strong.

Pizza has achieved a status among kids as being good tasting and good for them. "My friends and I eat pizza every day," says a boy, aged 11. "Pizza is good for you," says a 10-year-old boy. "It has tomato sauce, cheese, and bread. Only the grease is not good for you. My mom, dad, and me and [sic] my little brother go out for pizza every week."

Where Marketers Come In

The children of the 1990s, then, are active consumers and influencers for themselves and for the family. They are independent and worldly but devoted to family and generally hopeful. They're not, in sum, the easiest market for marketers to keep up with.

 Marketing, in its basic form, is the process of finding a need that is not being met and creating a product that fills it. The product that results can be a short-term fad, but the greatest successes are products that endure for more than one season and provide a meaningful benefit.

LEGO's yellow, red, blue, and white plastic, snap-fit building blocks, for example, have enabled children for generations to build elaborate castles, space stations, and cityscapes—without the fear, that children always had with wooden building blocks, of falling down. Barbie dolls let little girls imagine what it is like to be a teenager and fantasize about being whatever they want to be. McDonald's standardization of hamburgers and fries made it possible for millions of households to eat out without breaking the bank.

Where in the World Is Carmen Sandiego? has harnessed the entertainment values of the personal computer to teach children about geography in a fun, fast-paced manner.

We are only beginning to see the possibilities from computer technology. Marketing is going to be playing catch-up to the vast changes in society for some time to come. In the pages to come, we hope this book will help you make a difference.

We are still learning the basics about marketing to kids. Research is showing that their influence and power reaches across most products and services and the money they control is enormous.

Kids as a group are no less complex than adults. They segment by age, sex, region, and lifestyle. They need a sense of independence and freedom, as well as structure and limits. Children and teens are constantly experimenting and developing brand loyalties, which could last into adulthood. But, to understand today's kids, you will have to lose some of your adult preconceptions and learn to think like a kid. As one boy in a focus group said, "How do adults think they can rule the world? They can't even play Nintendo!"

Summing Up

1. Kids are a major consumer market. Their total spending power is around $150 billion a year. About $7 billion comes from weekly allowances, which average $3 per child. They directly spend on average an additional $7 a week with money given to them as needed by their parents. Additionally, they influence family purchases ranging from groceries to consumer electronics and vacation destinations.

2. The number of children in the United States has been growing. The number of live births has risen from 3.1 million at their nadir in 1973, to 3.7 million in 1984, and 4.2 million in 1990. There were 53 million kids under 14 years old, according to the diennial 1990 Census.

3. The number of children will continue to grow in the 1990s, as baby boomers pass through their childbearing years and economic and social factors influence the baby-bust generation behind them not to delay childbearing as late in life as the boomers did.

4. Changes in family life are vesting children with more responsibilities than kids had in the 1950s. With 70 percent of mothers working, children are handling more shopping and household tasks than kids in the privileged years of the 1950s and 1960s.

5. Kids are more aware of brands and advertising, and they see themselves as consumers. They are receptive to new products, new technologies, and new styles.

6. Despite the proliferation of two-income households, parents are highly involved with their children. Most parents say they spend more time with their children than their parents spent with them. Parents are also more likely to involve their children willingly in family decision making.

7. Kids are growing up in a far different world. They are part of America's most ethnically diverse generation: as of 1990, 38.6 percent of kids were nonwhite, compared with 28.4 percent for the total population. Mass media has made kids acutely aware of global problems from recessions to the greenhouse effect to the nuclear threat. They are exposed to sex earlier than their parents were. But kids are very family-centered. Family is an anchor of security.

2
Influence

How Kids Get What They Want

Pop Quiz

1. What percentage of kids say they influence the brand of cold cereal their family buys?
   (*a*) 45%, (*b*) 55%, (*c*) 60%, (*d*) 90%.

2. How many kids say they influenced the type of car their family bought?
   (*a*) 5%, (*b*) 10%, (*c*) 12%, (*d*) 20%.

3. In general, kids mind, or even prefer, using the same brands their parents do.
   (*a*) true, (*b*) false.

4. What does *divide and conquer* describe?
   (*a*) a method that politicians have used to hold on to power, (*b*) a technique kids use to get one of their parents on their side when they want something, (*c*) both.

5. Parents are generally satisfied with the choices of toys available to their kids.
   (*a*) true, (*b*) false.

Answers: 1. *d*; 2. *d*; 3. *b*; 4. *c*; 5. *a*.

The Baseball Kid

Max likes science fiction, LEGOs, mathematical problems, and swimming. But, like a lot of 8-year-old boys, his true passion is baseball. He owns two baseball mitts—a Wilson brand Pro Special, autographed by outfielder Kirk Gibson, and a Wilson brand Fieldmaster, with New York Yankee great Ron Guidry's autograph. He has six baseballs, five baseball bats (all Louisville Slugger), a Cosom-brand batting tee, a complete set of rubber bases for backyard games, and two Oakland Athletics baseball caps—one a vintage 1960s model and the other a current style.

He sleeps in Oakland A's pajamas. At least once a week, he goes to school in an Oakland A's jersey—purchased with proofs of purchase from Dow Consumer Products, Inc. Texize Spray 'n Wash Stain Stick. Every couple months he talks his mom into renting *Field of Dreams*, his favorite baseball movie, at the video store.

When summer comes, Max plays Little League baseball. He also makes it out to three or four big-league games (according to major league baseball, about average attendance for a family), and if his dad's feeling flush, Max comes home with a souvenir in addition to the usual hot dog, Cracker Jack, and soda.

Max also collects baseball cards—all year long. He has his eye on the cards his dad collected as a kid, especially the Nolan Ryan cards. But, whereas his dad collected his cards for fun, Max collects them for their investment value. He keeps track of his cards' rising value in *Beckett's Price Guide*, an index of the current market value of every baseball card from the past 40 years, and can rattle off quotes of the going price of the top cards like a budding Wall Street takeover artist.

Baseball is no idle hobby for Max. It represents fitness. It represents a social outlet; the game is the glue of conversation in the hallways at school and recreation for his gang of pals after school and on the weekends. And it represents money. The baseball mitts, gifts from Max's parents, cost $40 each. Bats, balls, caps, and other gear run $4 to $25 each. A weekly pilgrimage to the baseball-card shop can easily exhaust a $2 allowance on new cards, or—if he's saved up—even more for a prized rookie card.

As the late Sen. Everett Dirksen said of the federal deficit, a million here, a million there, and pretty soon you're talking serious money. And that doesn't even include the birthday party Max had last year, when a dozen pals came over for a baseball game, which included two ringer party attendants from the local high school team, a cake in the design of the card of Max's favorite player, and official major league baseball team T-shirts for all the kids.

Influence in Action

How did all this start? The answer is a microcosm of how brand influence works. It's something all marketers of products for children *and families* should understand. In this chapter, we'll tell you how it works. The fact is, children have a degree of influence that extends farther than you probably think. How far?

In a focus group of 12- to 14-year-old girls, Children's Market Research asked what their favorite commercials are. Unprompted, one girl piped up that her favorite commercial is Michelin Tires. The ads show babies in a Michelin tire, the point being, of course, that Michelin is a brand you can trust your children with. "The little babies are so cute," the girl said.

Do you think dad couldn't help but think twice when he mentions over dinner that it's time to replace the tires, and his "baby" becomes a Greek chorus to Michelin's babies?

Kids probably already know a lot more about your product than you think they do. In the same focus group, another girl said she tries to get her family to eat at the restaurants she likes when they go out—and she often prevails. Of those who eat cold cereal, more than 80 percent of kids aged 6 to 14 exercised "a little," "some," or "a lot" of influence over what kind of cold cereal the family buys, according to the CMR KIDTRENDS REPORT, based on The Simmons Kids Study. (See Table 1.) More than one-fifth of kids say they exerted at least "a little" influence on their parents' decision on what kind of car to buy, according to other research. Another study found that almost half influenced the decision where to go for the family vacation.

Several of the adolescent girls in focus groups have told Children's Market Research that they had told their moms about the detergent commercial that features a young hunk disrobing (not all the way, of course) and flinging his clothes into the washer.

If you market a brand that kids aged 6 to 14 have a vested interest in, it's important to know how much influence kids have over purchases in

Table 1. Amount of Influence Child Has on Purchase of Cold Cereals
(by percent)

	Total	Total boys	Total girls
Child eats cold cereals? Yes	90.3	90.4	90.1
Child's influence on brands purchased:			
A lot of influence	40.2	38.5	41.0
Some influence	31.0	32.1	29.9
A little influence	12.4	12.7	12.0
No influence	7.1	7.3	6.8

SOURCE: CMR KIDTRENDS REPORT, based on data from The Simmons Kids Study (1991).

your product category, what is motivating kids to lobby for one brand over another, and how the process of influence works.

> *How'd I hear about Sony? Everything's Sony. They make TVs. They invented Walkmans. They make all kinds of electronic stuff. It's what my friends have. If I have a choice, I'll buy Sony.*
>
> Girl, aged 12

Making Choices Is Important

Explorative play is the "work" of a toddler. It's been said by sociologists that the "work" of a youth is defining his or her own identity—deciding who he or she is. From the early years until children reach adulthood, they will decide what they will stand for, what their interests are, where their passions lie, what subjects they will pursue in school with the most vigor, what musical instruments and sports they will try to excel in, and, maybe, the seeds of what they will want to do in their career and the rest of their lives. The decisions they make will influence everything from their interests in reading and entertainment to what styles of clothes they wear, what kind of car they'll drive someday, what kind of house they'll live in, even how they talk. The choices they make are part of the process of self-definition. Your brand is part of that process.

If you've been around children, you know they are natural at type-casting: They describe themselves, their peers, and their family by their interests. "I'm a Giants fan." "My dad's a Mets fan." "I'm into skate-boards." "I love science." Or—as Mattel has advertised its ubiquitous fashion doll—"I'm into Barbie."

When you spend time with children, you also learn quickly that their reputation for curiosity is genuine. If they find something that interests them, but which they do not understand, they will tug at their parents' sleeve, asking questions. If they find something that intrigues them—a cereal box, a baseball card, a story in a schoolbook, an article in one of their parents' magazines—they won't just read it. They'll devour it. Donna Sabino, research manager at *Sports Illustrated for Kids,* says children are "natural information seekers."

Their twin preoccupations with defining themselves and seeking information come together in choices from what they'll wear to school in the morning to what they want for their birthday. Each decision that aligns them with a brand of toothpaste or cereal—like deciding what kind of music they like (rock, pop, rap, jazz, opera)—becomes an exercise in self-definition. The brand becomes part of their identity.

A brand can even be a force in the generation gap, such as preferring Madonna or Prince to Frank Sinatra or the Beatles. "Mom eats Shredded Wheat. I eat Cocoa Pebbles." The products don't have to be products for which they are the primary users. Sometimes, that's not the point.

Kids like to be the experts. For example, Nickelodeon, the children's cable television network, has gotten pet-food advertising on the basis that kids like to think of themselves as the experts on the family pet. Many times they are. With two-income households, kids often are the primary caretaker for the family dog or cat.

"Kids have their own opinions on brands, and very often they're very independent from their parents," says Marshall Cohen, executive vice president for corporate affairs for Nickelodeon. "There are a lot of areas where you wouldn't think kids would be influential—computers, television, grocery products—but they are." (See Table 2.)

If there is an added incentive to buy a product, such as a premium offer that tweaks a child's imagination, the motivation is stronger still. It is important, then, for you as a marketer to talk to kids, listen to them, and understand how your product fits into their lives. Only then will you know how to address them.

Max and Baseball

To give you an idea how influence works, let's go back to the anecdote about baseball with which we started this chapter. Like all kids, Max is

Table 2. Amount of Influence Child Has on Purchase of Frozen Entrées/Complete Meals
(by percent)

	Boys			Girls		
	6–8	9–11	12–14	6–8	9–11	12–14
Child eats frozen entrées? Yes	48.5	49.9	54.4	49.0	45.9	49.8
Child's influence on frozen entrée brands						
A lot of influence	12.3	14.8	14.5	11.6	10.5	9.0
Some influence	18.1	15.4	19.2	16.2	16.3	15.6
A little influence	9.5	9.7	11.7	12.0	9.9	13.8
No influence	8.5	10.0	8.9	9.2	9.1	11.5

SOURCE: CMR KIDTRENDS REPORT, based on data from The Simmons Kids Study (1991).

surrounded by a universe of influences, from parents and relatives, to television, peers, and his heroes. From there, he—again, like all kids— crunches the stimuli, like a long-limbed personal computer in sneakers and grass-stained blue jeans, and sifts out the stuff that will help him to fit in with his pals, satisfy his sensual and intellectual cravings, and, most of all, be fun.

For Max, baseball does all that. The Oakland A's baseball organization probably planted the seed. Through the 1980s, the team made families a top priority, with Disney theme parks as its model. It kept the ballpark meticulously clean. It banned cigarette smoking and clamped down on drunkenness to create a family atmosphere. It developed a busy schedule of sponsored giveaways tied to game days. It installed picnic areas and booths that let kids get their pitches "timed" or call half an inning of the game on a cassette tape in the Fantasy Play-by-Play Booth. Even if the A's lost the game, the team wanted its fans to have fun. Max, like a lot of Bay Area kids, became a regular attender.

Today, Max looks for baseball everywhere. He studies box scores and the back side of baseball cards to stump his dad with statistical arcana. He's lobbied on everything—actual baseball gear, pajamas in the local department store, and 12-packs of Coke and boxes of Cracker Jack that offered the premium of a collector's edition baseball card.

Take the Spray 'n Wash A's jersey. Max spotted the offer while browsing through the coupon section of the Sunday newspaper for new candy and breakfast cereals.

Like a lot of kids, Max knows that coupons introduce manufacturers' new products. Along with the comics and the sports section, the coupon insert is one of his favorite parts of the Sunday paper. If he finds something he likes, he quickly alerts mom and dad.

Manufacturers who sell products to children and families, therefore, would be advised to recognize the presence of kids in the audience, from television, to coupons, to the retail shelf.

My mom told me I could spend $200 on her credit card. That's really a stretch. I could only get a skirt, pants, and two blouses at the Gap and have enough left over for sneakers and school supplies.

Girl, aged 14

I have three girls, 7, 9, and 12. None of them will wear hand-me-downs the way I did when I was a kid.

Mother

> *My son won't wear a pair of jeans or a shirt if it doesn't have the right label.*
>
> Mother of 9-year-old boy

Peer Pressure

There are thousands of products that compete for kids' attention—and tens of thousands more adult products that kids can't help but notice when they watch TV or go into a store. How do kids decide which ones they want to have? Product packaging; advertising; and endorsements from athletic heroes, movie stars, and other role models all contribute to making a product stand out from the pack. But the most important influencer for kids is their own peer group.

As we noted earlier, the "work" of kids in determining their own identity includes developing relationships with their peers. This ranks in importance with multiplication tables, rules of grammar, the states in the union, and the other things they do in the classroom. Friendship is a vital part of life for kids. "I like to be with my friends," an 8-year-old boy told a Children's Market Research focus group. "I like recess and three o'clock, when we get out of school."

Almost everything—including the clothes they wear, the toys they play with, the shows they watch on TV, and the food they pack in their lunches—can be a medium of communication of how they perceive themselves and their relationship to others. Kids look to their friends as sources of information on what's in and what's out in activities, entertainment, styles, and language. Wearing the same styles of clothes can be an expression of feeling part of the group. Sporting different clothes—at least, in a child's perception—can put them at a social disadvantage. The child wants to be part of the group.

A mother in a Children's Market Research focus group once described going to three different stores to find a pair of sneakers for her son. "It wasn't that the other stores didn't have the brand of sneakers he wanted," she said. "He had to find the exact color and style worn by a certain tennis player. It was either those sneakers, or he'd wear his old ones." The shoes cost $110. "As soon as he walked on the tennis court the next day," the mother said, "his friend accurately identified the sports figure associated with the shoes. I couldn't believe it."

Another mother recalled having to buy a new bike for her son under similar circumstances. "Luis had a perfectly good bike, but he wouldn't ride it because it wasn't what the other kids have."

Basketball shoe companies, shooting to establish their shoes as the in shoe, have distributed pairs to young stars on inner-city playgrounds, in the knowledge that fashions in athletic apparel tend to be set in urban areas and spread out to the suburbs.

Video game companies enjoy enormous word of mouth from selling their games to early adopters, usually by advertising in enthusiast magazines like *Nintendo Power* or by developing point-of-sale at video game counters of toy stores. The early adopters spread the word to other kids.

How do you get to the early adopters? The easiest way is to ask kids what's cool. They are astute observers of what constitutes a trendsetter. The ingredients, as a matter of course, are in continual evolution. As everyone else catches up, what's cool moves ahead. With some relief, for example, researchers are reporting that antisocial behaviors, such as drug use, that used to be cool in the 1970s, have become uncool as kids have seen the light about their dangers.

Fashions are always changing. Television shows come and go, and musical performers rise and fall. Sports has stayed fairly constant as a general indicator of what is cool. Within that, basketball has become increasingly popular. And some specific activities—such as skateboarding and Rollerblading—have moved quickly into the mainstream.

To stay ahead as a marketer, you must keep pace with the market through focus groups, quantitative research, or just keeping your ear to the ground. And you must be flexible enough to change your product and communications. In essence, you must join the peer group—at least as an interested observer.

I watch TV, mainly sports.
Boy, aged 11

NIKE's Full-Court Press

By understanding how to make a product that satisfies kids' basic desires, how to use endorsements from sports heroes, and how to create attention-grabbing advertising that appeals to kids' senses of play and humor, NIKE, Inc., has put itself near the top of many kids' lists of brands.

In the process, the company has become synonymous with its athletes. The result has established NIKE, early on in children's lives, as a performance-oriented brand for those who aspire to be athletes. NIKE has invested well with its chosen athletes. In Michael Jordan and Bo Jackson in particular, the company has aligned itself with the heroes of a generation. Jordan is not just regarded as a tremendous athlete. Kids, like grown-ups, regard the soaring, slam-dunking basketball star as the greatest athlete in the world. Jackson, despite his career-threatening hip injury, is not just thought of as a great athlete. By being a record-setting pro-football running back and an All-Star, power-hitting outfielder, he has become a symbol of every kid's desire to excel at *every* sport.

According to Tom Phillips, who managed NIKE's marketing to kids in the growth period, the company learned as it went along. "We basically started out taking a few of our real classics and scaling them down to kids," he says. Each shoe got a kidlike name. Wally Waffle was a children's version of NIKE's breakthrough waffle-soled running shoe. Corky Cortez was the NIKE tennis shoe. Bert Bruin was the NIKE basketball shoe.

Parents responded enthusiastically. Kids' tastes, in turn, quickly grew more sophisticated. "The big shift we've been seeing is away from unbranded to more sophisticated, branded athletic shoes at younger and younger ages," Phillips said. By the early 1990s, about 40 percent of kids' sneakers were branded. Kids grew from zero to about 14 percent of NIKE's business.

As tastes got more sophisticated, NIKE redesigned its product line to make the shoes more sophisticated. Borrowing on the equity of basketball star Michael Jordan's Air Jordan adult shoes, NIKE came out with a line of kids' Jordans at different price points, from $50 to $90, to make them more accessible to kids. The goal was to offer a price point that would open up the market for as many kids as possible to be able to own the shoes. "We tried to focus in on taking shoes from the adult world that are exciting to kids and creating different levels of the shoe for kids, to let them get in," says Phillips.

NIKE didn't create exact duplicates of adults' shoes. Instead, it focused on the elements of the shoes that would most appeal to kids. The company has found that younger kids in particular love a shoe's look and feel—the combination of graphics, materials, colors, and other features that appeal to a kid's senses. The company updates styles as often as every six months, to satisfy kids' taste for variety and something new.

"The things that are important to a kid are what's new, what's innovative, and what's a genuinely exciting product," Phillips says. "About the last thing a child wants to do is buy the same shoe in a bigger size." Durability is also important. "Kids are very literal and true consumers."

You'll hear us repeat that line many times: "Kids are very literal and true consumers." Children live in the here and now. They expect you to be truthful and accurate; what you show in your advertisement should be what they get. They go on their first-hand experience.

"If a child gets excited about your product and goes out and buys and wears it and is not satisfied with how it holds up," says Phillips, "it's going to be very difficult to get them [sic] back."

Because of the guidelines for children's advertising, NIKE cannot use its celebrity endorsers on advertising for children's programming. Instead, the company has promoted the idea of athletics in commercials that encourage kids to go out and "just do it." But kids know the shoe companies' athlete ads, because they see them during sporting events.

NIKE's wonderfully imaginative ads have shown strong appeal to both adults and kids; most of the ads work on both adult and kid levels. Sometimes kids may not appreciate the nuances of the humor. Phillips notes, for example, that "Bo Knows" ads with Bo Jackson, the multital-ented professional football star/professional baseball slugger who endorsed NIKE cross-trainer shoes, often had lines that flew over kids' heads. One spot with multiple Bo Jacksons playing football, shooting baskets, riding race cars, and playing golf played off the "Bo Knows" slogan with a cameo by 1960s pop star Sonny Bono. Kids didn't get it, but they loved the commercial's special effects.

For marketers, there are several lessons. Try to learn from your expe-riences. Your first effort probably will not be your best. Popular brands, like Air Jordan, should be a big tent. It's important to price a product to encourage trial, the building block of brand loyalty, by as many kids as possible. And it's important to be able to offer variety and new items and features in everything from the product to its advertising.

I like Bart Simpson, because he's cool. He's always getting into trouble. He's a typical bad boy. He's always getting into trouble.

Boy, aged 12

Outside Influences

When kids watch television, they're not only looking for entertainment. They're also studying the kids, sports stars, and entertainers for fash-ions, language, and activities. Kids try on all sorts of personalities and fantasies while they go about constructing the identity they will wear in life. It's only natural for them to seek out role models. When they see a baseball player wearing a certain brand of sunglasses, they figure that that kind of sunglasses would look cool on them, too.

Arnold Schwarzenegger, for example, became a favorite of little boys, who admire his muscles, his slightly clipped accent, and his icy-cool personality. "He's a guy you'd like to have as a big brother," says one 9-year-old boy. Sports stars are another favorite. Girls adopt Olympic gymnasts like Mary Lou Retton and figure skaters like Dorothy Hamill and Kristi Yamaguchi as role models.

"Michael Jordon and Bo Jackson are my favorites," a 10-year-old boy says. "I want to be a baseball star," says an 11-year-old boy. "They get money and lots of girls."

As we said, celebrity endorsers generally cannot be used in advertising directed toward children. (We cover this subject more in Chapter 9 on advertising regulations.) Nevertheless, children see these endorsers on television, in movies, and in licensed products.

A celebrity can give a product instant validation, but it's only one of the outside forces that influence a child. Television programs, movies, videos, and advertising do also. When it clicks, a phrase can become part of the popular culture. "You got the right one, baby," "Hasta la vista, baby," "Just do it," "It's the real thing." The words become a switch that instantly create an image of the product or character behind them.

Every week, I tell my mom I want something. But she doesn't always buy it.

Boy, aged 9.

You should put it in the cart when she's not looking. Just throw it in the cart. Kool-Aid. Fruit Roll-Ups. When she gets to the cash register, she'll turn around and say, "Hey, where'd that come from?" But she never makes me take it back.

Boy, aged 10

How Do They Do It?

How do kids get what they want? Let's ask some experts—a focus group of girls conducted by Children's Market Research. "I just keep talking about it and say that all my friends have it until my parents buy it," says one girl.

"I tell them, 'I'll never ask for anything again!'" another girl says.

"I just keep asking them," says a third girl.

"You mean nag?" The girls respond with a conspiratorial smile.

Nagging, begging—the techniques are pretty basic. The most common is the war of attrition—wearing down the parent with the request until the parent throws up his or her arms and gives in to regain peace and quiet. "My brother and I wanted to go to Florida," one 11-year-old girl says. "We asked my dad. We just kept on asking. My mom wanted to go, too. We went." (See Table 3.)

Some kids prefer the divide-and-conquer method, going separately to each parent with the request in the hopes of winning an ally who will make the case for them with the other parent.

There's the fitting-in argument. All parents want their child to fit in with his or her peers; not having the right pair of sneakers, or jeans, or video-game system, the child argues, will put him or her on the outs, and who knows what the repercussions will be: long-term therapy, the life of a no-good. Horrors! And then there's the keeping-up-with-the-Joneses argument. Not buying the right label, the child argues, will bring the whole family down in the eyes of the world!

Knowing this, a marketer might consider turning out ads urging kids to nag and beg to get the desired products. It's not a smart idea. First, encouraging kids to nag their parents violates the Better Business Bureau's rules for marketing to kids (see Chapter 9 on advertising). Second, it's the kind of gratuitous behavior that makes parents regard marketers as money grubbing, exploitative villains.

Our advice, which we repeat in the pages ahead, is that if you want to have long-lasting success in this market, work on creating a product or service that kids will want, instead of pouring all your energies into *selling* dreck. If you create a good product, if you use your advertising and promotions to inform the market, and if the product offers benefits, the kids will make sure their parents know about it.

Table 3. Amount of Influence Child Has on Vacation Plans (by percent)

	Total boys and girls				
	A lot of influence	Some influence	A little influence	No influence	No answer
Activities	19.3	31.2	15.8	21.6	12.1
Destination	10.1	19.1	18.2	40.6	12.0
Restaurants visited	9.7	25.7	24.6	27.8	12.2
Selection of hotel/motel	4.8	7.8	11.6	63.7	12.1
Transportation means used	3.5	6.5	8.1	69.8	12.1

SOURCE: CMR KIDTRENDS REPORT, based on data from The Simmons Kids Study (1991).

Influence on the Toy Shelf

On what do kids exert influence? Practically everything that's part of their lives. Let's take a few minutes to survey three broad categories: toys, food, and apparel.

You'd expect kids to have a high degree of influence on toys. The numbers bear that out. Let's start with boys. Boys aged 6 to 14 who were interviewed for the CMR KIDTRENDS REPORT, based on The Simmons Kids Study, say they lobby harder for action figures than any other toy. A whopping 87 percent of boys exert influence on the brand and type of action figures that wind up in their toy collections.

The number shows the enduring play value of action figures, including G. I. Joe—Hasbro's toy soldier, who has gone from fighting World War II, to Vietnam, to terrorists since his introduction in the 1960s—licensed movie and comic-book characters like Batman and Superman, *Star Wars* movie idols, and Teenage Mutant Ninja Turtles. These types of toys do not go out of style; only the names change.

Boys exert influence on other toys as well, according to CMR KIDTRENDS REPORT, based on The Simmons Kids Study. Some three-quarters of boys exert "a little," "some," or "a lot" of influence on cars, racing sets, and trucks, branded through the years by Matchbox, Mattel, Inc.'s Hot Wheel line, and Galoob's Micromachines, among others. A comparable percentage also say they exercise influence on building sets— testimony to Lincoln Logs, Erector Sets, and, for today's generation, LEGOs. Not far behind are video games and remote-controlled cars, showing that new technologies can easily break into the must-have list of toys.

Surprisingly, toy guns, while frowned upon by grown-ups, still have a strong following. More than two-thirds of boys say they lobby for toy guns. The sentiment has created a market for "compromise products" that satisfy children's desire for the conflict and resolution guns offer but do not offend parents. Some such products have emerged—to great success. The new generation of pump-powered water guns, such as Larami Co.'s wildly successful Super Soaker, appear to be riding this wave.

What do girls lobby hardest for? Stuffed animals and dolls come in first. That's certainly reflected on toy-store shelves, where Barbie commands enormous amounts of space; collector dolls like Dakin, Inc.'s Ginny Doll have gained large followings; and a steady stream of lovable stuffed bears, dogs, cats, and even endangered species move from toy stores to toy shelves.

More than 80 percent of girls exert influence on the types of dolls and doll clothes that wind up in their toy chests. Close to three-quarters of girls, meanwhile, exert influence for arts-and-crafts products. Makeup, like toy guns among boys, has a surprisingly strong audience among girls. More than half of girls aged 6 to 14 influence the purchase of makeup. We think marketers have only begun to realize the potential for "down-aging" teenage and grown-up cosmetic brand names and products for girls.

Influence in the Supermarket

It's no surprise that kids are the "experts" in the family on the toys they play with. What marketers have not realized, until recently, is how far kids' influence extends. The CMR KIDTRENDS REPORT, based on The Simmons Kids Study, shows that kids aged 6 to 14 are very particular about the food they eat. Of those who eat cold cereal more than 78 percent of kids in that age bracket exert "some" or "a lot" of influence on the type their family buys; another 12 percent say they exercise "a little" influence; that leaves *only* 7.1 percent who exercise "no influence" on what kind of cereal winds up in their pantry. (See Table 1.) Cereal marketers know they have to talk to kids to get into the home.

In other food categories there is also a high degree of influence. Soft drinks, only rarely marketing themselves to kids, enjoy one of the highest scores of all food products whose purchase kids influence. About 2 in 3 kids exercise "some" to "a lot" of influence on cola soft drinks, for example, and a little more than 1 in 5 exert "a little."

Fifty-seven percent of kids also exercise "some" to "a lot" of influence on activity drinks and "thirst quenchers." That means two things. First, Hi-C and Kool-Aid, both big advertisers in kids programming, have created a following. Second, we think it's an indication that Gatorade, which has inched into marketing to moms, would probably meet a receptive audience if it spoke more directly to kids—and that one of the many high-powered competitors to Gatorade that have sprung up could pose a threat to the brand by taking its case to kids.

Snacks and treats also get a big share of voice from kids at lobbying time. More than half of kids say they exert "some" to "a lot of" influence on chips, Fruit Roll-Ups, frozen desserts, and snack pies.

And Beyond...

So which do you think kids would care the most about: the building sets they play with, the kind of cereal they eat, or the kind of sneaker they put on their feet? You probably guessed wrong. Sneakers are the clear winner. A CMR KIDTRENDS REPORT, based on The Simmons Kids Study, shows that more than 80 percent of kids say they exert "some" or "a lot" of influence over the kinds of sneakers they wear, and another 11 percent say they exercise "a little" influence.

In fact, according to the KIDTRENDS REPORT, based on The Simmons Kids Study, kids aged 6 to 14 care a lot about the brands and styles of clothes they wear. Some 78 percent say they exercise "some" to "a lot" of influence over the kinds of jeans they wear, 77 percent say they lobby "some" to "a lot" on casual pants, and 72 percent lobby "some" to "a lot" on sweats. We don't expect this influence to diminish. Many of the brand names and styles that have created phenomenon among teens and grown-ups—such as NIKE's and Reebok's highly stylized basketball shoes, The Gap's back-to-basics fashions, Levi's jeans, and neon colors—have migrated quickly down to the playground set. Kids always look up to teens and grown-ups for role models.

Toys, food, and clothes are the basics. But kids' influence can be seen in other categories. Two-thirds of kids in CMR KIDTRENDS REPORT, based on The Simmons Kids Study, said they exert "some" to "a lot" of influence on the family's choice of restaurants (Table 4). "We take turns," one 11-year-old girl told a Children's Market Research focus group. "Sometimes my mom and dad decide. Sometimes I do. I like Red Lobster. I also like Italian food." In a national survey of 1000 children aged 6 to 14, 47.4 percent of kids told Children's Market Research that they had influenced their family's vacation destination. (See Table 3.) As we note in an upcoming chapter on boys and girls, many kids exert influence over consumer electronics purchases, from calculators and computers to getting their own phone.

Polaroid's "Snap" Thinking

Instant photography is something adults have grown used to. But Polaroid Corp. realized it held a special appeal for children. Kids generally love having their pictures taken. They get to smile, goof off, make funny faces, or vamp like movie stars. The person with the camera can be the center of attention—particularly with a Polaroid because of the instant gratification of a photo's popping out of the camera and developing before everyone's eyes. "Having a camera makes a kid more interesting to the kids around him or her," a Polaroid executive says.

Most kids don't have access to a video camera. But, with a little streamlining, Polaroid realized, the cost of an instant camera could easily be brought down enough to make it an affordable present for a child. Polaroid dubbed the resulting camera, priced at $69, the Cool Cam. The company invited kids' input on the colors and packaging. The kids

Table 4. Amount of Influence Child Has on the Type of Restaurant Family Visits

(by percent)

Fast Food and Drive-In Restaurant			
	Total	Boys	Girls
A lot of influence	32.2	29.0	35.6
Some influence	35.3	36.5	34.0
A little influence	17.4	17.1	17.7
No influence	9.2	11.0	7.3
Did not visit in last 30 days	5.9	6.4	5.4
Family Restaurants and Steak Houses			
	Total	Boys	Girls
A lot of influence	11.4	9.8	13.0
Some influence	21.6	21.4	21.8
A little influence	18.6	18.3	18.9
No influence	18.6	20.6	16.5
Did not visit in last 30 days	29.8	29.9	29.8

SOURCE: CMR KIDTRENDS REPORT, based on data from The Simmons Kids Study (1991).

chose red and black, and pink and gray as the colors. And, at the kids' request, the company packaged the camera with sunglasses.

Goodby, Berlin & Silverstein, the company's ad agency, took the concept of empowerment a step farther by creating an ad campaign that invited kids to make their own commercials for the Cool Cam. The ad agency set up a contest for kids to come to designated locations (usually shopping malls) to shoot their entries. The winners of the contest were run on a national cable-TV campaign to promote the Cool Cam.

"Fish," the winning entry from a 14-year-old from Manassas, Virginia, was about a fish looking out a fishbowl at the kids in his house. "The only thing cool about these nerds is that they have a Cool Cam!" sneered the fish.

Whether it was the idea of control, the immediate gratification of instant photography, the notion of kids-produced ads for a kids' camera, or some other fact is probably not important. The bottom line is that Cool Cam's first-year sales exceeded Polaroid's projections by 30 percent.

My parents complain if my shoes don't look nice. So they go out and buy me a new pair. She says, "I don't want you walking around school with old sneakers on."

                                                       Girl, aged 11

Parent-Led Purchases

The caricature of pleading children and soft parents underestimates the power of parents. In most cases, parents set the parameters for their kids' choices. What the child "chooses," then, usually has the parents' implicit blessing at least. This is important for marketers to take into consideration. Parents are part of the purchase decision, particularly for items such as bicycles, skateboards, sneakers, and video games that are out of reach of a child's allowance.

Parents are generally satisfied with the products and services they buy for their children, according to research by the Roper Organization. About 9 in 10 parents say they are satisfied with the children's books on the market. Eight in ten express satisfaction with the toys, games, sports equipment, restaurants, and family vacation choices available to them.

The major areas in which there is dissatisfaction are video games and television programming. About 1 in 2 parents said they were unhappy with video games on the market, and 4 in 10 didn't like the networks' offerings for family programming. If video game companies and television programmers really want to maintain their respective sales growth and audience levels, they should ask parents what they want.

What they'd find is that parents want the media to do more to involve and educate children, Roper says. Parents want entertainment to go hand in hand with learning. The majority don't want their kids to just sit back and relax.

Part of the appeal to parents in Club Med's efforts to attract families is that the resorts offer activities like sports lessons, clown classes, and arts and crafts to pull kids away from the boob tube.

The explosion in children's books, for which parents have a high degree of satisfaction, shows how potent a force a motivated parent can be. In the 5 years between 1980 and 1985, children's book sales doubled. Between 1985 and 1990, they doubled *again*.

Sometimes a child can introduce a product into the house that the rest of the family will want to buy. We know a family, for instance, in which a son purchased an electric guitar. The father was a little interested when the guitar came into the house. Then the father got a little more interested. Before long, the dad had invested in an instrument and a sound system of his own, and the two were filling the house with music.

The Bible Goes Video

Parents' desire to educate their kids and instill values and traditions has created enormous demand for products that can directly or indirectly fill that need. Even the Bible is being packaged to meet contemporary needs. Hanna-Barbera's founder Joe Barbera, a devout Christian, led Hanna-Barbera to come out with a series of children's videos putting Noah's ark, the story of Moses, the Christmas story, and other Bible stories to animation.

Paulist Press says sales of children's religious titles has increased 50 percent in 3 years. Doubleday has published illustrated versions of Bible stories. Dover has come out with a pop-up Bible. Antioch Publishing of Yellow Springs, Ohio, created a line of miniature books called the Little Treasure series, which pair Bible stories with little keepsakes.

Allison Gallup, associate editor of the Princeton Religion Research Center, says the books and videos fill a need for today's parents. With the pressures of two-income households, many families don't make it out to church on Sunday morning. Church attendance, to be sure, has been level at 41 to 42 percent for the past 20 years, although church membership has slipped from 73 percent to 69 percent since the 1960s. Still, the vast majority of Americans continue to say they have strong spiritual feelings. As much as 75 percent of adult Americans say they have "a commitment" to Christianity, up from 60 percent in 1980. Organized religion may not be as strong as it was in the 1960s, but "individual spiritual experience" is rising, Gallup says. "Americans have more of a private faith than an organizational faith today."

When Joe Barbera suggested putting the Bible on video, "the typical response was 'The Bible?!'" says Wendy Moss, senior vice president and general manager for Hanna-Barbera Home Video. "'Why would that work?' People said, 'It's not a licensed product, like the Care Bears or Transformers.'" As it turned out, Barbera was in touch with the market. Hanna-Barbera has gone on to sell more than 2 million copies of *The Greatest Adventure*, a series of Bible stories, at $14.95. Distribution has expanded from direct mail and religious bookstores to general-interest book stores and consumer-sensitive mass marketers like Wal-Mart and K mart. "It's a nice way to learn about the Bible in a creative way," says Moss. "I guess you could call it a starter kit."

Grandparents

The generation that nurtured today's baby boomer parents through Barbie, Howdy Doodie, Duncan yo-yos, and the other products representative of the first real explosion in children's products are today's grandparents. They are taking an active interest in their grandchildren.

Benefiting from their mortgages being paid off and the investment income and pension distributions flowing from the fruits of their labors in the workplace during the golden years of the 1950s and 1960s, they have the discretionary income to buy things for their grandchildren.

There are about 50 million grandparents. According to some estimates, a quarter of toy purchases are by grandparents. Grandparents tend to be less price conscious than parents. Although most children do not press their grandparents as aggressively as they do their parents, most grandparents listen closely to the kids' requests.

Summing Up

1. Children exercise a surprising degree of influence on purchase decisions, on both products that they are the primary consumers of and those that are used by the whole family.

2. Statistics bear out children's interest in influencing purchase decisions. Of those that eat cold cereal more than 83.6 percent of kids aged 6 to 14 say they exercise "a little," "some," or "a lot" of influence over what kind their family buys.

3. Perhaps the biggest task kids have as they grow up is defining themselves. Making choices and influencing choices are part of that process.

4. Influence usually comes from peer groups or from outside influences, such as television or movies. Some marketers try to shortcut the traditional, time-consuming brand-building methods of mass marketing by trying to align themselves with the early adopters who are the trendsetters for other kids.

5. Parents lead purchases on some decisions and play a role in others. It is important to gauge whether you should be addressing both parents and children.

3

Talking to the Market

Focus Groups

Pop Quiz (True or False)

1. A good market researcher never lets kids horse around in focus groups.

2. It's important to make children sit around a conference table, to communicate to them the seriousness of the event.

3. Smart marketers use the same kids over and over for focus groups. It saves time and money.

4. A box of crayons and a drawing pad can help children express thoughts and feelings they cannot express with words.

5. Asking kids to vote on a product or advertisement by secret ballot can protect a researcher against the possibility that one child will dominate a group.

Answers: 1. false; 2. false; 3. false; 4. true; 5. true.

And the Children Shall Lead

The notion that children should be seen and not heard may have made for proper Victorian etiquette, but it's a formula for failure in marketing. If you take the time to listen to children, you can come away with a terrific and original new product idea, product positioning, or advertising

38

campaign. Keebler Co., wowed at kids' love affair with pizza, for example, set its elves to work to create a snack chip based on pizza dough with authentic pizza toppings like cheese, pepperoni, and green pepper.

Pizzarias, the resulting product, rang up $75 million in first-year sales and won an Edison Award for new-product innovation from the American Marketing Association. Heinz discovered that young people eat one-third more catsup than adults and, quite frequently, pick the brand of catsup their family uses. The company redirected its ads, with executions featuring teenagers, and sales went up 2 percent.

There are all kinds of ways for companies to talk to kids. Levi Strauss & Co. once sent a team of market researchers to poke around in children's closets. The jeanswear giant was sure that the clothes, toys, athletic gear, and miscellaneous odds and ends the modern-day Margaret Meads found would give the company insights into the purchase decisions kids make in blue jeans. Other marketers have followed kids when they go on shopping trips with their parents to department stores, have tracked children down at swimming pools, and interviewed them in fast-food restaurants.

But the most popular form of market research is the focus group. In it, a moderator interviews six to eight children, while the marketer watches from an adjacent room with the aid of a two-way mirror. Done right, a focus group can yield insights on a full spectrum of issues, from brand preferences, to lifestyle patterns, likes and dislikes, reactions to advertisements, and comparisons of competitive products.

Focus groups are undertaken before launching new products, creating new advertising campaigns or promotions, or changing the positioning strategy for an existing product. Many times they are the basis for more extensive, quantitative research studies of 150 to 2000 or more children. Focus groups can give you a general impression of how kids feel. They also can turn up pearls of wisdom.

video programming ?

The Birth of a Blue Jeans Ad

Sifting through the comments that kids make, marketers have turned up many surprises. Levi Strauss and its ad agency, Foote, Cone & Belding, once noticed that the children they talked to always seemed to classify themselves according to their favorite pastime. "I do all kinds of things," a typical child would say. "I play sports. I have different interests. But what I really love is skateboarding. That's me. That's what I do."

The insight led to "Wild Creatures," a rib-tickling series of kinetic, hip television commercials that "announced" the discovery of new species of kids, with the stylized photography and breathless language of TV nature programs. (See Figure 2.) The ads were unlike anything else on television. One spot featured Slimus Pursuitus, a species of kids that collects worms, bugs, and other things slimy, icky, and yucky. Hoopis Alley-Oopus examined basketball fanatics. Zoomis Skatis was about skateboard freaks. (See Figure 3.) Hippis Hoppus Rappionus focused on youths who love rap music. The groups were connected to each other by one thing: their devotion to pursuing their youthful preoccupations in Levi's jeans.

If it sounds like the jeans maker and the ad agency had fun, it's because they did. There's an infectious energy that comes from talking to kids. Many marketers talk about getting a high talking to kids. The reason is simple. Kids are fun to talk to. They don't have the pretenses and worldliness of grown-ups. They're not uptight. And, given the chance, they will dazzle you with an honesty, charm, and insight that adults could never anticipate.

> *Is this orange juice the real thing or the cheap kind?*
> Boy, aged 11

"You always get wonderful, surprising things when you talk to kids," says Tim Price, the creative director on the "Wild Creatures" campaign for Levi's youth wear. "They're just fantastic." Many times, Price says, kids will reveal a degree of subtlety that grown-ups in their day-to-day life could never guess exists. "Wild Creatures" speaks to one such wrinkle: "Kids want to be accepted and be part of a group," Price says, "but they want to be individuals, too." So, they form groups that will express their own individual uniqueness.

Starting Out

You don't get those kinds of insights from sitting down with a group of your grown-up colleagues over a cup of coffee in the conference room. Adults don't know the language of children. They don't understand kids' motivations. They don't know how toys, sneakers, games, snacks, and cereals—much less individual brands—fit into a child's lifestyle.

Marketers need a liaison to the world of kids. Market research is intended to fill this void.

Research has not been given the priority it deserves in children's products and services. Marketers who are new to dealing with children's products often think they can get away without it. Many times Children's Market Research is called in to unravel what went wrong

Figure 2. Levi Strauss found in research that kids identify themselves by the activities they enjoy. So it created a whimsical ad campaign describing pseudo-anthropological subgroups like "Horrorflickus Addictus"—a creature that "dwells principally in darkened movie theaters" in the company of bats, "man-eating slime," and aliens. (Courtesy of Levi Strauss & Co.)

Figure 3. Other "subspecies" of kids "discovered" in the Levi's campaign ranged from skateboard enthusiasts to basketball fanatics, video game lovers, gadget freaks, and creepy-crawler fans. The hook, of course, is that each pursues its beloved activity in Levi blue jeans. (Courtesy of Levi Strauss & Co.)

when, not surprisingly, it is the unresearched approach that doesn't work. For example, Children's Market Research was recently called on to design a study on a food product for a major packaged-goods corporation. The product had been marketed primarily to mothers. The company had taken a stab at advertising on Saturday morning cartoons, but it wasn't registering. The company hadn't done its homework. "What do I do to reach kids?" the brand manager asked in frustration.

Many marketers are intimidated by children. They react to them like the uncle or aunt who breaks out in a cold sweat at the prospect of entertaining his or her precocious niece or nephew on a Saturday afternoon. "Kids don't express themselves verbally," some marketers moan. "Kids are fickle," say other executives. "You never know when they'll change their mind. You're better off guessing."

Children communicate in play, activities, fantasies, and images. Words are only one of many ways they communicate. What they say with words, moreover, is very often not what they feel but what they think the adult they are talking to wants to hear. That doesn't mean you shouldn't talk to children. It just means you must observe their behavior and interaction with other kids. With kids, actions truly do speak louder than words.

Undertaking market research with children not only requires skill in framing questions, analyzing responses, and utilizing the other tools of the trade. Market researchers are selected on the basis of experience and reputation. Generally, a company will interview two to three researchers and choose the one who is most appropriate to the project. The researcher will then prepare a written proposal. The document describes what the rsearcher is going to cover and how much the project will cost. The researcher will spell out the objectives of the project and the methods to be used.

A good market researcher must be comfortable with children. Kids goof off, make noise, or sometimes laugh so hard they fall off their chairs. That's OK; it's what kids do. Adult values, interests, and thought processes can't be distilled down into a kids-sized questionnaire. Kids inhabit a different world. They take spontaneity seriously. Marketers who venture into their world shouldn't squelch that—it's in those wonderful, spontaneous moments that smart marketers make the most amazing discoveries.

I have expensive tastes. I pay about $40 or $50 for my sneakers... like Reeboks, Keds, and L.A. Gear.

Girl, aged 12

The Ground Rules

Ages

The most common mistake companies make is to think all kids are alike. "After all, there's not much difference between people who are 45 to 54 years old," they say. "How much difference can there be between 6-year-olds and 10-year-olds?" Spend an afternoon looking at a playground at recess time, and you know the answer is "a lot." Companies don't realize that if they show 6-year-olds in advertising, the 8-year-olds who are watching will tune out. "Too babyish," they say.

Before you start, you should decide exactly who you want to study in your focus groups. It's important to talk to kids of different ages. Older kids will often feel differently about an issue you raise than younger ones; 6-year-olds live in a very different world from 4-year-olds. Physically, they're more capable. They're more mature emotionally. And, having entered the world of school, they're more adept socially.

Children's Market Research does most of its focus groups with kids aged 6 and up. It is very hard to conduct focus groups with 2-, 3-, and 4-year-olds. If the nature of a product or service requires Children's Market Research to talk to kids that young, we often will encourage them to bring a friend. "Friendship pairs" can help a child open up and feel more comfortable. An alternative is to hold minigroups of three kids. Little ones will feel more at ease in a smaller group.

Kids should be grouped with kids of similar ages. For example, 6- and 7-year-olds should be put in one focus group, with 8- and 9-year-olds in another, 10- and 11-year-olds in another, and so on. A 6-year-old will always defer to a 10-year-old. Keeping children with peers of their age will ensure they will be more open and spontaneous.

Sexes

Just as 6- and 10-year-olds will have different things to say in a group, boys and girls will offer different insights and observations. Because of this, market research tends to follow a rule of separation of the sexes.

Whether it's in the classroom, on the soccer field, or in a social setting, boys tend to be more active than girls. Focus groups are no different. Boys kid around. They fall under the table. They roll around on the floor. They cackle. They shout. They horse around.

Girls, in comparison, are more reserved. If you have boys and girls together in a focus group, the boys will dominate. The girls will giggle, while the boys act out. Alternatively, the girls will sit back and look with disdain on the boys' boorish behavior. Either way, you get a distorted view.

The Suburbs Are the Middle Ground

The major point is to keep a group as homogeneous as possible. This puts the children at ease and gives you true, honest responses. For that reason, suburbs are the most popular site for focus groups. In cities you generally find greater extremes of lifestyle, attitudes, incomes, and wealth. As a result, a random selection of children easily could produce a focus group of kids who are not familiar with each other and, as a result, would not be as comfortable or talk as freely as you would wish.

This is not really a matter of race as much as income. Because suburbs are relatively self-selected communities, people of different race are generally united by a common set of values—belief in education and community, for example. The suburbs are homogeneous. When you bring suburban children together to talk about a product in your focus group, they'll be less distracted by each other and more likely to focus their attention on the marketing questions you want to ask them.

In addition, suburbs are pretty similar from one part of the United States to another. The same basic set of attractions—schools, community, greenery, security—draws people to the suburbs in one geographic region as in another. For market research purposes, that means you'll get a fairly projectable cross section. You can match income and lifestyle characteristics to produce an apples-to-apples comparison of how kids in different markets will respond to your idea.

Suburbs also have a built-in magnet—the shopping mall. Families naturally gravitate to the mall on weekends to buy school clothes, pick out a gift for an upcoming birthday, people watch, and so forth. In addition, many malls are equipped with focus-group rooms for market-research purposes.

> *My mom pays for my clothes, but I pick them out.*
>
>   Girl, aged 11

Setting Up

Your first job is to decide whom your target is. Do you want mainstream, middle-income kids? Some products or services might be more upscale. Is it for boys? Girls? Both? Market researchers normally recruit 10 kids to ensure they will wind up with 6 or 8 in their focus groups. If the product is to be marketed nationally, it's wise to conduct focus groups in different geographic regions. Tastes can vary in the

Northeast, the Midwest, the South, and the West Coast. Costs vary somewhat, but $2500 to $3200 per focus group is a good rule of thumb. Participants are given a fee of about $35 to $40 to reward them for the time and effort they took to attend.

Participants in focus groups are recruited through companies that specialize in arranging and hosting focus-group sessions. The researcher contacts the facility and outlines the number and kinds of kids he or she is looking for, by age, sex, household characteristics, and so forth. The facility is responsible for contacting, screening, and recruiting the subjects.

You can find focus-group facilities (as well as market researchers) through the *International Directory of Marketing Research Companies and Services*, known popularly in the industry as "The Green Book." The directory is published by the New York Chapter of the American Marketing Association (310 Madison Ave., New York, NY 10017. For information: (212) 794-0983).

It's important to check out the facility to make sure it does not use the same children over and over. You want virgin respondents. Why? Many times a child who has been in a focus group before will be influenced by his or her prior experience. He or she will be savvy. The child will anticipate what the focus-group moderator wants and offer that up instead of his or her own opinion. Needless to say, that distorts your results.

The Work Environment

The setting should be warm and friendly. Most focus-group rooms have a big conference table. Children's Market Research normally pushes the table to the side of the room. That way the kids can sit on the floor, as they do when they're in the comfort of their rooms. And they need plenty of room so they can role-play, play games, and move about freely. (See Figure 4.)

Sometimes, they'll sit on chairs. If they do sit on the floor, the moderator will sit on the floor, too. It's a small thing, but it communicates to the kids that the moderator is part of the group and not an authority figure, like a teacher or parent. You want kids to be free to say things they may not say around parents or teachers. You want to have a moderator who can come down to the kids' level—both literally and figuratively.

> *I like running up and down the aisle of the supermarket with the shopping cart.*
>
>   Boy, aged 11

Figure 4. The key to a successful focus group is putting the children at ease, so they will talk freely and openly. That can mean sitting in a circle, instead of around a table, encouraging each child to talk, or having children draw or play act. Selina Guber is the group moderator.

The Warm-Up

Children's Market Research opens up with a warm-up of about five minutes. The moderator goes around the room and asks a question to help the kids relax and encourages them to talk openly and freely about themselves. The moderator then talks a little about himself or herself and about why they are all there today.

At the outset it's important to assure the children that their opinions are very important. "This is how we get our information to make products and advertisements that appear on television," the moderator may say. "There are no right or wrong answers. We want to know what you think."

If it's Christmas or Hanukkah, the moderator might loosen up the group by talking about the holidays. "What's happening at your house?" "What presents do you want?" If the kids just came from school, you might ask what they did at school that was fun today. If you're trying to get opinions on a snack food, you might ask them what they did after school. Did they watch TV? Did they have something to eat? Milk and cookies? Chips? That can then lead you into a discussion of what snack foods they like and what they think of particular brands. The goal throughout is to make it as spontaneous as possible.

Younger children often start out with more physical activities. With 5- and 6-year-olds, for example, you might sit them in a circle and play a game like duck-duck-goose. Then you might do a march. Let them burn off a little physical energy, and then you can get down to work. And everyone has some fun.

> *When my father shops, my mom wants me to go along*
> *so he will get what she wants.*
>   Boy, aged 8

Drawing Pictures

One way to keep things fun and get work done as the session proceeds is for the moderator to ask the kids to draw pictures of the subject he or she is talking about. Drawings can be invaluable tools for market researchers. First and foremost, the use of pictures ensures that each child will at least start out with an independent opinion.

That's important. There will always be one or two dominant members in any group. Pictures can dilute their influence. Using pictures is not the only way to get opinions on the record. You can have kids write down their views on secret ballots. One marketer recently told Children's Market Research that he wished he could do secret votes with grown-ups, too!

Drawings do more than get kids on the record. They offer a window into feelings that kids may not have the words to express. Psychologists refer to this as a projective technique. "Can you draw how you feel about the product?" the moderator might ask. "Draw a picture of a person who might use the product or the family that has the product." We've seen kids draw rainbows around products. We've seen lots of pictures of happy family members sitting at a dinner table with a great, big box of the product in the middle of the happy scene.

Drawings are a projection of the child's emotions. From looking at the position of the images on the page, the number of people in the scene, the use of colors, and other elements, an experienced market researcher can sift the emotions and thoughts a product or service elicits.

CMR once saw a child draw a picture of the product's being dumped into a trash can. This sort of reaction can be upsetting, but it can and does happen. Marketers often go into a focus group determined to prove themselves right. Focus groups aren't done to champion causes. They are a real-world test of the idea you have nurtured in meetings in your company.

Play Acting

Children have boundless energy and limitless imaginations. The clever moderator will harness those resources in the focus group. A moderator may, for example, ask the children to playact a child describing the product to a friend on an imaginary telephone. A moderator may ask the children to role-play what it's like to go buy the product, with one child as the consumer, another the store manager, and another the marketer from the company. Alternatively, a moderator may have children act out going to "a store" that has been set up with different products and ask them to pick out the one they like best and explain why.

The moderator might ask one child to play himself or herself and another child to assume the role of the child's mother. The activity lets kids act out how moms react when children ask them to buy a product. The result is often cascades of giggles, particularly if it's a product kids love and parents disapprove of. Often a child will articulate feelings when they can act them out that they wouldn't express directly. Kids love to put themselves into their parents' shoes.

> *When we rent a video, we get a big pizza, put a blanket down, and eat pizza when we watch the movie.*
>
> Girl, aged 12

The Discussion Guide

What has transpired looks spontaneous, but the moderator has been following a careful script all along. If it's a focus group on a cheese snack, the moderator will not bring out the product until everyone has had a good opportunity to talk about snacks and cheese. The point is to prod the children to verbalize their feelings, build up anticipation, and then see what the reaction is.

Discussion guides cover the relevant areas the moderator will cover. They are the outlines for how the moderator will probe the dynamics of the product or service on the child's life, what experiences the child has had with the product or service, how the product or service fits into the child's life: what the child likes and dislikes about the product or service, and why he or she likes or dislikes those things. Use of a discussion guide helps to focus on individual brands and their qualities, the impact of advertising and promotions, and the factors that enter into the choice of the brand.

Are there any points of leverage that differentiate the product that have not been brought to bear in the past? Are there any things that have not been done that would make sense? With children, the bottom line is exactly how much influence they have in the purchase of a product or service and how that influence is exercised.

The fun and games serve to loosen up the kids and, at the same time, elicit answers to the questions the business wants and needs to know.

The Process

You only have about an hour to an hour and a half for your focus group, so you can't load it down. It's crucial to stay with one or two important goals you want to accomplish. Sometimes the nature of the focus group is purely exploratory. But, even then, you have to be careful not to pack too much information into one session. You need to keep in mind what questions will bring out the marketing implications.

Frame the questions in a simple way. Kids don't really relate to the nuances of adult language. You should be clear and direct. Talk kid talk. That doesn't mean trying to sound trendy or "fresh"—or, worse still, talking down to kids. It just means using words kids understand. "What do you like about the product?" "What don't you like about it?"

If you ask kids to rate a product, don't ask them to do it on a scale of 1 to 10. Make it a scale of 1 to 3, or 1 to 5.

A good moderator will use humor a lot. Kids, after all, relate to each other with humor. If a child is being shy, the moderator will softly encourage him or her to open up, for example, about a drawing. Never assume quiet children have nothing to say. They often have a lot to say. The moderator should create an atmosphere that will encourage them to open up.

Likewise, if one child starts to dominate, the moderator should try to use subtle diplomacy to soften him or her. The dominant child can be "promoted" to an assistant, who is "responsible" for helping to draw out the others.

Kids tend to be very enthusiastic, so the moderator might have to play devil's advocate. For the most part, kids will try to please. So, if you get a totally unanimous "great!" you might prod them. "This can't be that great." "Are you sure?" Make them argue their point. Sometimes it will strengthen their position. Many times it will flush out the real issues.

I paid $175 for my skateboard. I'm talking complete.
My mom put it on layaway from my dad's paycheck.

Boy, aged 11

Analyzing the Results

Everything in focus groups is recorded on an audiotape. If possible, you should use a videotape as well. Sometimes you can hear a kid say on an audiotape, "Yeah, I love it," but when you see everyone's faces, you'll see one or two kids recoiling in disgust. Obviously they don't love it. Remember, gestures and expressions can be as important as words. Kids are expressive and action-oriented. A videotape will tell you how enthusiastic they really are.

The tape should be fully transcribed. (Very often, they're not. That is a mistake. Sometimes the most valuable insight you dig up is in the type of words a child uses. Some things are never noticed the first time through.) At Children's Market Research, if we're following an outline, we want to know each child's snacking habits. So we'll select the taped conclusions from each group about their favorite snacks, followed by what brands they like, their reaction to advertising, and so forth. If there are important regional differences, they will be broken out. The same applies to age groups, sexes, and so forth.

Very often, to elaborate on what they have found in talking to kids, researchers will recommend that marketers interview mothers of children of a comparable age in separate focus groups. Their comments will be compared and contrasted with those made in the first focus group.

Look for the nuances. Simple yeses and noes don't tell you much. What are the reasons behind the stands the kids take? Just saying they don't like gray or green on the package leaves you hanging. You want to get at the underlying feelings. "I don't like gray," one child once said in a focus group, "because it reminds me of a gray day."

---

*I vacuum the upstairs and sometimes the downstairs
and feed my doggie.*

　　　　　　　　　　　　　　　　　　Girl, aged 6

The Management Report

Watching kids express their thoughts and feelings in a focus group can be an exhilarating experience. With all their excitement, your mind races with ideas. Keeping track of all the things the kids say and sifting out the bottom-line conclusions is enough to make your head spin.

Fortunately, you don't have to rely on what you retain in your mind's eye. After conducting the research, the market researcher should compile the results in a management report. This document puts on record the answers to all the questions you started out with: how your target market feels about your product; how much they use the product; who actually buys it; how it's purchased; and how the product, the company, and the advertising promotions are perceived.

Most importantly, the report summarizes the marketing implications. Do kids think this new product is a good idea? Do they find the advertising persuasive? Should everyone go back to the drawing board and start over again?

A summary begins the management report. It details the basic findings. The summary is followed by pages of verbatim quotations from the kids. Many managers don't look at them. That is a mistake. As you've seen from reading them in this chapter, the actual words the kids say can be the most fun part of the project.

A Word of Caution

As we said at the outset, focus groups will give you a basic sense of how kids should react to a product or service, an ad campaign, or a sales promotion. You'll get a sense of the language kids use to describe your product. You'll learn a little about a lot of things, but you won't get results that are statistically representative of all children. You'll have the opinions and attitudes of, say, 32 kids—that is, four groups of 8 kids in each—a very small sample.

If you want to end up with a projectable opinion, you should move onto a quantitative study. Many companies use focus groups as a starting point for surveys of 150 to 1000 or more kids. The focus groups can clarify the issues you will address in the larger study; that is, they give focus to the issues. We discuss quantitative research in more depth in the next chapter.

> *My mom makes me do my homework first. Then I can play Nintendo.*
>
> Boy, aged 11

One-on-Ones

Individual in-depth interviews with children, called one-on-ones, are used when a researcher wants to probe each child's response in detail.

The sample size is usually 10 to 30 children with each interview lasting an average of 30 minutes.

While this method lacks the spontaneity and benefits of group interaction, there are studies in which an in-depth understanding of each child's responses is important. The decision to conduct focus groups or one-on-ones is based upon the nature of the study. In some studies both methods are applied.

As in focus groups, it's important to start with a list of questions you want answered. But don't be afraid to take a detour down a road that the child is interested in talking about and that you find fascinating. Just make sure it's relevant to your research—and make sure you get your other questions answered, too.

I like to sneak things into the grocery cart, like hair spray, potato chips, pretzels, and candy.

Girl, aged 11

Anthropological Alternatives

According to one of the clichés of marketing, some of the best ideas come from "mother-in-law research." That refers to what you see your mother-in-law, child, pal, or neighbor doing. Although market research hasn't yet institutionalized the mother-in-law, it has gone down some exotic paths in recent years in the quest for new ideas.

Swimming pools, baseball diamonds, shopping malls, and grocery stores are just some of the spots Children's Market Research has gone to interview kids. Recently, CMR suggested to a breakfast cereal marketer that interviewers stand in discreet locations in supermarkets to observe and question parents and kids as they came to the cereal aisle.

By observing people in the so-called native environment, you sometimes pick up things that may not come across in the structured environment of a focus group. When shopping carts wheeled down the cereal aisle, for example, kids would break away from mom or dad and make a beeline for a specific brand. Sometimes it was their long-standing favorite. Other kids went for the prize inside that was advertised on the side of the box.

Most of the parents gave in immediately. Only one flat out stood her ground and ordered her child to march back to the display, put back the sugar-coated cereal, and come back with the raisin bran instead. Several mothers adopted bargaining stances: "You can have the sugar-coated cereal," they'd say, "if you'll get this healthier one and eat it some mornings." Or, "OK, but we're going to buy raisins for you to eat in your lunch this week instead of cookies." The interactions—the negotiations, crocodile tears and all—brought to life the tradeoffs parents make to get their offspring food that is good for them—and food they'll eat.

Early in the 1980s, Levi Strauss noticed anecdotally that little boys were becoming more fashion conscious. They were ripping their jeans like teenagers did, wearing their jeans baggy—or tight, and topping them off with Hawaiian shirts or oversized T-shirts and accessories like friendship bracelets and porkpie hats. The insight led to a series of commercials that showed kids talking about how they like to wear their jeans. To refine the idea, the jeans maker's researchers sought out permission from a handful of families to peek into boys' closets to see what kind of clothes they had and what other possessions defined their lifestyle.

A few years later, Levi built on another research-born insight (noted in the opening pages of this chapter) to create its "Wild Creatures" ad campaign. In 1991, curious to see just how kids make the purchases they do, Levi gained permission from a handful of parents to observe when they went out with their kids on shopping trips. What the researchers found confirmed their gut feeling. Kids, in fact, were making the decisions on the brand and style of clothes they wore. The parent wasn't irrelevant, however. The child would turn to him or her for approval of the clothes the child picked out.

Summing Up

Questions to Consider

Are you undertaking a focus group? Before you start, make sure you can answer these questions:

1. What questions do you want answered in your research?

2. Describe all that you can about exactly whom it is you want to reach, by age, sex, household type, region, and everything else you can think of.

3. Is the market researcher/moderator you are working with comfortable and experienced in talking with kids?

4. Exactly where are you going to find these kids—focus-group facilities, shopping malls, or supermarkets?

5. What tools can you use to make sure the kids will feel at ease and express their true feelings? Can you ask them to make drawings, vote by secret ballots, or do special activities?

6. Have you gathered enough information for your research so that the results can be acted upon? What do you want in your final report? What is your bottom-line goal?

4

Surveying the Landscape

Quantitative Research

Pop Quiz (True or False)

1. To get a statistically representative sampling, you need to interview 3000 kids.

2. It's a good idea to let Mom or Dad sit in while you interview a child for a research study to ensure you get the right answer.

3. Market researchers have created various gimmicks to help keep kids involved, such as asking them to choose between smiling faces and frowning faces, or sorting cards into boxes.

4. When asking grown-ups to rate a product, it's common to use a scale of 1 to 10; because kids are less sophisticated, they're usually asked to make ratings on a scale of 1 to 5 or less.

5. As in focus groups, it's a good idea to let kids sit on the floor, play games, and do other things to feel as comfortable as possible.

Answers: 1. false; 2. false; 3. true; 4. true; 5. false.

Why Do Quantitative Research?

As we said in the last chapter, focus groups will give you the basics about how kids will react to a new product or service, line extension, a name, an ad campaign, or a sales promotion. You might get a general sense of what kids think of your product and maybe the words they use to describe it. You might get their gut reactions, but it's limited. Even if you've done an intensive round of focus groups, you've still talked to only 30 or 40 kids. With close to 30 million kids aged 6 to 14 in the United States, you can hardly go to the bank with conclusions you have drawn from that few kids. If you're making a money decision—particularly on the introduction of a new product—you should add to your base of knowledge with quantitative research.

Quantitative research gives you just that: quantity. Through a market-research firm, you will survey a large number of children to find out what a segment of the population thinks of your idea. Quantitative research studies vary in size. They start as small as 150 kids, and go up as high as 2000 children. The size of the study is usually subject to the project needs, regional variations, age differences, and, of course, cost to the client.

Obviously, the larger the study, the more representative your results will be. If you interview 300 to 400 kids, you will have a margin of error of 3 to 5 percent. That is, you can be confident of being 95 percent accurate in your conclusions if you interview 300 kids. The conclusions from a larger sample will have a lower margin of error.

What Quantitative Research Can Tell You

Marketers use quantitative research for a variety of tasks. A quantitative study can be used to check the assumptions you have developed internally and tested in focus groups on the wisdom of the new-product decisions, line extensions, or product names you have chosen. It can further be used to see whether kids get the basic product points you are making in your advertising and whether they will respond to a new marketing promotion program.

Quantitative research can also work in reverse, bringing in information to spark new ideas within your product group. Marketers often use quantitative research to learn what activities kids are interested in; what brands they use; whose advertising they remember; what music, programs, and sports they like; how they feel about their parents and families; where they like to go on vacation; and what their feelings are about other lifestyle issues.

You can use that information to identify areas that will offer you opportunities for new products. You can use it as a starting point for deciding how you will position a new product or reposition an old one.

And you can use it to get ideas for what kind of setting to use for your ad—California surfer beach, major league baseball stadium, classroom, the mall, what colors you should use, what kinds of words to use, and what lifestyle cues to put in the ad.

Advertising copywriters and art directors often bristle at quantitative research, saying it stifles creativity. To some extent they have a point. However, as a marketer you have to be thinking foremost about the effectiveness of the marketing dollars you are investing. Therefore, it is wise for an advertiser to invest in up-front research prior to launching a new product or advertising campaign that might miss the mark and cost millions of dollars. You have to make sure your audience understands your message. That is true not only for an ad campaign but also for new products, pricing, promotions, names, packaging, and line extensions of your products.

Custom Research

There are two basic options you have in quantitative research. The first—and most valuable to finding out specific information about *your* product—is to commission a market-research firm to conduct a study for you. This is called custom research. The results will be kept proprietary. No other companies—particularly competitors—will have access to them.

Custom research offers many benefits. You can ask exactly the questions you want, and you can ask them in the way you want. If you have a specific question to answer, a custom study will provide you with the specific answer. The cost of a project can be as little as $10,000. Considering the hundreds of thousands of dollars that launching a new product can cost, it is a pretty small expense. The cost can go up, depending on how many people you want to interview and how many regions of the country you want to include.

Companies usually husband their budget lines for custom studies for the most important questions. Children's Market Research, for example, recently was asked to conduct a custom study for a major marketer to determine which of a list of names for a new product for children would be greeted with the most enthusiasm in the marketplace. A name is one of the most important features of a new product, and you can't very easily go back and change it after spending millions of dollars to launch the product. It's a decision you have to get right from the beginning.

A company that is launching a new product or a million-dollar campaign should conduct a custom study to make sure kids will remember the product's name, the slogan, and the key selling points.

Syndicated Research

The second option you have in quantitative research is to purchase syndicated research. Syndicated research is conducted on a periodic basis on a variety of issues. It will tell you about the market, but it will not give you very much information about your specific product. The market-research company that conducts syndicated research sells the results to companies on a one-time basis or on a regular basis to companies that subscribe to their service.

CMR KIDTRENDS REPORT, based on the Simmons Kids Study, which we have cited periodically in this book, is an example of a syndicated study. Children's Market Research, Simmons Market Research Bureau, and others conduct research on various markets and sell the results to corporations.

Syndicated research won't answer your specific question about how consumers will react to your new product or ad strategy. However, it will provide an information context for you to learn more about your market: what brands are consumed, how much influence kids (to take an example) wield on product purchases in specific categories, how and where kids buy products, what lifestyle options are in or out, how children feel about major issues, where their values lie, and what their aspirations are.

Since market-research companies are able to spread the research costs over a number of clients, syndicated research is generally less expensive than a custom study. Specific reports on market topics or select demographic groups can cost as little as $1000 to $2500. However, if you need specific information about your product, custom research is the route to take.

Sometimes ad agencies, media companies, or other vendors will provide clients with syndicated research that they have done in-house as part of the relationship with a client.

As marketers have begun to demand more information about children and teenagers, the number of options in syndicated research has grown. Several market-research companies that have not previously offered children's syndicated studies have added them in the past several years. So you, as a marketer, have a reasonable variety of choices.

Custom Research: Starting Out

The first decision to make, after finding a research firm, is to determine exactly what you want the research to tell you. What do you want to find out? What is the validity, for example, of coming out with a cookie with a soft middle versus a regular cookie? Which two of the five flavors under consideration are liked most by children? How will kids respond to the proposed packaging? What do they think of the commercial?

As in focus groups, your time with your interview subjects is limited. In fact, it is more limited. Most quantitative research interviews with kids run 10 to 20 minutes. By comparison, you can run a focus group to 60 minutes without undue strain. Since there are six to eight kids in the group, no one gets too tired. However, in quantitative research you do get individual readings on each child with one-on-one interviews.

In quantitative research interviews, then, you must use your time wisely. You have to make sure you get your most important questions answered before you ask the interesting but ancillary queries you've been curious about.

Mall Interviewing

There are two basic techniques for conducting quantitative research with children. The first, and easiest, is to hire a market-research firm who will work with a market-research facility in a shopping mall. Children will be recruited in the mall and escorted to the research facility, where the interview takes place.

There are several specific wrinkles in conducting mall "intercepts" with children—that is, intercepting kids in a mall, to ask them questions. The first is in the questions themselves. Questionnaires in quantitative research rarely ask open-ended questions. This is in marked contrast to focus groups, where the point is to open up the group and encourage participants to be expansive. Instead, quantitative research asks the child to make a choice. "Do you like the taste?" "Yes" or "No." "Which package do you like best?" "A, B, C, or D."

"Is this a product you would ask you mom to buy?" Researchers ask children to rate a product, taste, ad, and so forth, on a scale of 1 to 5. The scale is smaller than it is for grown-ups, who are normally asked to rate a product on a scale of 1 to 10. The consensus of child researchers is that 10 choices is too confusing for kids.

It's important to phrase the question in a way that the child will understand it. You can't use words that the child is not familiar with, and it's important to look for secondary meanings that could throw the child off course.

Likewise, it's important to weed out leading questions. The objective of your research is not to get the child to say what you want to hear. It's to get an objective response to the questions you have.

The second hurdle in doing quantitative research with kids is to get the permission of Mom or Dad before you escort a child to the interview room. That proviso, of course, doesn't apply to market research with grown-ups. You can show the parents the room so they'll know what it's like. But once the interview with the child begins, they should not be in the interview room.

A Children's Market Research researcher once was observing an interview with a 10-year-old boy whose mother was seated right behind him in the research room. Every time the poor boy opened his mouth, the mother chimed in to "correct" him. It was like having a back-seat driver in the interview room. The boy wound up totally confused, and the answers had to be discarded. The goal of research, after all, is to find out what children—not grown-ups—are thinking.

One Frog or Two? Making It Fun

It's easy to see why the marketer is excited about the interview. He or she is about to find out from the child whether the company's marketing brainstorm is a great idea. But put yourself in the child's shoes for a moment.

Interview rooms are pretty businesslike settings. The child sits in a straight-back office chair across the table from the interviewer. Unlike focus groups, there is no sitting on the floor. There's no jolly camaraderie with other kids. You're all alone with a grown-up. There's no time to playact. There's no time to let the conversation detour into whatever is interesting to you at the moment. Instead, there's a list of 10 to 20 questions to answer.

Pretty boring.

One of the biggest challenges during an interview, then, is to keep the child's full and undivided attention. Interviewers trained in working with children have come up with various innovations to help do that. Personal computers, for example, have become an increasingly popular research aid. Kids are intrigued by computers, and most kids who come into interview rooms know them from school. Some software programs let kids self-direct the questionnaire, pushing keys to answer the questions and proceeding to the next one.

Children's Market Research often uses familiar or funny icons to help kids with written questionnaires. Instead of having to answer "Yes," you can ask the child to choose a happy face. Instead of "No," you can ask the child to choose an angry face with its tongue sticking out.

Rather than ask them to choose on a scale of 1 to 5, you can ask them to choose 1 frog to 5 frogs. Children's Market Research often uses a cartoon of a happy kid holding a balloon; that is the company's logo. An alternative is to show a graded scale of faces that go from a happy face, to a face with a blank expression that is neither happy nor sad, to an angry face.

Another way to keep a child involved is to use flash cards. The interviewer asks the child to choose the card and put it into a box.

It shouldn't be too hard to get the child interested. Kids generally like to participate in interviews, especially if they're told that the opinions they express are important to the company and will influence the decisions the company makes. That makes the child feel important. The interviewer should be experienced in working with children to develop a rapport with the child. Some researchers are "pencil people." They sit at the interview table, pencil in hand, and check off questions one by one, rarely even looking up at the respondent. The ideal researcher has a warm, helpful personality. At the end, it's good to give the child a toy, goodie bag, or cash payment to acknowledge your appreciation.

How One Company Did It

Children's Market Research was called on by one company that wanted to see which name on a list it was considering for a new product was most popular with kids. The company had generated the list of names internally. Which would work best?

CMR began with a pretest of 50 kids in the Northeast. The pretest afforded an opportunity to run down the questions to make sure that kids would understand them. It also offered the opportunity to winnow down the total number of names under consideration.

CMR then interviewed 100 kids in each of three more regional areas.

Because of the number of names under consideration (there were 12 in all at the pretest stage) the best method for assessing the relative strengths of the names was to sort them into boxes. The interviewer had two boxes. The interviewer welcomed the child and then described the product. The interviewer then handed the child 12 cards, each with a different name. Which names did the child like for the product? The child put the names he or she liked in one box and the ones he or she did not like in another.

The researcher then emptied the box with the names the child liked and, pencil in hand, asked the child which one the child liked best, second best, third best, and so forth. The same was done with the box of names the child disliked, to find out which names the child hated most.

The pretest yielded five names. The study was then conducted in three other regions to find which name kids liked most. Why go to several regions? It's important to have geographic diversity. A name that has a particular connotation in one part of the country might have a completely different meaning in another part; it might not even be a word in common usage at all. Although that's not likely, it's possible enough to warrant checking. Regional differences are most important in foods. The United States continues to have distinctive regional cuisines that are based on spiciness, availability of vegetables and fruits, and ethnic tastes.

Phone Surveys

You can also conduct quantitative research with older kids by telephone. The methodology is basically the same as it is for adults, but the questionnaire must be simple and understandable to kids. Market researchers can generate a list of households to call in-house or acquire a list from companies that specialize in list management.

The researcher places the phone call and asks a parent for permission to speak to the child. Then the interview is conducted.

Generally, you can't ask a child as many questions as you do an adult in a phone interview. Since you do not have the one-to-one personal contact that you have in an interview room, it's hard to keep the child's attention for as long a period of time. While the child is talking to the interviewer, he or she is being distracted by things he or she cannot see in a focus group facility, such as the family's dog or cat, the television, Mom, Dad, and siblings. As a result, you have to be more prudent in the questions you ask and how you as them.

It's best to ask short, simple questions: How much allowance do you get a week? What do you spend it on? What commercials do you remember? What are your favorite foods? What are your favorite snack foods?

You also have to be more careful in telephone surveys about the age of the children you use. It is very difficult to interview children younger than 8 years old on the telephone because their communication skills are still fairly unsophisticated.

Children generally feel uncomfortable talking with people they do not know, and they are particularly uneasy talking with people they don't know over the telephone. It's much easier to establish contact when your interviewee can see you.

Tabulating the Results

After the research is completed, the results are tabulated by computer. The report, in some respects, will be similar to the report you get at the end of a focus group. It will begin with a summary of the basic findings.

The report will give you the top-line finding. It should break out how different segments of your market responded. It should also have space for the researcher to make observations that he or she has discovered in the process of analyzing the data.

For example, consider the name research that Children's Market Research conducted, which was described in the previous section. If 6- to 8-year-olds liked a name but it fell flat with 10- to 12-year-olds, it would do no good to choose that name. The goal was to find a name that would appeal across a broad section of the market. Since older children are usually the trendsetters, it was particularly important to find a name that would appeal to them.

The report will then go on to give specific results. The numbers in this section are reported as raw data. It may be intimidating, but it can be worthwhile to explore the numbers to look for nuances in the responses among different groups. It is in those kinds of insights that you often find your next big idea.

Summing Up

Questions to Consider

1. What, in descending order, are the most important questions you want to have answered by a quantitative study? Can they be answered by existing syndicated research, or do you need to commission a custom study?

2. How large a survey do you want to conduct? What are the key market segments you want covered? Will it be important to talk to kids in a variety of geographic regions?

3. Have you created a questionnaire with nonleading questions that will give you objective answers? Has the research firm written the questions in straightforward terms that will be easy for kids to understand?

4. Has your research firm created an environment that will help make the interview proceed efficiently, with a minimum of interferences? Has the firm incorporated techniques that will involve the child and keep his or her attention?

5. Will the report you get at the end of the study answer your most important questions, tell you how key market segments responded, and include additional observations the researcher has made after analyzing the data?

5

Boys and Girls

The Differences and Similarities

Pop Quiz

1. What are the most popular toys for girls aged 6 through 14?
   (*a*) dolls and makeup, (*b*) bicycles and skateboards, (*c*) crayons and stuffed animals.

2. After watching television, what is the favorite leisure-time activity among girls aged 6 through 14?
   (*a*) shopping, (*b*) playing with dolls, (*c*) sports.

3. How common is ownership of a hand-held calculator among 6- to 14-year-old kids?
   (*a*) twice as common among boys as girls, (*b*) significantly higher among boys than girls, (*c*) virtually the same for boys and girls.

4. Since little girls tend to emulate their mothers and little boys emulate their fathers, does it stand to reason that girls aged 6 to 14 are the household "experts" on food?
   (*a*) true all the time, (*b*) true most of the time, (*c*) generally false.

5. When shopping day comes around, who's more likely to go along on the shopping trip?
   (*a*) most girls aged 6 to 14 but not most boys of the same age, (*b*) most girls aged 6 to 14 and most boys of the same age, (*c*) very few boys or girls.

Answers: 1. *c*; 2. *c*; 3. *c*; 4. *c*; 5. *b*.

It's a Modern World...

So, let's get this straight. According to our pop quiz, drawn from the CMR KIDTRENDS REPORT, based on The Simmons Kids Study, the favorite toys of girls aged 6 to 14 are crayons and stuffed animals. But little girls' favorite leisure-time activity is sports. Girls are about as likely to own hand-held calculators as boys; about 4 in 10 boys and girls own one (we'll tell you more on this subject later in this chapter). And they're no more likely to be the household "experts" on foods they like than boys are—*and* no more likely to go along on the weekly shopping trip to the grocery store than the boys are. What's going on here? Have we achieved equality of the sexes?

Yes—and no. Being a girl is very different than it was a generation ago, but in many fundamental ways it has not changed. According to the research, opportunities have opened up considerably for girls over the past 20 years. Girls are participating in a broader range of activities. According to *Sports Illustrated for Kids*, which conducts an ongoing omnibus study that includes interviews every other month in shopping malls with 300 kids aged 8 to 12, the most popular participatory sport for both boys and girls is *basketball*. More than 40 percent of girls report they have played basketball in the past year; volleyball, softball, gymnastics, baseball, and soccer come next.

Girls are getting greater opportunities to follow whatever interest they want in school. Many parents reject the notion that math and science aren't for little girls. Girls' sports are more popular than they used to be. In some states, girls' basketball games are as well attended as boys' games. There's less pressure for girls to suppress themselves intellectually. There's more encouragement for girls to dream of being whatever they want—be it a mother, an astronaut, a rock climber, a computer scientist, a world-class bicyclist, the head of a company, a U.S. senator, or the president.

...With Traditional Values

But—and this is a significant proviso—the abiding belief of some members of the women's movement in the 1970s that the differences between the sexes could someday be eliminated if children were brought up in a nonsexist environment has, in fact, not come to pass. There are still meaningful and important differences between boys and girls that are manifested in things from the way they think, to how they express themselves, to what they value, the toys they choose to play with, how they play, and how they assess products and services from clothes to potato chips to sporting events and rock concerts. If you want them as customers, it is your obligation to understand them.

In many ways, what's going on with children is a mirror of the adult world. Grown-up men and women are refining the redefinitions of the women's movement of what it means to be a man and what it means to be a woman. This process has seen motherhood reelevated in status in recent years and family values elevated into a middle ground that both Democrats and Republicans claim as their own. For all the changes that they have made, girls still tend to be nurturing, creative, and expressive and are drawn to products that reflect those qualities. Boys, on the other hand, are drawn to physical, competitive, outward activities.

As a marketer, then, two questions you should address when you begin a project is whether it's for boys or girls and what difference that will make in how you carry out your task.

In this chapter we guide you through the sexual maze of childhood. We tell you what has changed, and we detail some opportunities we think have been created by those changes. We give you an idea of what the differences between the sexes mean for you. This will get you thinking about issues that come up in later chapters as we discuss conceiving a product, creating names, designing the package, deciding how and where you want to sell the product, coming up with advertising and promotions, and looking ahead to what trends will create new opportunities for you.

Blue for Boys, Pink for Girls

A friend of ours had an urgent need for sleepers for her baby. The little fellow had just recently had a growth spurt and had outgrown his infant clothes. The nursery was a veritable horn of plenty of rattles and activity boards, but there was a shortage of 12-month-old-sized clothes. The mother proceeded to the children's section of the nearest department store and bought all the terry cloth sleepers in stock, including—over the heated protests of the salesclerk—the *pink* ones. The mother was miffed. "What difference could it make to a little child?" she huffed to herself.

Time passed, and little things started happening. For example, every day the nanny religiously removed the baby doll the mother had bought the boy in her commitment to raise the child in a nonsexist manner. When she dropped her son off at play groups, it seemed like the little boys were always off in a corner banging things—banging each others' metal trucks together in a cacophony of metal, banging wooden mallets into the pegs on the workbenches, banging cardboard bricks and wooden blocks onto the floor. Meanwhile, the little girls were gathered at the playhouse area, cuddling the baby dolls or dressing up in the moms' recycled high heels and fancy hats to go out for a pretend lunch at a fancy restaurant.

By the time the mother was dropping off her son for first grade, the boys and girls had hardened into different groups at opposite ends of the playgrounds—with occasional forays of one group swooping down on the other to chase the opposite sex around the slides, swings, and climbing structures. The worst insult her son could give or get was to be compared to a girl. The son cut short the time he spent saying good-bye to Mom when she dropped him off at school because the other boys had teased him for letting his mom hang around. If you talked to girls—even moms—you were considered a sissy. And if the son happened to dress in the same unisex sweater as a girl in his class, he'd shrink in embarrassment and swear never to wear the sweater again. Pink? No way!

In an earlier time, the parent probably would have been convinced she'd done something wrong. But, after hearing the same story from her friends and acquaintances for years, she knew that her experience was not unusual. Boys and girls separate at a fairly early age as part of their process of defining who they are and who they aren't—the process of finding their own identity. In the marketing universe, the separation is not always clear-cut. There are some products that boys and girls partake equally, particularly foods. But, in toys especially, kids generally define products and activities by sex.

The marketplace offers up a resounding affirmation to this reality. Take a look at the 10 most in-demand toys from one recent Christmas. For little girls, there were two dolls from Mattel, Little Miss Singing Mermaid and Ariel the Little Mermaid. There was also Baby Wanna Walk, a baby doll for little girls from Hasbro, Inc. For boys, there was Bigfoot Crunch Arena from Mattel, which was based on the car-crunching "monster" trucks that prowl through real-life stadiums. Parker Brothers offered Nerf Bow and Arrow. Sears, Roebuck and Co. was seeing brisk sales for a collector's car set, the Official Commemorative NASCAR race-cars set. And Nintendo of America and Sega were seeing big sales for their Supernintendo and Sega Genesis video-game systems, in which the story line of a typical game involves a male figure who saves a female in distress from bad guys, monsters, or both.

The Enduring Barbie

She uses Rollerblades. She drives a fast car. She saves endangered species. She wears fashions from the leading designers. Sometimes she plays in a rock 'n' roll band. And, for more than 30 years, she's racked up big, big sales for Mattel. Barbie, the world's top-selling fashion doll, may be the gold standard for success in the toy business.

She has her faults. Her body is too picture-perfect; some sociologists

Figure 5. Barbie dolls have become one of the enduring toys for girls. Part of the reason for their success is that Mattel regularly comes out with new models of the fashion doll, and new clothes and accessories, to keep Barbie contemporary, maintain interest, and encourage additional purchases. (Courtesy Mattel, Inc.)

say she makes girls feel self-conscious if they don't have a buxom chest, a tiny waist, and skinny legs, too. Some critics have called her a consumerist and a bubble-headed blond, as well. Parents say her exaggerated fashion-model body makes it hard for girls to pull her clothes on. But the criticisms do not seem to have tarnished Barbie's image among little girls. Barbie continues to thrive, despite the critics and a parade of rival fashion dolls from Mattel's competitors.

One reason why Barbie continues to do so well lies in Mattel's understanding of its audience. On the one hand, the company has skillfully created enough accoutrements for Barbie to stimulate little girls' imaginations. On the other hand, they have not weighed her down with so much stuff to inhibit how girls play with the doll. Barbie can be whatever little girls want her to be—a singer in a rock 'n' roll band, a horse trainer, or a high-powered corporate executive. "We've always believed that little girls fantasize through Barbie about how they will be when they are older," a senior marketer in Mattel's girls toys division told an *Adweek's Marketing Week* writer. "The doll is the prop on which young girls project their very private dreams."

The second factor in Barbie's continued success is Mattel's ability to reinvent her to keep up with the changes in the world around her. Mattel has always drawn Barbie's fashions from the top designers in the fashion world—from high-fashion designers of the 1960s and 1970s to the colorful, global contemporary outfits of United Colors of Benetton.

Mattel introduces as many as a dozen new line extensions of Barbie every year. Some have reference points to familiar names from the real world, such as the Benetton Barbie and Ice Capades Barbie. Some respond to girls' individual fantasies. For example, one of the most successful Barbies in recent years was Totally Hair Barbie, a Barbie with tresses that come down almost to the ground. (The doll came with a packet of Dep hairstyling gel to encourage girls to style the doll's hair.) Sun Sensation Barbie was conceived with a beach theme. For younger girls, Mattel introduced a "beginner's" Barbie, My First Barbie, with proportions and clothes that are easier to put on and take off.

Usually the Barbie has a corresponding Ken, for example, Totally Hair, My First Barbie..., or some other brand extension. Mattel sometimes brings out corresponding dolls of Barbie's little sister, Skipper, and of Barbie's various friends.

The strategy encourages girls to continue to collect Barbies. One of the biggest marketing problems Mattel faced with Barbie was that because the doll is so popular, it could easily saturate its potential market in the United States. According to some industry sources, more than 90 percent of girls 3 to 10 years old have a Barbie. The goal of Mattel, then, is to encourage them to buy more. And it has wildly succeeded. The company has introduced a variety of accessories, as well. They range from the small (ski equipment) to the large (a Barbie dream house, a Barbie Ferrari or Porsche, a Barbie Hawaiian Flower Shop, and a Barbie swimming pool).

Mattel's attentiveness has enabled it to keep up with the changing demographics of its market as well. The company has astutely introduced a series of African-American and Hispanic dolls that reflect not only the changing racial hue of the nation but also the nuances in fashion and culture in those markets. The dolls—particularly Shani, Mattel's African-American doll, her boyfriend Jamal, and her pal Nichelle—are, in our view, some of the most beautiful and interesting new fashion dolls to be introduced in recent years.

For marketers, there are various lessons that can be learned from Mattel's success with Barbie. First, Mattel understands how children's minds work—particularly, their sense of fantasy and play. The toy becomes a prop for children's own imagination. Second, Mattel doesn't try to change the market; it changes the product to fit the market. Third, Mattel gives children variety. Products are updated regularly with line extensions that help kids get more play value out of the toy.

Boys' Products, Girls' Products

As a marketer, it's in your interests to be aware of the differences between the sexes and how those differences evolve as children grow up. For some time, Mattel has split its product line into separate divisions, one for boys and one for girls. "Any child psychologist will tell you that at a certain age boys and girls have different developmental patterns," Robert Sansone, at the time president of Mattel's American operations, told a *New York Times* reporter. "It's natural that toys reflect the sex that uses them." (See Table 5.)

Hasbro splits its product line into boys and girls products, but only where appropriate.

The Kenner product line is organized into three groupings: products for girls, products for boys, and activities. Care Bears—one of the most

Table 5. Toys and Games Child Owns or Uses

(by percent)

	Total	Boys	Girls
Crayons	59.2	55.0	63.5
Stuffed animals	51.1	40.2	62.5
Puzzles and games	45.8	44.0	47.7
Plush toys	32.6	25.6	40.0
Dolls and dolls clothes	31.7	7.6	57.0
Cars and trucks	31.5	51.3	10.6
Building sets	31.3	43.3	18.7
Riding toy/tricycles	29.7	32.9	26.3
Frisbees	29.3	32.0	26.5
Radio-controlled toys	28.9	46.0	10.9
Play guns (including water guns)	27.7	42.7	11.8
Reusable compound (such as Play-Doh, Silly Putty)	23.8	22.3	25.3
Action figures, robots, and accessories	22.6	38.1	6.4
Bubbles	22.4	18.5	26.4
Play makeup	18.1	5.3	31.5
Figurines (such as army dolls)	17.9	24.4	11.0
Super-hero figures	17.6	29.0	5.7
Auto racing games and track	16.9	28.7	4.5
Sewing and needlepoint crafts	13.5	4.2	23.3
Trains	12.8	20.1	5.1
Toy appliances	10.1	4.2	16.4
Laser action toys	9.0	14.1	3.7
Other	11.7	12.0	11.4

SOURCE: CMR KIDTRENDS REPORT, based on data from The Simmons Kids Study (1991).

popular toys of the past decade, with more than 40 million in unit sales and 97 percent awareness—are a product for girls. Virtually everything about the stuffed animals seems to encourage little girls to act out their own natural tendencies to nurture, care, share, and love. It plays out in the bears' bright colors, which range from pinks and purples to bright blue. It also influences line extensions. For example, the Precious Heart Bear has a special treasure chest that opens up in his heart for little girls to store their prized possessions. It influences the different bears' names—Funshine, Share Bear, Friend Bear, Love-A-Lot Bear, and so forth. It even influences the language the company uses to describe the bears: "Caring keeps the world beautiful!" "Full feelings ahead!"

Now let's look at the products for boys. There's Batman, which includes a line of action figures and dress-up equipment that bring the caped crusader to life. The product line revolves around active, outward-directed fantasy play, such as fighting crime and saving Gotham City from harm. Look at the product names; they all use active words. For example, Air Attack Batman is a figure who swoops through the air on a hang glider that is shaped like bats' wings and equipped with projectiles. Deep Dive Batman dives into the murky depths. Thunderwhip Batman comes with martial-arts-like weapons. The Batman Batcave Command Center is an elaborate home-outpost for Batman to plot his next deeds. The Turbojet Batwing and Sky Blade Vehicle carry Batman through the air. The Batmobile roars him to the scene of the crime. In contrast to the Care Bears' bright, friendly colors, the Batman uses dark, ominous colors.

The sexual divide is evident in the rest of the lines as well. The products for boys range from Starting Lineup collectible baseball, basketball, and football action figures based on real-life athletes; to action figures and toys based on the sci-fi action-adventure movie *Terminator II*. The products for girls are mostly dolls—Baby Talking Alive talks ("I love you, Mommy." "Let's play."): Baby Alive sucks her thumb, eats her food, and dirties her diaper; transformerlike dolls such as Cupcakes can be manipulated (fold down the paper wrap, and lift up the icing and a doll emerges); and miniatures like The Littlest Pet Shop serve as collectibles.

The sexual divide is still pretty evident in Hasbro's activities products. Some products like the Speedy-Make Ice Cream Maker, the Spirograph spiral-drawer, and the ColorBlaster and T-Shirt design product lines draw on both sexes. They are packaged in basic primary colors, such as red, yellow, and blue, and show both boys and girls in the package photos. The Easy-Bake Oven, on the other hand, is all pinks and purples and generally shows pictures of little girls.

As with Mattel, there are specific lessons you can learn from Hasbro's success. First, Hasbro, like Mattel, has proven it is keenly interested in children's sense of fantasy. The company creates toys that help children act out their individual style of fantasy play.

Second, the detailing of the physical product is exact. Batman and Terminator, for example, are reproduced from the movie characters with a high degree of precision. Poor imitations and fakes are turnoffs.

Third, by extending its detailing to the language and design of its packaging and ads, Hasbro builds myth into its toys. Hard consonants—Bs, Ts, and Ks—communicate the action of boy's toys like Batman. The colors of the packaging are consistent with the colors from the movies. That tells kids that this is the real thing. When the customer buys the toy, he or she isn't just buying a piece of molded plastic; the customer is buying a whole mythology of Batman as a heroic character in a troubled, forbidding world.

Nature and Nurture

The process that results in children's adopting sexual roles and behavior appears to come from both nature and nurture, the interplay of genetics and socialization. In toddlerhood, children are eager to imitate everything they see in the world around them. Boys delight in cooking at a toy stove or washing clothes in a play laundry, just like Mom. Little girls pick up a toy mallet and pound at a toy workbench, just like Dad. Both boys and girls, at certain stages, may experiment with Mom's makeup.

Toys for younger children reflect the open-endedness of kids' lives. Instead of color coding toys in soft pink or blue, toy makers emphasize simple, bright colors, like red, blue, yellow, and green. The color coding that does exist—pink sleepers for girls, blue for boys—is arguably more for the benefit of the parent than the child. The open-endedness of the color and design encourages a natural curiosity that leads young children to explore and experiment.

Sexual differences start to emerge in preschool. Boys play house, but they also delight in aggressive play. The behavioral separation of the sexes accelerates when kids begin school. Kids start to form peer groups on the basis of sex. On the playground, boys compete for dominance in games of football, tag, and, sometimes, out-and-out wrestling. Girls, meanwhile, form cliques to talk about their stuffed animals, their art projects, makeup, and other shared interests. If you are marketing a product to children, it is at this age that you will want to manifest the sexual orientation of your product. (See Table 6.)

Table 6. Entertainment/Activities Child Participates in (by percent)

	Total	Boys	Girls
Swimming pool	67.9	67.2	68.7
Beach	50.8	50.3	51.4
Carnival or state fair	49.4	49.5	49.2
Amusement park (such as Six Flags)	46.8	48.0	45.6
Circus	44.7	44.8	44.6
Overnight camp	24.9	25.6	24.1
Day camp	21.3	22.8	19.7
Professional sporting event (other than professional wrestling)	19.8	24.6	14.7
Ice-skating show	18.1	15.5	20.7
Concert (other than a rock concert)	17.9	18.3	17.5
Rock concert	16.5	12.5	20.6
Professional wrestling	11.3	15.1	7.2
Other	19.8	18.5	21.1

SOURCE: CMR KIDTRENDS REPORT, based on data from The Simmons Kids Study (1991).

What the Numbers Say

Market research bears out the differences between the sexes in toys. Action-oriented playthings dominate the toy chests of American boys, according to the CMR KIDTRENDS REPORT, based on The Simmons Kids Study. (See Table 5.) After crayons, the one universal plaything found in both boys' and girls' toy collections, cars and trucks are the most prevalent toy for boys aged 6 to 14. They are found in 51.3 percent of homes.

Radio-controlled cars come in third, with a 46 percent market penetration. Puzzles and games are a close fourth, at 44 percent, followed by building sets and play guns, at 43.3 percent and 42.7 percent, respectively. The significance for marketers is that the types of toys boys play with have changed little over the years—only the technology has gotten more advanced.

Boys do have a soft spot: stuffed animals rank seventh in market penetration at 40.2 percent, with action figures, robots, and accessories next, at 38.1 percent.

What we think of as classic toys—cars and action figures, for example—peak between 9 and 11 years old. Some 54 percent of 9- to 11-year-old boys, for instance, have radio-controlled cars. By the time a boy hits 12, he begins to move into teenage pursuits. Athletic equipment, for example, becomes more compelling. Frisbees, for instance, are most popular with this age group. Only 40 percent of 12- to 14-year-old boys have radio-controlled cars.

Girls tend not to go through such dramatic twists and turns from age 6 to 14. Instead, their tastes stay fairly constant. They evolve. Girls do not turn wholeheartedly away from their stuffed animals, as boys do with toy cars and trucks. More than 50 percent of girls in the 12 to 14 age group still have stuffed animals. Some 42 percent still have crayons, and 35 percent have dolls, doll clothes, and puzzles.

After the ubiquitous crayon, stuffed animals are the most popular toy among girls aged 6 to 14, at 62.5 percent. Dolls and doll clothes are close behind in third place, with a household penetration of 57 percent. Puzzles and games follow, with 47.7 percent. Plush toys are next, at 40 percent, followed by play makeup, Frisbees, bubbles, and riding toys.

As girls grow up, sewing and needlecraft become more popular, as do athletic pursuits. But the shifts in girls are less dramatic than in boys.

For marketers, these numbers should serve as a road map for developing products. Cars, trucks, action figures, and building sets will continue to be mainstays for boys. Dolls, arts and crafts, and related products will be popular for girls; some products, like stuffed animals, will likely always be found in both boys' and girls' toy boxes (though the older guys may be a little less willing to admit to it). Be aware of what toys—such as crayons and arts and crafts products—are universally enjoyed by children so that you don't unintentionally stereotype yourself into a corner.

The Movement to Control Toy Guns

Toy guns used to be one of the classics, too. A replica Colt 45 or Civil War musket seemed to be a standard-issue prop for children in the 1950s who played cowboy or the North against the South in their backyards. It was easy for parents to give their children toy guns in the 1950s and early 1960s when the violence of real guns was as far away as the Wild West or even World War II, a war already becoming a distant memory in the rush toward the future.

But the assassinations of John and Robert Kennedy, Martin Luther King, Jr., and Malcolm X; the attempted assassinations of Presidents Reagan and Ford; the wrenching experience of the Vietnam War; and the violence that is all too present on city streets combined to make the violence implicit in toy guns all too real. Toy guns—like the television shows based on World War II and the Wild West—faded into the shadows.

The continuing violence from random crime and drug wars—some of which has claimed innocent children as its victims—will continue to make many parents feel revulsion at the sight of a toy gun. Some guns, primarily water guns, will still continue to come into the home. Fifty-two percent of 9- to 11-year-old boys still have a toy gun of some sort, but guns are not as actively promoted as they once were.

In response to the tragic deaths of young children who pointed toy guns at police or at criminals with real guns, some toy-gun makers use bright, fluorescent colors for their product so it won't be mistaken for the real thing. Some toy marketers have been able to give kids the same kind of emotional release that they used to get from toy pistols and rifles, in products that only bear passing resemblance to the real thing. For example, the *Ghostbuster* movies spawned Ghostbuster ghost zappers. The Super Soakers became a high-powered squirt gun.

Nevertheless, controversy has never been far behind. The accidental shootings of children carrying toy guns that were mistaken for real guns resulted in calls for banning all toy guns. The escalation of several Super Soaker water fights into real gun battles in troubled neighborhoods led to a bombardment of condemnation of the toy's maker in newspapers and television.

Many parents, following the recommendation of some child psychologists, take the deliberate position of not buying children guns. A protest movement has sprung up periodically to picket stores that carry toy guns. Until the violence in our society ebbs, companies that make toy guns are courting controversy.

The Fitness Movement

In the place of Wyatt Earp, Jessie James, and other gunslingers from the Wild West and the battlefield heroes of the Normandy invasion and the Battle of the Bulge, the idolization of athletes has increased commensurately. *Sports Illustrated for Kids'* research has shown that Michael Jordan, the Chicago Bulls basketball star, is better known among 8- to 12-year-olds than *the president of the United States!*

Both boys and girls have caught the sports bug, although they express it in different ways and to different degrees. We noted earlier that basketball is one of the most popular participatory sports of both boys and girls. In general, however, their interests diverge. Boys tend to pursue sports, while girls lean toward *activities*. Asked to choose a favorite sport or activity, boys choose baseball, football, and basketball. Girls pick swimming, roller-skating, and gymnastics.

The *Sports Illustrated for Kids'* study showed that baseball is the most popular sport for boys to participate in; about 2 in 3 boys say they have played baseball in the past year, followed by football, basketball, and soccer. Among girls, basketball is most popular, although, at 43 percent participation, it draws considerably fewer players than boys' sports.

Where boys tend to be more active participants in competitive sports, girls have higher participation levels in many activities. Among girls, 83 percent say they've been swimming in the past year—the most popular activity for both boys and girls—compared with 79 percent for boys. Girls are also more likely to roller-skate, 75 percent do it, compared with 52 percent of boys. And girls are more likely to ice-skate.

Boys are more likely than girls to go fishing, go skateboarding, go for a hike, or take karate lessons. Both boys and girls are active bicyclists; about three-quarters do, making it the second most popular sport.

The findings of Children's Market Research complements those of *Sports Illustrated for Kids*. When CMR asked girls to list their favorite leisure-time activity, apart from television (the universal favorite), the number one response was sports, with 49 percent. The answer trailed boys, but only by 10 percent.

We think there's a potential market in sports and activities for products geared to both boys and girls. We think the rapid growth of Rollerblades—which has spread from grown-ups to a growing number of kids and has evolved into a burgeoning number of dolls and toys with Rollerblades—is an indication of the potential. The phenomenon should be of interest to marketers beyond athletic goods.

Sports Illustrated for Kids teamed with Kellogg Co. and D.C. Comics to produce a series of instructive and entertaining comic books based on sports stars. The most impressive one, about the Olympic heptathlete Jackie Joyner Kersee, illustrates how marketers can bring girls into the equation. For girls, the motivation isn't only success. Girls, like their mothers, have told CMR in focus groups that they see being fit and athletic as keys to being healthy and attractive.

Fashion-Conscious Fellows

What about boys? From our research, they haven't changed as much as girls over the years, but boys have changed in two ways. Like men, boys are more conscious of their appearance. Also, while they don't do so as much as girls, they are more involved in choosing food, shopping, and housecleaning than their dads were when they were young. In other words, you don't have to confine boys to the baseball diamond when you create settings for commercials. You can show them going to the corner store, dusting the mantel, or taking out the garbage.

You also can show them preening. Snips and snails and puppy-dog tails may still be in the formula, but there's also a fair amount of *GQ*. Boys in the 1980s began to deck themselves out in dayglo sneakers, surfer shorts, neon T-shirts, and fad hairstyles. They have stayed in tune with fashion. Many 11-year-olds borrow their fathers' and older brothers' hairstyling gels, underarm deodorants, and colognes.

All this attention to appearance doesn't necessarily say they're going to be more forward with the opposite sex than their dads were when they were kids. The mating dance is complicated and confusing, as parents know. At certain ages, boys want nothing to do with girls. A little later, they may want girls to think of them as cool but not want the girls to know they want them to think of them as such. They may be outright opposed to actually talking to a girl, for fear of being teased by their peers.

Whenever kids are unsure of their own identity, the concept of a relationship with someone of a completely opposite identity can be downright frightening. Kids may ape their parents' language ("I like Jay, but I'm not really ready for a *commitment*," one 8-year-old we know remarked recently), but they're still just kids.

So, while an occasional knowing nod to the mating dance might show you understand a child's world, don't assume the fashion sense is directed outward. To some degree, it is another outward sign of children's trying on different identities, on the road to deciding who they're going to be.

Brand awareness is high, a Converse executive says. "Our dealers say boys down to age 2 are telling their parents what they want on their feet," he says.

According to a study in the late 1980s for the Nickelodeon cable television network, 85 percent of kids aged 6 to 15 exert influence over the brand of apparel they wear. More kids lobby for brands in clothing than in any other area—17 percentage points more than in breakfast cereal, 24 percentage points more than in toys, 25 percentage points more than in soft drinks, and 34 percentage points more than in videotapes.

Out of 40 percent of boys aged 9 to 17 who got blue jeans for Christmas, 67 percent hinted at them, asked for them, or picked them out, according to a survey for *Boys' Life* magazine. Only T-shirts, guitars, and drums got more intensive lobbying.

Companies, in turn, have heightened the fashion component in boys clothes and sought opportunities to get out the message. V.F. Corp's Lee jeans, for example, sponsored a special edition of *Scholastic News* magazine on the bicentennial of the U.S. Constitution. Converse All-Stars, the canvas sneaker that for generations was available only in black and white, has exploded into a fashion line with more than 20 colors and styles, from turquoise, yellow, and raspberry to dinosaur shapes.

"My son spends at least an hour on his hair," one mother says. "He won't even eat breakfast until every last hair is in place."

The lessons? Marketers who used to target the pitches for their apparel to moms are now talking more directly to kids. Even if you're not marketing apparel, hair gels, or other such products, you should know what your audience is doing so you'll know how to portray them. We would not be surprised to see boys or adolescent boys' personal-care products arrive on the market.

Makeup

There already have been a growing number of cosmetic products introduced for little girls. More than one-third of girls aged 6 to 14 have their own makeup at any given time. More than one-half of 6- to eight-year-old girls said they wanted to buy makeup.

We expect to see a growing number of companies bring children's makeup and fragrances to market. It would not be surprising if some are junior versions of grown-up brands.

There's good reason for reformulating makeup for kids. Girls have softer skin and like different fragrances than women. Babar and Celeste children's fragrances, a popular product in Europe for both girls and boys, were introduced to kids in the U.S. in jasmine, lemon, and other flower and fruit fragrances. Children, after all, relate more to flowers than musk.

The Babar and Celeste products were formulated for sensitive skins, in low-alcohol and alcohol-free versions. Their name and package design were based on Jean de Brunhoff's internationally beloved children's stories.

Hello, Kitty, the ubiquitous Japanese brand, is on everything from stuffed animals, to stationery, makeup kits, and miniature snap-shut boxes with little makeup brushes inside. The brand puts tiny kittens and hearts on lipstick and attaches a perfume bottle to a cord that girls can wear around their neck.

Going Out on the Town

So, beyond sports, television, and play, what do kids do for fun? (See Table 6.) Movies are the universal form of entertainment. Virtually all children are frequent (once a month or more) moviegoers, and the generally universal presence of videocassette recorders make children one of the leading markets for video rentals and sales.

Both girls and boys like amusement parks and circuses. Close to half of all kids have been to an amusement park, and almost 45 percent have been to a circus. This is an area of strong influence: 37 percent of both boys and girls lobbied to go to these activities. After these activities, there are some interesting divergences between boys and girls.

Boys are more likely than girls to prefer live sporting events. In the past year, 24.6 percent of boys have been to a professional sporting event, such as one featuring major league baseball, the National Football League, or the National Basketball Association. That's about 10 percentage points higher than girls.

Rock concerts are girls' favorite live entertainment. A total of 20.6 percent of girls have been to a rock concert, compared to 12.5 percent for boys. Most of the girls said they had gone in the past year. Even when they get a little older, girls remain the primary audience for rock concerts. Girls aged 12 to 14 are twice as likely to have been to a rock concert as boys. Girls are also more likely to have gone to an ice-skating show.

New Kids on the Block, Menudo, Partridge Family, Jackson Five, Monkees, and Beatlemania weren't an anomaly. There has been a long parade of teen idols that will continue on into the future. The reliable route to a boys' heart, meanwhile, is a sporting event. And if you want to draw in both, better try the circus.

Supermarket Surprise

Because kids have generally been an afterthought to marketers of packaged goods other than cereals, sweets, and salty snacks, it would be easy to conclude that they exert little to no influence when their parents go on the weekly shopping trip.

However, both boys and girls are highly involved in supermarket shopping. Most of both sexes accompany parents when major food shopping is done. A total of 52 percent of boys "sometimes" or "always" accompany parents when they go grocery shopping. Sixty-four percent of girls "always" or "sometimes" do. Fewer than 20 percent of boys and girls never go shopping with parents.

There is not a big drop-off as they grow older. Fifty-five percent of 6- to 8-year-old boys go grocery shopping with their parents. By ages 12 to 14, 48 percent still do. The same is true of girls. Seventy-one percent of girls aged 6 to 8 go shopping with their parents; 61 percent of girls aged 9 to 11 continue to go on supermarket trips; and 59 percent of 12- to 14-year-old girls go grocery shopping instead of their parents.

Household Experts on Food

Boys and girls are not passive shoppers. On many items, they are the household "expert." Fully 47 percent of girls and 46 percent of boys are household "experts" on cereals.

You'd think that girls would influence grocery shopping more than boys. Girls naturally emulate their mothers, and in most households Mom continues to handle the weekly grocery chores. But both boys and girls are the household "experts" on a number of products. Boys, at 49 percent, are slightly more likely than girls, at 44 percent, to be the household "expert" on cookies.

Meanwhile, girls, at 44 percent, are slightly more likely than boys, at 37 percent, to be the household "expert" on candy and gum. And also they're slightly more likely to be the "expert" on salty snacks: 30 percent of girls are the "expert" here, compared with 25 percent of boys. But these are not dramatic differences. In corn chips, macaroni and cheese, ice cream, and soft drinks, there's virtually no difference. It makes sense. Both boys and girls consume the foods.

Given the trends, most marketers of products consumed by kids should at least give some consideration to studying how involved kids are in the purchase decision. If they are highly involved, marketers should at least study whether to address them or not.

Both boys and girls should be taken into consideration in most food marketing. In addition, both should be taken into consideration in product development. The makers of canned spaghetti for kids, for instance, have come out with a series of line extensions of spaghetti shapes to appeal to boys and girls both—shapes such as dinosaurs, teddy bears, alphabet letters, numbers, Where's Waldo, and circus animals.

Equal Opportunity Walkmans

Traditionally, boys are associated with gadgets. However, the CMR KIDTRENDS REPORT, based on The Simmons Kids Study shows that there's equal opportunity in consumer electronics. Marketers should bear this in mind when they create advertisements and promotions, decide on colors for products, and develop new products.

Some products are, in fact, more likely to be owned by girls. Cameras, the most popular item in consumer electronics, are owned by 53 percent of girls, compared with 46 percent of boys. More girls than boys own boom boxes as well. A total of 45 percent of girls own their own boom box, compared with 43 percent of boys. Girls trail boys only slightly in

Walkman ownership. Forty-one percent of girls own Walkman portable sound systems, compared with 42 percent of boys.

Calculators are another stereotype buster. They are universal class-room tools now. Some 47 percent of boys have their own calculators, only slightly more than 44 percent of girls. Generally, it seems that con-sumer electronics companies think of boys first when they market their products. That's a mistake.

As we noted at the outset of the chapter, the opportunities for girls to achieve in math and science have opened up whole new areas where personal computers are standard equipment. Music, meanwhile, is a part of all kids' lives. That could be a microcosm of the tradition-rooted, but outwardly expanding, worlds of boys and girls today.

Summing Up

Questions to Consider

1. Do boys and girls respond differently to your product?

2. Can you create a product or position your product to target the changing activities and attitudes of boys and girls?

6

Bottling Magic

How to Create a Product

Pop Quiz (Essay Questions)

1. What was your favorite toy as a child? What was it about the toy that made it special? What did it let you do? Did you learn anything from it? What?

2. Describe something that you've bought lately that you like a lot—a new suit, a compact-disc recording, a living room sofa, whatever. What is it about that product that makes it special? What does it enable you to do that you couldn't do before?

3. Compare your answers from question 1 and question 2. Are there any similarities in the answers? Is there anything in the second product, the one you bought recently, that a child might like? How would you redesign the product to make it appropriate to children? What are the qualities in the product that could be distilled for children?

Note: These questions probably won't lead you to a product idea. Instead, it is an exercise to help you expand your thinking about new products.

The Big Idea

It was unavoidable. Keebler was looking for new ideas for salty snacks—something that would stand out from Frito-Lay, Borden, Inc., Eagle Snacks, and the dozens of regional companies fighting for shelf space in supermarkets and convenience stores. No matter where it searched, from consumer surveys, to newspaper and magazine stories, to government statistics, the same thing kept coming up: pizza. It was the fastest growing food and the favorite of kids and teens, the core market for salty snacks. That, in itself, was important. "They're the opinion leaders in the household," says Bob Dillon, vice president of new product development for Keebler. "They're hard to please. But if you can capture them, you can get everybody else in the family."

So why not make a snack based on pizza? And, while they were at it, use real pizza dough? Keebler did. Pizzarias, in pepperoni, cheese, and supreme flavors, went on, as earlier noted, to win the American Marketing Association's Edison Award for new product of the year.

Larami, a small company in Philadelphia, created the marketing sensation of the early 1990s by applying a bit of modern science to an item that has been a staple of summertime play for generations. The result, the Super Soaker, was a neon-colored pump-action, air-pressure-propelled next generation squirt gun capable of shooting a jet of water up to 50 feet. The invention led to a line of products, from tiny hand-held minisoakers to a giant-sized model that requires the wearer to don a backpack's worth of water. Kids couldn't get enough. At many stores, the whole line sold out.

Pleasant Rowland, a can-do former TV anchorwoman, schoolteacher, and entrepreneur, found her moment of inspiration while shopping for a doll for Christmas for her 8-year-old niece. Instead of the lovely dolls she remembered from her childhood, she could only find garish, licensed dolls. Rowland turned her frustration into a business—The American Doll Collection, a series of historically appropriate, accessory-laden dolls and storybooks that would let contemporary girls recreate the lives of little girls like them in Colonial America; on the prairies of the Midwest in the nineteenth century; in the exciting, bustling cities in 1900; and on the patriotic American home front in World War II.

In four years the Pleasant Co. zoomed from zero to $50 million in sales and spawned a legion of devoted fans. A tea party at historic Williamsburg, Virginia, to introduce Felicity Merriman, "a spunky, spritely Colonial girl," drew more than 10,000 little girls and their families—forcing Pleasant Co. to expand to three days worth of teas. Ernst & Young named Pleasant Rowland one of America's top 12 entrepreneurs. The American Booksellers Association, the International Reading Association, and the International Women's Forum honored her as well.

Where do ideas come from? What's your idea? It is the most important question we will ask you in this book. And it is the most important determination you will make. Studying the demographics, and conducting your first round of focus groups will identify areas of interest.

A clever television commercial, backed by massive amounts of media dollars, or an off-the-wall gimmick might get your name in front of your market. It might even prod the market to try your product—once or twice. However, without an idea the best you can hope for is a flash in the pan, a fad. Or a dead end, where, six months or a year from now—if you're lucky enough to still be in business—you will have to start all over again. Or, at worst, a bomb.

Your Goal: To Fill a Need

Probably the biggest conceptual problem for marketers of children's products to overcome is the perception that children are a volatile, unpredictable market where products rise like rockets and then, inevitably, tumble back to terra firma with a resounding crash. We would like to suggest that that reputation has come about in part because of the failure of companies, through a lack of desire or resources, to understand children. The successes of companies like Mattel and Hasbro show that a traditional, astute, packaged-goods marketing sensibility can be applied to children's products.

In part, the problems associated with children's products probably arose because children's products originated as a retail-driven business. What worked was what sold at the cash register. Serious marketers tried to go to work for big packaged-goods companies. The business, in turn, operated more on assumptions, faith, and blind luck than market research. In addition, companies may have been reflecting society. Many people believed that children were simply blank slates. There was very little serious research about children's motivations, behavior, perceptions, and attitudes anywhere.

That's changed. As a society, we are gradually learning that children are complex, intelligent, and subtle persons. Moreover, successive generations of executives have brought stronger management and marketing skills to companies, with the result that some of the ups and downs of cycles are being smoothed out. Some of the best-run, most admired companies in America today are predicated on products and services for children—Disney, LEGO, Mattel, Hasbro, Nintendo, Nabisco, Fisher-Price.

Their products are surrounded by auras of quality, fantasy, imagination, and excitement. Think of Walt Disney Co., and you think of "Sleeping Beauty," "Snow White," "101 Dalmations," "Little

Mermaid," and clean, predictable, friendly theme parks. LEGO brings to mind bright red, yellow, and blue plastic building blocks; and mind-opening, sophisticated environments based on contemporary cities, medieval castles, pirate ships, and science-fiction space ships and outer-space colonies. Hasbro and Mattel are associated with dolls and action figures that let children act out their fantasies. Nintendo's reputation for creating the best mix of technology and game software has given it the extra edge to surpass competing video-game systems that have won critics' plaudits.

The companies are competently managed. Moreover, the products fill a market need. LEGO's molded, interlocking building blocks let kids build more interesting, sophisticated, and colorful things than traditional wooden building blocks. Fisher-Price, Inc., and Playskool produce durable, educational products that kids enjoy and parents appreciate. Disney and Nickelodeon stand for entertainment. Nintendo offers the challenge of traditional board games, with a kinetic, high-tech edge. Even baseball cards fill a need, offering a connection between kids and their heroes on the baseball diamond.

The baseball card investment craze, which has led to the bidding up of old baseball cards and dozens of spinoffs, from hard-plastic display cases to baseball card price guides, is not pointless either. It offers lessons in how to make and husband your investments to a new generation that—from the standpoint of the country's economic difficulties—already has a practical attitude toward life.

Pleasant Co. is one of dozens of companies that have sprung up to offer toys that combine educational values with traditional, classic toys.

Larami's Super Soaker water guns, conceived by a rocket scientist, took a treasured summertime toy of generations, gave it two high-tech spins—a pump-action barrel to increase pressure and a water tank to hold a larger supply, and took off.

In traditional marketing terms, your most important task is to figure out what "problem" you want to solve. That is where your product will begin.

The Basics

There is a word in the toy business for products that have been so well conceived and are so well marketed that they can be expected to sell well year in, year out. The word is *evergreen*. We like the word. We think it is a standard to shoot for. Mattel's Barbie is an evergreen. It's the one toy that has managed to stay at the top of lists of best selling toys, despite the advances of video games. Barbie has been the favorite doll of little girls for almost 40 years. Mothers had Barbie dolls when they were little girls. It's only natural, when they have children, for them to buy Barbies for their little girls. As we move into a global economy, Barbie seems to be one of America's most exportable dolls.

There are certain basics to creating a product that will be an evergreen. First, the product should be durable. That is, it shouldn't break the 1st, 2d, 3d, or even the 50th time that a child plays with it. Barbie is sturdy enough that a little brother can bang it on a table or throw it out the second-floor window without doing damage.

Barbie also has the second quality basic to kids' products: she's easy to play with. Mattel's designers have carefully planned her clothes so they can be pulled on and snapped shut with Velcro, simple buttons, ties, or other things a little girl can manipulate. For younger girls, the company has even created "starter" Barbies that are easier to dress and undress.

The third, and maybe most important, quality is that the product should be engaging enough for a child to want to pick it up a 2d, 3d, or 50th time. The sheer, maddening, excruciating difficulty of getting within inches of advancing to a next level in Nintendo—or even winning—ensures that a child will come back again and again.

All the classic children's games—Monopoly, Parcheesi, Clue, Mouse Trap—have that element. They also have the benefit of surprise—the sheer exuberance of the plastic mousetrap rattling down the rickety plastic pole upon the trapped mouse that climaxes the process of building a crazy contraption in Mouse Trap as the players move around the board, the terror of landing on Boardwalk with four hotels, the exhilaration of finding the secret brick in Mario Brothers that will give you special powers.

It's probably too much to hope for a product that cannot be easily duplicated. Knockoffs in children's products sometimes beat the original from test market to store shelves. But the product or service should be something that will rank high on at least one family member's list for priorities. Several years ago, there was a flurry of banks for kids. But there was not enough of a compelling reason to go to a bank specifically for children. Parents could easily get a piggy bank for kids to keep small amounts. Or, if they were dealing in larger sums, they could open an account where the parents banked—a more convenient prospect then schlepping across town to a different bank, when life is already complicated enough.

The lower down a product is on the priority list, the more likely it will get the ax in a down economy when the family has to tighten its budget.

How Do You Define Success?

The question seems obvious, on the face of it. But how you measure success—and what your standard is for it—is one of the key decisions you will make. Some products have garnered enormous popularity, but the companies manufacturing them have failed.

For example, Teddy Ruxpin, the talking, gesturing teddy bear from Worlds of Wonder (WOW), of Fremont, California, was *the* hot toy for one Christmas in the mid-1980s. Children clamored to get the bear. The company's founders built overnight fortunes. But WOW was not able to maintain its success. Like many young toy companies that find themselves with an unexpected overnight sensation, it faced an incredible challenge in just keeping the pipeline filled. Furthermore, success put pressure on it to come out with more big hits. The company rapidly expanded. Growth tapered off, and it found itself in bankruptcy.

The most admired makers of children's products are companies that have evergreens—products that are nurtured into successes year in, year out. It takes smart management—not expanding too quickly, not overextending yourself in leases, learning to smooth out the boom-bust cycles.

Children's Toothpaste: A Study in Flexibility

Smart marketers learn how to adapt. It's been proven over and over in the past 10 years. In the frenzy to clamor onto the bandwagon of the explosive growth in population of young Americans, marketers rushed out line extensions for children the same way they had earlier for the needs of an aging population. What they've found—despite the bells and whistles of cute, kid-friendly designs and big ad campaigns—is that other markets are not predictive of kids.

For example, marketers have gone back to the drawing board several times on children's toothpaste. On the surface, it had looked liked another can't-miss product that would fit neatly into industry trends. In the 1970s, when young singles were a booming population, marketers created line extensions using toothpastes with brightening formulas to help consumers impress the opposite sex. Likewise, a decade later, to meet the needs of an aging population, packaged-goods companies introduced tartar-control formulas to fight gum disease.

The push for kids' toothpaste started in the mid-1980s, when SmithKline Beecham, one of the companies that had reaped the benefits of brighteners, introduced a line extension of Aquafresh for the children's market and received a positive response. Aquafresh for Kids boosted SmithKline to an 11 percent share of the $1.2 billion dentrifice market.

Soon after, Procter & Gamble came out with Crest for Kids, and Gillette Co.'s Oral-B unit came out with Muppet brand toothpaste. Colgate-Palmolive Co. followed with Colgate Jr. The products had kid-pleasing hooks, such as sparkles and flavors like fruit and bubble gum. They also got splashy $5 million to $10 million Saturday morning TV ad campaigns. Brand managers liked the demographics: 30 percent of households in the United States at the time had kids under the age of 12, but only 6 percent of oral-care products were focused on kids' needs.

The products got a lot of trial, but purchases tapered off. Children's toothpastes amounted to 6 percent of the dentrifice market in 1988, 5.5 percent in 1989, and about 5 percent subsequently. Five percent is a pretty fair niche. It's a $50 million-plus business. About a quarter of households with children are buying kids' toothpaste. But it's not 30 percent of the toothpaste market.

Companies have made some interesting adjustments. Procter & Gamble, for instance, modified the name of Crest for Kids ever so slightly and came out with Sparkle Crest—playing up a product attribute, the toothpaste's colorful, sparkly appearance, and dropping *kids* to a smaller type. We know of some grown-ups who like the taste of the product; no doubt, for them the name change is appealing. And it probably makes the product seem less like kid stuff to a lot of kids.

Meanwhile, Tom's of Maine, which has gained up to 2 to 3 percent of the market share in some areas of the country with natural-ingredient toothpastes, introduced a natural line extension for kids, in "silly strawberry" and "outrageous orange" flavors. Tom's attributes, such as no saccharin and no artificial flavors or colors, plus the line extension's efforts to soften the baking soda tastes that some kids don't like, might give Tom's a chance for success on the basis of product attributes.

"Kidsizing" Grown-up Stuff

It is, of course, a gross oversimplification to say that products for children boil down to a few, simple formulas. Saying so negates the very individual ideas, innovations, and energies that lie behind a Nabisco, Keebler, Mattel, or Nintendo. Recognizing that risk, however, we think it is still possible to say that most new products for kids fall into eight basic categories.

The most recognizable category contains items that are downsized or, to coin a word that we consider more accurate, "kidsized" versions of a product that has been successful in the grown-up marketplace. Kids' toothpaste is one example. A more successful example is children's electronics.

Sony Corp.'s and Fisher-Price's lines of consumer electronic products for kids have downsized adult electronics for kids, incorporating kid-friendly changes in the process. Buttons for operating the equipment were simplified to make them easy for kids to operate. Corners were rounded to prevent injuries. Instead of black or gray, the colors most found in adults' consumer electronic products, the products used bright, inviting reds, yellows, greens, and blues.

The combination of benefits gave Sony and Fisher-Price durable, high-quality products and filled a market need. A generation ago, children had record players. But, with the rough handling kids gave them, the records soon popped, skipped, or broke. Tape recorders and CDs are easier and more convenient for kids to handle. A growing library of musical and story-telling tapes and CDs for kids offers corroboration.

Levi Strauss regularly differentiates itself from its competition in fashion by transporting styles popular among teenagers down to younger kids. When teens started to favor fuller-cut, baggy pants in the early 1990s, Levi introduced Big Jeans, which had a looser, fuller-fit cut for boys.

Worlds of Wonder, before its financial collapse, had a minor success with an answering machine designed to fit in students' school lockers. Kids have proven themselves to be at ease with phone products: about 1 in 5 have their own telephones. Kids Cuisine and Snoopy's Choice, the ConAgra products described in Chapter 1, are examples of food products that have been revamped for the kids' market.

A growing number of companies have kidsized personal-care products, with mixed results. DuCair Tsumura has found a niche in licensed-product shampoos and bubble baths that offer milder formulas for kids' sensitive skins in packages carrying the images of the Little Mermaid and Miss Piggy, among others. SC Johnson, likewise, has found a niche alongside industry stalwart Johnson & Johnson, with a line of children's shampoos based on Fisher-Price's Little People. However, William & Clarissa, a start-up company in San Francisco that launched a line of upscale, sensitive-skin shampoos and bubble baths made with aloe, chamomile, and other all-natural ingredients, was forced to liquidate its product line a short time later. Its products were too expensive.

Research, Research, Research

Having a good idea is not enough. You have to follow through with commonsense decisions on ingredients, components, pricing, packaging, marketing, and sales strategies. We cover some of these topics in upcoming chapters. We would like to take time now, however, for an anecdote about a company that had a good idea but poor follow-through.

The company, which will go nameless, was coming to market with a line of children's cologne. The company called Children's Market Research to conduct the initial research. CMR found three things. First, kids were receptive to the concept. Although CMR had expected that answer from girls, it had not expected to discover that boys as young as 7 years old said they already were using their dads' after-shave. One boy said he splashed some on every day.

The second finding was not such good news for the company. The company had decided to make unisex colognes. The focus groups were enthusiastic about the scents. Everyone loved bubble gum. Boys liked the lemon scent. Girls liked strawberry. The boys, however, were uncomfortable with the notion of wearing the same cologne a girl was wearing. They liked something more macho.

Third, there was a problem with price. At almost $10 a bottle, the cologne would be beyond the reach of weekly allowances. Grandmothers might pick it up, but parents thought $5 was a better deal.

The product hit the market, but it didn't last. The lesson to be learned is that it is important to go back to the market as you are developing the product to find out if your execution is on the right track. A good idea is not enough.

"Straddle" Products

Some products straddle two markets, meeting both children's desires and parents' concerns. As health has become more of an issue with grown-ups, an opportunity has arisen for products that straddle adults' hopes of giving healthy foods to their children and kids' goals of finding foods that are fun and taste good. Snoopy's Choice is one example. Another example focuses on Continental Baking Co., which, after finding that a sizable percentage of the low-fat line of snack cakes it created for grown-ups were being bought by moms for their kids, decided to go all out and create a healthier snack cake specifically for kids. The result of the effort was Hostess Grizzly Chomps, a 97 percent fat-free chocolate cupcake that was designed to appear as though a bite had been chomped out of it. The company created a hip "spokesbear" on rollerblades, Grizzy B., to claim responsibility in ads and packaging. "I start 'em, you finish 'em," Grizzy would declare.

Dannon's Sprinkl'ins yogurt for children is a third example of a straddle product. Through the 1960s and 1970s, as Americans woke up about health and diet, yogurt was a growth category. By the late 1980s, however, it was showing signs of flattening out. Dannon, convinced that yogurt was nowhere near to being close to its market potential in the United States, looked for areas of opportunity. One of the obvious candidates was kids, who had never quite developed a taste for yogurt.

Dannon did a little investigation. First, it found that kids had specific problems with yogurt. Yogurt wasn't "nearly" as much fun "as green slime pudding and other snacks kids have to choose from," as Dannon vice president of marketing, Bob Wallach, puts it. Second, Dannon found, as other companies had, that kids exercised surprising autonomy over what they put in their mouths. The company found that 1 in 3 kids makes his or her own breakfast and that 1 in 5 makes his or her own lunch.

Dannon tested 48 concepts "ranging from the interesting to the absurd," Wallach notes with a smile. "We really stretched at this stage and applied few constraints." With the help of focus groups of kids and moms, the company winnowed the list to four. Quantitative research then took the remaining four down to one.

The most intriguing notion was a yogurt cup that would come with a packet of multicolored sugar sprinkles like those that children often put on ice-cream cones. The kids would mix up the resulting snack themselves. Dannon went back into testing for a name: Sprinkl'ins won. Meanwhile, it asked kids how they could change yogurt to make it better. The kids told them to make it thicker and to give it brighter colors, "stronger flavor delivery," and kid flavors. Dannon responded with eight flavors. It set a price that would fit Dannon's "price-value" equation and rolled out advertising support. It's too early to project Dannon Sprinkl'ins success, but as we were going to press Wallach said the initial results were impressive.

Old Product, New Technology

Early in this chapter, we cited LEGO and Larami's Super Soaker. They are two examples of new products that took long-accepted products—building blocks and squirt guns, respectively—and gave them a new, technological advance. This is a third category of products for children.

This category includes a lot of common-sense advantages. Because the product category has been around for a long time, there is no need to educate consumers about it. They already are familiar with it. In fact, familiarity has probably bred a certain degree of contempt for the first generation of technology. When Larami came out with the Super

Soaker, it was welcomed with open arms by a generation of kids who had gotten bored with regular squirt guns.

Hasbro's Go-Go My Walking Pup, a fluffy, white battery-operated dog that rolls backward and forward at the push of buttons in the handle of its leash, updated kids' interest in animal toys. New generations of toy dolls talk, crawl, walk, eat, relieve themselves, and do all manner of other things that their predecessors could only hint at.

Nerf, the soft, squishy foam rubber toy line of Hasbro's Kenner unit, has built a substantial product line by casting about for new product segments to recreate in Nerf. The original Nerf ball, billed at its introduction in 1969 as "the first indoor ball," was a small round orb about the size of a softball. A Nerf football and minibasketball with hoop soon followed.

In the mid-1980s, under Kenner's guidance, the product line exploded. Nerf Turbo Footballs, in a new spiral-cut shape, made it easier for kids to throw longer and better than a standard football. That was followed by a Screamer football, containing a small plastic whistle, that made a sirenlike noise as air whistled past it in flight. Nerf followed up with Turbo disks—one-upping Frisbee—and Turbo Screamer Boomerang. A "pro" line, for older kids and teens, offered the benefit of easier-gripping, durable footballs, basketballs, soccer balls, and volleyballs that were heavier than original Nerfs but easier handling than standard sports balls.

In addition to moving in on the turf of regular sports balls, Nerf invaded the toy-weapon segment with soft, pliable products that were designed not to look like traditional toy weapons and, thus, more easily win parents' approval. The line included a Nerf fencing set, Nerf Bow 'n Arrow, sci-fi guns that shoot Nerf balls and, for those interested in advanced weaponry, a Missile Launcher that fired Nerf arrows up to 50 feet through an air-powered mechanism launched by stepping on a "detonator" pad. The forays into new areas has put Nerf on the hottest-toys list at Christmas for many years.

Educational Products

Some parents would never buy their children a gun under any circumstances. They would rather spend their money on toys that educate their kids. This is the fourth category of new products for children. Chemistry sets, musical instruments, brain teasers, and computer learning games like *Math Rabbit* and *Where in the World Is Carmen Sandiego?* all fit into this category.

Most of the classic toys from Fisher-Price, Playskool, and Mattel's new Disney line that are introduced to babies and toddlers have educational properties. Activity boards, found in almost every crib, encourage babies to learn that they can effect a response by pushing a button, pulling a lever, or squeezing a bulb to make the brightly colored objects on the board emit squeaks, ring bells, or make things move back and forth. Fisher-Price's classic Little People plastic-person sets let young children act out how families, farms, airplanes, and cities operate.

There's unusual demand for educational toys from today's parents, but that's to be expected since today's parents are the most educated generation in U.S. history. According to the U.S. Census Bureau, 31 percent of 35- to 39-year-olds and 33 percent of 40- to 44-year-old Americans have had four or more years of college.

One client of Children's Market Research created a direct-mail activities club that encouraged kids to pursue their interests. If a child were interested in photography, for instance, he or she would get a new packet each month about photography.

Learning runs throughout Pleasant Co.'s strategy. For each of the four dolls in The American Girls Collection, the company has produced six storybooks about their families, schools, Christmas, birthdays, summers, and winters. Through the stories, the dolls' owners learn what it's been like to be 9 years old at different times in American history. The dolls' accessories—clothes, school materials, toys, dishes, and furnishings—are an extension of the history lesson. For example, for Kirsten Larson, the Swedish girl on the American plains in the 1850s, you can buy a pioneer school lunch—bread, sausage, a wedge of cheese, and an apple—in an engraved wooden box made to scale. For school time, you can buy a slate, school books, and even a school bench. The educational approach is a deliberate strategy.

Parents, hungry for quality, educational products for their children, agreed with their pocketbooks, shelling out $80 apiece for the pricey dolls and up to $300 more for doll clothes, doll furniture, and—for real verisimilitude—real little girls' clothes that let Pleasant Co.'s pint-sized doll collectors dress like their dolls.

Pleasant Co. knows it holds a special status in its owners' eyes. "We view our dolls as classics in the making," says Janice Blankenburg, the company's director of sales and marketing. "The characters let little girls compare and contrast their own lives with what it would have been like to be in history at a given point in time. Through play, we bring history to life."

With the collection, Pleasant Co. proved that education can be extended beyond the expected products, such as books, cassette tapes, and games, to the world of dolls.

Updating the Classics

Kransco toys has rediscovered the Hula-Hoop. Sales soar every few years as a new wave of parents buy their kids the 1950s fad that they remember from their own childhood. Actually, Kransco is not alone. Many of the classics from the 1950s and 1960s—Play-Doh, Crayola crayons, Frisbees, Slinkie, ant farms, Monopoly, Clue—have seen sales go up in recent years.

In response, many of the companies that own the brands have moved to leverage the equity of the brand into expanded product lines. Crayola, for example, now means not only multitudinous hues of crayons, but markers, pens, and paints. Play-Doh is a full product line of modeling clays and contraptions that mold them into sundry shapes. Milton Bradley has updated The Game of Life with new twists such as rewards for players who recycle or learn CPR. The proliferation of Nerf products is recounted earlier in this chapter.

There also appears to be opportunity in reviving brands and products that have faded away. Trolls, the slightly odd-looking little creatures that had a surge of popularity when baby boomers were young, have made a comeback in the past few years as have model trains. Erector Sets, the metal construction sets that many children enjoyed in the 1950s, have been resurrected by Tyco Toys. The company acquired the name from a French company and reintroduced the product—absent for 10 years—in the United States in 1992. Does that mean Pet Rocks are about to make a comeback, too? Stay tuned.

Licensing

Licensed products are the one area in which the boom-and-bust cycles and unpredictability that children's products are famous for still lives on. Licensing has created some of the hugest hits in recent years: Teenage Mutant Ninja Turtles was a monster success in action figures, video games, apparel—even food. The Ghostbusters movies and the Saturday morning TV series made Kenner—the licensee for Ghostbusters action figures and accessories—look good for years, as "Batman," "Star Wars," "Terminator," "The Simpsons," did for their licensees.

But licensing has also created some of the most colossal flops. The Disney movie "Dick Tracy" left retailers and manufacturers holding the bag after the movie failed to hook kids. "The Rocketeer" and "Howard the Duck" likewise were major flops. For licensees, the market is a crapshoot because deals are often negotiated before manufacturers and retailers can get a handle on how popular a movie or TV show will be. If negotiations are delayed until everyone begins to realize a TV show character, for example, has hit potential, it may be too late to start work on a licensed product. By the time it comes out, the character may have faded back into obscurity.

The secret seems to be to stay so close to TV shows, movies, and popular taste that you will be able to spot a phenomenon before it becomes one. It's no easy task.

Miniaturizing

A little while ago, we discussed shrinking down grown-up products for children's physical and lifestyle needs. There's another way you can use size: shrinking down kids' products into miniature products. Miniature toys have always held a special appeal for children. In recent years, marketers have expanded that appeal to a surprising number of items. For several years Lewis Galoob Toys had an enormous hit with Micro Machines, a miniature line of toy cars, trucks, planes, and ships.

A number of companies have introduced miniature dolls, dollhouses, bubble gear, and jewelry—some of which open up to reveal an even smaller toy. Kenner introduced a line of miniature pets in The Little Pet Shop.

The miniature craze has benefited food companies as well. We talk about Nabisco's discovery that it could do booming business in miniature cookies in Chapter 13. Fruit snacks from many companies can be found in various miniature shapes. Keebler has spun off Bite Size Chips Deluxe, Bite Size Rainbow Chips Deluxe, Bite Size Pecan Sandies, Mini Middles, Clubette crackers, Sweet Spots shortbread cookies, and Elfkins sandwich cookies. Eggo Minis, Frosted Mini Wheats, and Cinnamon Mini Buns have taken the phenomenon into the breakfast market.

Keebler's Pizzarias were designed to look and taste like a little slice of pizza. (See Figure 6.) The chip is made with real pizza cheese, meats, and spices. The new-product development team did all sorts of research to meet that end. It ordered pizzas from around the country. It also conducted consumer research around the country to find out what flavors of pizza, an intensely regional food, were most popular throughout the nation. Keebler's goal was to recreate "the pizza experience." It succeeded. The product, as noted, racked up $75 million in sales its first year.

Figure 6. Some of the best ideas for new products come from translating a favorite into a new category. Keebler Co., recognizing the popularity of pizza, came out with Pizzarias—a pizza-based chip—and won an American Marketing Association Edison for new product of the year. (Courtesy of Keebler Co.)

Topical Products

Keebler, as we note at the outset of the chapter, got the idea to create a pizza chip by scanning eating trends and discovering that pizza was the most popular takeout food and—most importantly—the favorite food of kids and teens, the key audiences for salty snacks. Other companies, in a similar vein, have found new-product opportunities by hatching new products that would play off of a topical trend.

Rising interest in physical fitness, for example, led gymnastics coach Al Fong and recreation-design expert Ron Matsch to sit down in 1989 with 50 cans of tinker toys and create a prototype for a physical-fitness center for kids. The brainstorming session led to Discovery Zone, a franchised indoor play center for kids that signed up 108 franchisees, including Billy Jean King, in its first year in business.

The typical Discovery Zone is 9000 square feet of brightly-colored, heavy-duty plastic climbing structures, spiral slides, "gerbil" tunnels, rope swings, vinyl mountains, and plastic ball "rooms," with party rooms attached. For $3.95 to $5.95 for the first hour, and $1 an hour thereafter (roughly the price of going to a movie) kids can climb over the play equipment, with adult supervision, without the hassle of rain, snow, or cold.

Jack Gunion, Discovery Zone's president, says an educated, involved generation of parents combined with declining physical-fitness levels in kids created an opportunity for a solution. The company points to TV viewing levels—25 hours a week for 5-year-olds, obesity—up 54 percent among 6- to 11-year-olds since 1963, and fitness levels—aerobic fitness levels have declined 10 percent among kids since 1980 and body fat is up 2 percent—for support. "We've raised a generation of couch potatoes," says Gunion. "There's a great deal of pressure on the American family. Discovery Zone offers an environment where a parent can spend time with a child. We get comments all the time from parents saying their kids sleep better, eat better, and behave better after trips to Discovery Zone."

Environmentalism, likewise, has given birth to nature books, arts and crafts kits, and toys and has affected the way other companies do business. Archie Comic Publications, for example, shifted to printing on recycled paper after getting letters from its readers requesting it. In return, the company, which sells more than 14 million comic books a year, got more than warm feelings from its buyers. It landed front-page treatment in *USA Today*. "Kids are so sensitive to environmental issues; they will demand our product over other comic books," marketing vice president David Silberkleit says. "That's what our business is about—listening to kids."

Summing Up

1. Products should fit a real need in the market and offer meaningful benefits. Research should be conducted periodically in product development to determine how significant a response the company can expect for the product, what qualities the consumer wants to see in the product, and how it should be priced and marketed.

2. New products defy strict categorization. But there do seem to be common threads to many of them, which can guide the development of further products.

3. Many new products take consumer electronics innovations, new fashions, and other trends from the adult market and redesign them to fit the demands of children.

4. Some products straddle the desires of grown-ups and kids. One example that we are seeing more of are foods that offer health benefits of lower salt or fat levels with a taste or packaging that kids enjoy.

5. Because today's parents are the most educated in the country's history, there is an unusually high demand for educational products for children and for products that combine learning with fun.

6. Products and brands that were popular in the past have a potential to be brought back today, particularly if they offer benefits that no other products do. Parents often find comfort in giving their children toys and foods that they enjoyed when they were kids.

7. Licensing has provided companies with some of the biggest successes of recent years, but they are also risky investments since it's virtually impossible to know ahead of time whether the movie or TV show in question will be popular.

8. Kids are fascinated by shapes and sizes. As a result, new products that do something new with an accepted object—for example, by shrinking a car or doll to miniature size—are often favorites of children.

9. Likewise, marketers who keep ahead of issues have found new-product opportunities in social trends, such as environmentalism, and health and fitness.

7
Getting the Look, Finding the Name

Naming and Packaging a Product

Pop Quiz (Essay Questions)

1. Think of your favorite toy, cereal, or snack from when you were a child. What was the product's name? What did the name mean to you? What comes to mind when you think of the name today? Was it an unusual name?

2. What do you see first when you pick up a package in a store? What's the second thing you see? The third thing? What draws you—if anything—to pick up the package and look closer? What stands out in the small type? What do you remember about the package after you have left the store?

3. How did the name of the product and the packaging work together? If they didn't, what went wrong?

Note: These exercises aren't intended to create a package, but rather to open your mind about the subject.

What's in a Name?

In the course of conducting focus groups for a client, Children's Market Research recently had occasion to ask kids about various product names. One name that came up consistently was *Nerds*. You may not know the product. It is a tiny, round candy in various colors that comes in a clever, sprightly done box and is made by a division of Nestlé. The product has done very well. Kids love it.

Why do they love it? The candy itself, obviously, is a large part of the explanation. But it's also the name. It doesn't particularly relate to the product. But the name, with its connotation of a playground insult, immediately brings smiles and giggles to kids' faces. The product was able to capitalize on the popularity of the word. Anytime a kid says "nerd" in any context, it's a de facto advertisement for the product.

Why Names and Packages Are Important

The product's success shows there's a lot to a name. The same is true of packaging. An exciting name and intriguing graphics can inform kids about what's inside, hint at the pleasures and revelations the product will bring, and stir up enough curiosity that the child will pick the product up off the shelf, buy it (if he has the money to do so), or remember it when he or she makes out the list of things wanted for a holiday or birthday, or from the weekly trip to the grocery store.

Ultimately, of course, a product lives or stands on its own merits. A head of broccoli, packaged in neon green and hot pink cellophane, with Lichtenstein graphics and a totally cool name, will still, when you unwrap it, cook it in the steamer, and serve it on a plate to a child, be a head of broccoli. If the child turned his or her nose up at it before, he or she can be counted on to do it again. A lousy product is still a lousy product. But, if it's a product the child already is predisposed to like, the packaging can push it over the top.

The name *Teenage Mutant Ninja Turtles* is a good example. It combines in each of its elements something that appeals to preadolescent boys—it's green, it's slimy, it's strange, and it has a martial-arts connotation. Karate is an intriguing sport to young boys.

The rules for what a name or package should do depend upon what kind of product it is. Generally, the more expensive the item is, the more information the consumer will want to have before making the purchase. If a child is buying a packet of chewing gum, for example, he or she will want to know basic information from the gum's name—the flavor or flavors of the gum, the number of sticks inside, and a brief description ("Super Sour!" "Extra Juicy!").

For a $25 doll, the consumer, be it a child or a grown-up, probably will want to be able to get a good, close look at what the toy is—preferably with a see-through package instead of a photograph or drawing. He or she will also want to know whether batteries are needed to operate the product and, more importantly, whether, for example, the doll crawls. The consumer may also want to know some basic operating instructions from reading the box, such as whether the doll does indeed crawl and how you get her to do it.

A well-considered name is the icing on the cake. Once established, it can create a tremendous amount of good will that can pave the way for future line extensions. Barbie, Mario, Oreo, LEGO—they all by their very sound, can bring a smile to a child's face.

The names even describe in a humorous way what the product is like. *Nerf* sounds like the noise a Nerf ball makes as it bounces crazily off an object. The same is true of *Koosh*, the spindly, soft rubber ball. The names *Barbie* and *Skipper*, the two Mattel dolls, both have strong, memorable alliteration. *Oreo*, like the oreo cookie itself, is surrounded by a pleasing substance—the rounded, smooth *o*, in the case of the name, and the crisp, chocolate wafer, in the case of the cookie. *Nutter Butter*, the peanut butter sandwich cookie from Nabisco, is a singsong rhyme on *peanut butter*.

Testing the Name

If you're uncertain, it's best to go to the experts. Product names are one of the easiest things to test about a product. Not testing a name can have serious consequences. Children's Market Research has been called in many times by companies that have chosen a name on the marketing director's or chief executive officer's gut instinct. Sometimes, you get lucky. CMR recently was contracted by a regional food company to find out just why the name it had chosen for a product had turned out to be so popular with kids. The marketers, in essence, wanted to know what they had done right.

In that case, CMR was able to offer an explanation, after interviews with kids, how the name had struck such a chord. The research suggested that the product's packaging should be redesigned to emphasize the name more. It also indicated that the company should consider a series of line extensions to capitalize more on the product's popularity.

Most times, though, the call that comes in is from a marketer who went on chance and found out in the marketplace, after the fact, that the name did not work.

Companies usually bring market research into the selection of a name well before a final name—or even set of names—is chosen. For example, CMR was recently called on by a major company that had a list of about two dozen names for a new product. In an initial round of research, conducted on 50 kids through one-on-one interviews at shopping center research facilities, the list was narrowed down to the top 10 prospects. CMR then traveled to shopping malls in two more cities for a second round of one-on-one interviews, with about 150 more kids, to decide which name kids liked best.

You don't have to choose the name that tests as the most popular with the kids. It's quite possible that name is a word that is in vogue at the moment and will grow stale by the time your product hits the market. But market research can show, quite clearly, what names kids *don't* like. You do not want to go to market with a product name that is universally disliked by your target market.

Where Do Names Come From?

Conceiving a name that another company does not already have trademarked—as anyone who has been through the process knows—is next to impossible. However, there are some advantages to creating names for children's products because children's language is constantly changing. Thus, a word can be transformed overnight from something undesirable into something funny or even desirable. *Def* which sounds like *deaf*, has become a word associated with hip, in, or cool.

Even *stupid* acquired an aura of being neat. *Wack* quickly was transformed from *wacky*, meaning offbeat or goofy, to a word that means stupid in the original sense, the farthest from hip one can get. A sociologist might offer the explanation that, in their search to define themselves in their own terms in a world that is run by grown-ups, kids will always develop their own language. As marketers, suffice to say that, if you're trying to communicate to kids, language is on your side in the search for words that have not already been legally claimed.

There are all kinds of different processes for coining a name. *Barbie* was the name of the daughter of the doll's creator (*Ken*, not surprisingly, was the name of her son). *Sara Lee*, likewise, was the name of the creator's daughter. *Ginny*, the long-successful collectible doll marketed by Dakin, likewise was derived from the name of a real little girl. Other names are nonsensical strokes of genius that struck someone as right.

Some names are straightforward attempts to describe the product. *G.I. Joe* is probably the simplest name possible for an action figure based on the hard-working, stolid soldiers of World War II—as Joe originally was before veering off into anti-terrorist crusades.

Choosing a name means making a decision about what you want your name to accomplish. Do you want to create excitement? Do you want your name to educate the market about the product? (If you're marketing a new idea, that makes sense.) G.I. Joe worked well for Hasbro because, when the action figure came out, it was the first fashion-sized "doll" for boys. It was the same size as Barbie. However, the name communicated that Joe was a macho doll that offered boys a new way to play war. In the years since, G.I. Joe's size has diminished. He is now standard action-figure size, but the name continues to differentiate him.

The Process of Generating a Name

We have sat in on formal name-generating sessions. Some open with New Age music or psychological exercises. Most are simple, straightforward meetings. One productive session we participated in brought together the marketing department of a major company. If people had not taken part in the development of the product, all the better. They could bring a fresh perspective. We describe this session in detail because it offers a basic outline on how you could create a name.

A moderator gave a brief presentation on what the product was, how the marketing staff felt it would fit into the marketplace, what the sales goals for it were, and what consumers had said about the product in initial research. The research was summarized in memos to be used as references later, and distributed to the assembled group. The group then broke up into small teams of four to five persons that were assigned to caucus on the subject independently. Some teams stayed in the meeting room. Some went into offices. Some went to conference rooms.

Their assignment was to come up with a list of suggested names. No one could hold back. No one could criticize anyone's idea. The goal was to free-associate. Some looked for names in the words on the memos they had been given—either single words; compound names formed from words in the text; or nonsense words that picked up a phrase, partial phrase, or partial word. Others tried to think of proper names that they could build an icon around, like Betty Crocker. Some thought up names of cities, towns, regions, and landmarks.

When the group reassembled several hours later, the moderator collected all the lists, read them, and wrote them on a chalkboard. Then, he invited comments—preferably, positive comments on the names people liked best. In time, he winnowed the list of 50 names down to a manageable number.

The marketing staff took the remaining candidates to focus groups to see what images and reactions they evoked among consumers. Then they took the four top candidates—which did not necessarily include all the ones the consumers liked—and submitted them to quantitative research. Generally speaking, you don't have to pick the one name that ranks highest. You may have a feeling in your gut about what's right. But the research can give you an assessment of what kind of task you will have in the marketplace building awareness for your brand.

The Two Kinds of Names

There are two basic kinds of names for children's products. The first, as we have noted, is one that describes the product succinctly and accurately, conveying a sense of the single emotional characteristic the product will evoke in the consumer.

Super Soaker, described in Chapter 6 on creating a product, for example, tells rather well what the product does. It soaks the target. In fact, it does a super job of carrying out the task. The name has the added kick of alliteration; the repeated *s* evokes the slippery, sopping sound of the heavy-duty, next-generation water gun. The rhythmic repetition of two-syllable words, with the repeated hard consonant (*p* in *Super*, *k* in *Soaker*), ending both times in *r* communicates a sense of fun, urgency, and excitement that works well for the product. (See Figure 7.)

Most children's products, on some level, fit this type of name. That is appropriate, particularly for younger children. As we noted earlier, and will come back to again in Chapter 9 on advertising, children are very literal consumers. They want to know what they will get. It pays, in all communication to them, to explain straightforwardly what you are trying to market to them. They want to know that a doll is a doll, a cookie a cookie, a video game a video game. One should not take much for granted.

Walk through a toy store, grocery store, or restaurant that depends on children for its business, and you will find that most of the products have descriptive names. The name *Go-Go My Walking Pup*, Hasbro's battery-operated walking dog, tells the consumer that the product is a puppy; that it walks or, if you prefer, really *goes*; and that, best of all, presumably, it can be yours. *Hot Wheels*, Mattel's long-successful collectible car line, are "wheels," in 1950s teenage parlance, that are "hot," that is, fast and neat.

Fisher Price's Little People *are*, in part, little people. Micro Machines are practically microscopic-sized machines. Matchbox cars are collectible cars that really could fit into a matchbox. Cupcakes are toy cupcakes that transform into dolls. Transformers, of course, are items that transform into robots. Baby Alive is a baby doll that does many of the things that live babies do. Talking Baby Alive is also a baby doll that does many of the things that living babies do—and talks to boot. McDonald's Happy Meals, of course, are meals that are supposed to

Figure 7. From the original Super Soaker pumpaction water gun, Larami Corp. developed a surprisingly large line of Super Soaker products such as the Super Soakerman. (Courtesy of Larami Corporation.)

make you feel happy. Mini Oreo cookies are indeed miniature Oreo cookies. Play-Doh is play dough. Teddy Grahams are graham crackers in the shape of teddy bears. Pizzarias are pizza chips. Easy Bake, that line of cookies, cakes, and toy ovens that has been around since the 1960s, makes it easy to bake things. Cabbage Patch Kids, in a slight modification, created a story around the dolls; they were kids who came from the cabbage patch.

The second basic type of name for children's products is the nonsensical name. Some are made up. Many communicate onomatopoeia—that is, they sound like the action or end result of the product. *Koosh,*

Nerf, and *Frisbee* all do that. *Koosh* and *Nerf* sound like playful, harmless sounds of the objects bouncing off surfaces. *Frisbee*—with its flying *f,* buzzing *s,* and whimsical *bee*—actually sounds like the flying disk as it cuts through the air to its target.

Other nonsensical names take existing words and turn them inside out. *Garbage Pail,* for example, hardly sounds appealing— until you append the word *Kids* and make it a fun, adventuresome tour with the kind of stories and jokes preadolescent boys tell, usually punctuated by blasting burps, around the lunch table at school. Nestlé took a rather derisive, humorous term—*Nerds*—and turned it into a candy.

Various companies have tapped into that sense of the gross, which appeals strongly to little boys. It's not particularly new. *Mad* was launched in the 1950s and developed a broad following through the 1960s with Alfred E. Neuman, its gap-toothed icon; Don Martin's offbeat cartoons; the "Spy v. Spy" series; and its twisted parodies of *West Side Story,* "Star Trek," and other movies and TV shows of the day. In the 1960s, boys collected Rat Finks, the miniature plastic-molded statuettes of a rather demented looking rat in coveralls, who raced hot rods. In the 1980s, Garbage Pail Kids trading cards delighted kids with their gross drawings and names of the kids. Topps Co., known for its baseball trading cards, developed a healthy side business with sick products like a candy dispenser in the shape of a sickly face that spit out candy. Not a pleasant sight, particularly to moms and dads, but it served a purpose.

Familiarity Breeds Security

It's important to remember that the world is a big, strange, and often confusing place that kids are learning how to come to grips with as they move from the ages of 6 through 14. In a world where there are so many new experiences, they take great comfort in the familiar.

It starts, of course, with their families, relatives, friends, and pets, but it extends also to their toys, *chatchkas,* eating habits (How many children go through periods of only eating Cheerios and peanut-butter sandwiches?), and experiences. Parents know that children love to listen to a favorite tape or watch reruns of a beloved television show, over and over until it seems they have memorized every word.

It's easy to understand, then, why so many companies look to licensed products for success, in categories from toys, to videos, stuffed animals, comic books, action figures, lunch boxes, cereals, and consumer electronics. The television character, movie celebrity, athlete, children's book hero, or pop-music star already has done the work of establishing awareness with the consumer. To the extent the character has a positive association, the purchase may make the child feel as though he or she has purchased a certain cachet. Often it's someone other than the child, such as a grandparent, who buys the product, knowing only that the kid likes the character.

Ralston Purina has developed an ongoing business in licensed breakfast cereals based on such pop-culture icons as Batman, Nintendo, and Barbie. Some survive for a couple of quarters; some bomb. The composition of the sugary cereals were all fairly similar, regardless of the licensed product. The key for Ralston appears to be to keep production costs low enough to survive the flops so they can cash in on the hits.

It stands to reason that the child, comfortable with the character, will be more likely to accept the product the character endorses. Seeing the character on the package and advertisements draws in the child.

As we noted in the previous chapter, however, licensing is a risky business, and it costs substantial amounts of money. You might find yourself buying into a star who has already peaked and begun the downhill slide or who will never reach prominence at all. You don't have to rely on celebrities to build familiarity into a name or a package. You can look at the market's own life—the rhythms of behavior, language, types of people and events—to find universal touchstones.

A French Catalog

Children's Market Research was contacted by a company that wanted to launch a catalog in the United States for children's clothes. The company planned to offer clothes that were designed in France. The executives figured that French clothes would have a certain cachet with American consumers. Many parents bought well-established European designer clothes for themselves. Given parents' desire to have their children put the best foot forward, it stood to reason that parents would buy the same, smartly designed, fashionable styles of clothing for their children—and pay a premium price for them.

What the company wanted to know was what to name the line. What would communicate the flair of the clothing without putting off consumers? Children's Market Research conducted studies on several options.

Consumers responded that they were confused by purely French words that they could not understand. French proper names sounded nice, but it appeared that the company would have to take extra steps to fill in the blanks for consumers on what the names *meant*. The choice that consumers preferred was a name that contained a French word that was part of the English language as well. Such a name could communicate the French heritage, but in a form that was accessible to Americans. Based on the research, the company chose a name and went on to enjoy immediate success.

Packaging: Make It Eyecatching, Keep It Simple

It's easy to get wrapped up in the aesthetics of packaging. With the evolution of new type faces and bold new colors, going to the supermarket in a yuppie, product-rich area of the country can be like going to a department store. But—and this is especially true for kids—it's easy to forget that the single most important task for packaging is to tell the consumer what the product is.

Many products do this with photographs and drawings. This enables the company to show the product in action. For some products, this is the best packaging. For example, Mattel often shows photos of its more elaborate Barbie sets, to give girls an idea of the kinds of stories they can act out if they buy the set. An 800-piece LEGO building-block set would just be a jumble of pieces without illustrations. The attraction for the consumer is to see what the product looks like when it is assembled. To excite the consumer about the little gadgets the product includes and, perhaps, to light the child's sense of challenge, LEGO products often include a flap, which lets the consumer lift up the box lid displaying photos of the finished product to see the hundreds of colorful pieces they may soon be putting together.

For other products, see-through windows are preferable. Some companies have found that they even save the package from damage. Before introducing My First Sony, Sony executives strolled consumer-electronics aisles in department stores, toy stores, and stereo stores to see how consumers shopped. They were surprised to find that parents, blithely ignoring the labels on packages instructing them not to open the box, tore off the sealing tape and pulled the product out anyway. With the size of investment they were making, the parents wanted to see what was inside. Sony subsequently designed its packages with windows so that consumers could get a good, clear view of what they were buying.

Colors and Design

There are tens of thousands of items in a typical modern grocery store or toy store. To make the leap from the store shelf to the shopping cart, the product has to say something compelling that will make it stand out from the products around it. A good name—which we've already covered—can accomplish at least some of the task, but the product itself certainly has to do a lot of the work.

Package design is also key to selling the product. It is the most important in-store advertisement, and, with research showing a growing number of consumers making their purchase decisions spontaneously after they're in the store, some observers argue that package design is a product's most important advertising, period.

A clever combination of colors and graphics, such as the bright colors, cartoon characters, and kid-friendly dishes on ConAgra's Kid Cuisine frozen entrée line, communicates immediately to a kid that *this stuff is for me!* Kids know their world intimately. If they see Mickey Mouse; Bugs Bunny; Saturday morning cartoon characters; familiar faces from their favorite sitcoms or movies; or even new characters like the Kid Cuisine bear, who look like they could be a character that kids would know, they recognize it.

Overall, kids show remarkable discrimination. Packaging, as a result, should reflect as tightly as possible the market that the product was created for. By the time kids have reached the age of 10, they start to emulate the product purchases of preteens and teenagers. A 10-year-old, then, may be less than receptive to a package that he or she considers babyish.

Kids will immediately decide from the product's colors, rightly or wrongly, who the product is for. So it pays to research the colors that you will use. Pink and lavender, as we noted in Chapter 5, immediately says "girls." Bright, primary colors say "younger kids." Blue generally says "boys." Neon colors, when they were trendy and new, said the product was for "cool" kids, perhaps even teenagers or preteens, who were slightly older and more sophisticated.

As neon has gone more mainstream, however, it has lost its edge. And it may be moving younger. Once elementary school students adopt a trend, it's likely the older kids will move onto something new, to set themselves off from the masses. The same may be true of the animated, surfer-style graphics and type faces that were associated with neon colors.

Kids also look to colors to describe the product. If a product is chocolate, they expect to see brown packaging. If it is strawberry or cherry, they want to see red. If it's lemon, they want to see yellow. Grape, purple; licorice, black; apple green, green. If they don't see the color they expect, it's disorienting. They may have less trust for the product.

Again, the key is to go out and talk to the consumer as you develop the product. The colors you choose will play a large role in defining the product. They should be as effective as you can make them.

How Much Should a Package Say?

How many words should be on a package? The answer depends on what the product is. Some packages stay around the house for a long time. It can help build brand equity to encourage the buyer to stop and take a moment with the item. The first rule should be that the words on the package should be clear and understandable to the market.

Breakfast cereals come immediately to mind. Kids haul them to the table every morning, and, quite often, pore over the stories, puzzles, and games on the back of the box while they eat with the same intensity that Mom and Dad pore over the morning paper. Most kids love to read—if not schoolwork, then comic books or the sports section.

Kellogg and General Mills do a terrific job of keeping kids coming back. The Big G went so far as to create a back-of-the-box basketball game, with Michael Jordan's endorsement, that folded out from boxes of Wheaties, keeping kids entertained while they ate. Kellogg's corn-flakes has become the baseball fan's cereal. The brand has produced holograph baseball cards of greats like Willie Mays. It also has little lessons about the game, such as one series that let kids "make the call" on specific plays and then explained what a real-life umpire using the major league baseball rule book would do.

Some packages will stay around while the buyer learns how to use the product. Toys that require assembly or have more than a mild degree of complexity often contain some kind of instructions or a troubleshooting guide. (A very complicated assembly, of course, should be included on separate instructions inside the box. Boxes inevitably get stepped on, chewed up by the dog, or destroyed.) To ensure that the instructions won't interfere with the brand name, the visual icon, or the description of the product, this information often is put on the back of the box.

But not all packages stay long. Candy wrappers, for instance, go immediately into the trash bin once the contents have provided the buyer the immediate gratification he or she was looking for. On these wrappers, then, the only really important elements are the brand name and the icon graphic design. They should be colorful enough and dis-tinctive enough to be immediately recognizable. The packaging should be simple and have impact.

Before deciding how much to put on the package, then, you should learn from your consumer how they will be using the product and how much time the package will stay around. The longer it will stay around, the more prominent a place it will have in the household. And the more time the consumer will spend with the package, the more information it can hold.

Kids, not surprisingly, read what is of interest to them. Children's Market Research has found little evidence that many kids read nutritional information on food packages. To the extent that many kids read such tables and charts, it's to find out how much of the ingredients that they love and their parents may be wary of, like sugar, are in the product. Interest in nutrition appears to rise among older kids, depending on how much kids have been exposed to the subject in school. By the age of 12, children appear to be familiar with basic health and nutrition issues.

Summing Up

1. The product itself, of course, will determine your ultimate success. But an exciting name and intriguing package can inform kids what's inside and hint at the excitement the product will bring.

2. Names and packaging depend on the kind of product you are marketing. Generally, the more expensive an item is, the more information the consumer will want.

3. There may be some advantages to creating names for children's products in comparison with ones for grown-ups. Because the language of children is fluid, new words and new meanings are continually taking shape.

4. There are two basic kinds of names for children's products. The first type describes the product succinctly and accurately. The second is a nonsensical name, often conjured from thin air, that communicates the emotional appeal of the product.

5. Kids are literalists when they venture out as consumers. As a result, they find comfort in familiar names and images. This accounts in large part for the appeal of licensed products.

6. The single most important task for packaging is to describe what the product is. This can be done visually through photographs, drawings, see-through windows that show the actual product, or a combination of techniques.

7. The number of words on the package should be determined by how long the package will stay in the house and how prominent it will be. Cereal boxes, for example, are prominent on the breakfast table every morning, so it is appropriate for them to carry stories, games, and puzzles that will keep kids' interest. More complicated toys often carry basic descriptions of how they work.

8. Colors and graphic elements are tip-offs to kids on who the product is targeted to. For example, kids generally assume that lavender and pink products are marketed to girls. It is important to research your packaging and names before going to market to make sure you and your market are on the same wavelength.

8

How Kids Shop

Where and How to Sell Your Product

Fast Facts

1. Children are shoppers. In all, kids aged 6 to 14 have about $7.3 billion in spending money a year.

2. Kids accompany their parents on a variety of shopping trips. They influence between $120 billion and $150 billion in purchases a year.

3. Most children accompany their parents when the major household food shopping is done. And many are influential in product and brand selection for themselves and for the family.

4. It can be anticipated that children's influence will continue to increase, in the aggregate, with the growth in the population of 6- to 14-year-olds.

The New American Family

Changes in the American family, such as dual-income households and kids' increased responsibilities in the home, are major factors affecting family lifestyles in the 1990s. As mothers have become less traditional homemakers, children have become more independent and have been given more responsibility and a greater input in family life and purchasing behavior. There is more discretionary income in dual-income families.

114

Children as Primary Consumers

Children aged 6 to 14 have about $7.3 billion in spending money. As a result, they have the means to purchase many things. Parents provide nearly half of their children's income in the form of allowance or money given out as needed. The other half comes from earnings from part-time work, household chores, and odd jobs. Children only save about 20 percent of their income.

Kids as Shoppers

By the time they reach 6 years old, kids have been introduced to being consumers. Shopping becomes almost a hobby. (See Tables 7 and 8.) It is a way to explore the world, make choices, husband your financial resources—and you get the reward of an object you want. Some are very enthusiastic shoppers. Said Lisa, aged 10, in a focus group, "I was born to shop!"

Starting Out: Convenience Stores

The first experience many children handling their own money have is in convenience stores. There are two basic reasons why. The first is location. For most kids growing up in a city, suburb, or small town, there is usually a convenience store within a short walking distance of home or school—either a mom-and-pop store around the corner in a city or town or a 7-Eleven in a small strip mall on a street a few blocks away.

The second reason is selection. The variety of goods that convenience stores carry—gum, candy, chips, cookies, soda, comic books, trading cards—fits what kids aged 6 to 14 typically spend the bulk of their allowance on. A young consumer can bike to the store, make a choice from a broad array of goods, and not bust his or her $3.50-a-week allowance.

The other goods a convenience store carries are the kind of items that a family buys in between major shopping trips. For example, a mom will send her 10-year-old to the store to buy items like milk, juice, bread, perhaps disposable diapers for our young shopper's little brother or sister. The age that parents give their children the responsibility to go shopping by themselves varies by family. Kids are usually trusted with this task by the time they are 11 years old.

Table 7. Stores Visited by Child in the Last Four Weeks
(by percent)

	Total	Boys	Girls
K mart	47.8	46.4	49.2
J.C. Penney	31.3	26.3	36.6
Wal-Mart	28.4	28.2	28.6
Sears	26.2	25.3	27.2
Toys R Us	22.4	23.0	21.8
Target Stores	14.9	13.4	16.5
Payless	14.5	12.3	16.7
Kay Bee Toys	14.2	15.1	13.3
Woolworth/Woolco	11.4	11.9	10.9
Montgomery Ward	11.3	11.5	11.1
Mervyn's	9.3	7.3	11.4
Ames	8.6	9.7	7.4
Kids R Us	8.6	8.2	9.1
Kinney	7.2	4.7	9.9
T.J. Maxx	5.8	4.6	7.1
Marshall's	5.6	4.7	6.6
The Gap	5.5	4.1	6.9
Fayva	4.9	4.6	5.2
The Limited	4.1	2.0	6.4
Disney Store	4.0	4.1	4.0
Benetton	3.6	2.7	4.6
Thom McAn	3.5	3.3	3.7
Esprit	3.0	2.7	3.3
Jordan Marsh	2.9	2.8	3.0
Marshall Fields	2.7	2.4	3.1
Foley's	2.5	2.6	2.3
Parkway	2.5	2.5	2.6
Young World	2.2	1.9	2.5
Richway	1.7	2.2	1.2
Mandees	1.7	1.6	1.8
Other	32.7	33.0	32.5

SOURCE: CMR KIDTRENDS REPORT, based on data from The Simmons Kids Study (1991).

The economic function the stores serve often creates a social function as well. Kids will convene at a mom-and-pop store after school to buy a Marvel comic, suck on a packet of Jolly Ranchers candy, play a video arcade game, and socialize with their friends.

Convenience stores, despite the fact that they deal in small change, can offer lessons on customer service for larger retailers. The owner usually knows what the customers like most and groups those items accordingly to make it easy for the kids to find what they want. At a

Table 8. Amount of Influence Child Has in Choosing
Department or Discount Stores Where Shopping Is Done
for Him/Her
(by percent)

	Total	Boys	Girls
A lot of influence	15.7	11.8	19.7
Some influence	26.6	26.0	27.2
A little influence	22.9	21.4	24.4
No influence	28.5	33.2	23.4
No answer	6.3	7.6	5.3

SOURCE: CMR KIDTRENDS REPORT, based on data from The Simmons Kids
Study (1991).

well-established corner store, the owner and sales help will know the
regulars who come into the store.

They greet them by name, ask about their parents, talk about a subject
of interest to the kid ("How was your little league game?"), and maybe,
if they are a "preferred" customer, give them a break if the child comes
up a couple pennies short on a purchase. The interaction builds up a
relationship that will keep the kids coming back week after week.

Grocery Shopping with Mom

The second place where children get an introduction to shopping is the
grocery store. Most children aged 6 to 14 accompany their mother or
father when the major weekly food shopping is done for the household.
They learn from watching their parents—how to draw up a grocery list,
how to make choices between competing brands or different heads of
lettuce, how to use coupons, maybe how to read a label, and, usually,
how to impulse shop. It's an invaluable experience.

At some point—very often, by the time a child is able to articulate his
or her own wants—the child will take the initiative to ask for a product
or, if they have climbed out of the cart, toddle over and pick it out himself or herself. Grocers know this happens; that's why children's brands
are usually on the lowest shelves in the store.

Mom may protest at first, but on some level she's also proud to see
her child making choices. And, given the cost of food, it's a relief to see
her boy or girl pick out a food that he or she will eat. Along the way, the
kids usually come to take responsibility for picking out certain products—the breakfast cereals, the juice, fruit rolls, fresh fruit, ice cream, or
salty snacks. And, in many families, the kids come to influence the pur-

chase of a broad range of products, from bread, to fruit, vegetables, meat, and fish.

By going into the grocery store with their parents, kids are guaranteed at least a chance at getting most of their favorite foods. They love to walk up and down each aisle and throw an item into the cart. Sometimes there is negotiation, as we have seen in earlier chapters, but the child often gets what he or she wants.

Many children become *the* household expert on specific categories of food. CMR KIDTRENDS REPORT, based on The Simmons Kids Study, showed that the types of foods children are most likely to be experts on are snack foods, such as cookies, candy, potato chips, crackers, soda, and ice cream. (See Figure 8.)

Anywhere from 25 to 40 percent of 6- to 14-year-olds are deemed the experts when it comes to selecting these types of foods. And 47 percent of kids are the family experts in the selection of breakfast cereals. That means the kids are deciding what is bought. For marketers, then, advertising and promoting products to kids as well as parents should be a basic component of these products' marketing mix.

Figure 8. As anyone who has pushed a shopping cart through a supermarket knows, children actively influence purchases of food. Here, Dr. Guber interviews two kids in the snack-chip aisle.

Toy Stores: The Kid Mecca

Less frequent, but infinitely exciting, are trips with Mom and Dad to the toy store. A trip to the toy store can be more than a journey to make a purchase. It is an outing.

Going to the store is entertainment, like going to a movie. The child gets to see what's new and to touch and experience what he or she has seen in commercials on television and at their friends' houses.

Stephanie, aged 5, and Todd, aged 8, say they love going to the toy store. They describe the trips as two-hour minivacations. This week, Stephanie was begging for a new bike, preferably pink. Todd was insistent on a new Super Soaker. For the parents, the trip is fun, too. Toys R Us, F.A.O. Schwartz, and other toy retailers are expert at tapping into the little kid inside grown-ups as well as marketing to the children. To the parents, going to the toy store and buying something new for the children is a reward for making it to the weekend.

Often, the kids come out with more than the one major toy they set out for, for example, adding baseball cards, a Nintendo cartridge on sale, or a new Barbie outfit.

In-Store Displays and Promotions

Promoting a product to children inside a store is a sensitive issue and should be undertaken with caution, care, and respect toward both children and parents. Children and parents have limited amounts of money they can spend. Overwhelming a child with urgent demands to buy, buy, buy is both unethical and bad business. It can reduce a child to tears and get you an angry parent who will retain a sense of anger and resentment toward your product and the store.

It's advisable for retailers and manufacturers to test your ideas with parents and children. Parents in some parts of the country, for example, may protest stocking candies next to the checkout line at the supermarket. In response, the retailer may want to set out an equivalent selection of sugarless gums and candies, trail mixes, or other noncandy items popular with both parents and children—such as Golden Books, children's magazines, crayons, and other arts and crafts products.

As we've said before, children are visually oriented. That is why television and movies are such popular forms of entertainment for them. They bring that same visual acuity to their shopping expeditions. Upon entering the stores, kids are attracted by visual stimuli as well as actual products. The stimuli can be anything from a sign to a character, a poster, the colors on a box, or a display of products.

The manufacturer can help the retailer create an atmosphere that appeals to kids by supplying displays with colorful graphics and familiar images. It could be a life-size poster of a popular athlete such as Michael Jordan or characters from a children's book such as *Where The Wild Things Are* (an obvious visual cue for the location of the children's section of a bookstore).

Live appearances by popular characters or celebrities can supplement an ongoing program. An appearance by a Disney character or the Teenage Mutant Ninja Turtles is an obvious draw. But it doesn't have to be a movie star. Stew Leonard's, the popular northeastern dairy-store chain, created its own store spokescharacters to make the grocery shopping experience fun for both children and parents. A worker dressed up as a cow, for example, passes out cookies. Animatronic characters sing songs from the top of grocery aisles.

Sampling: A Small Taste

Sometimes a child or parent will not be familiar with a product. Offering free samples of the product can introduce the consumer to it. It can also tap into children's desires to try something new and their delight in receiving something for free. Kids enjoy being able to taste a food before deciding to buy it. It makes them feel important to be courted.

Sampling can be an effective technique for drawing attention to products such as food, snacks, treats, and cosmetics. It's another way of generating word-of-mouth advertising. If the child likes the product, he or she will tell parents and friends.

Obviously, sampling is more difficult for a toy. The corollary in toy stores is to set up displays to give room for children to touch and play with a display model. F.A.O. Schwartz, the famed New York toy store, is a model for this. The store gives ample space for children to play with toys from musical instruments to stuffed animals to race-car sets.

Arranging the Goods

When they enter a store, children look for visual cues that point out the section that is for them. At Blockbuster Video, visual cues include an arrangement of brightly colored children's furniture and games that marks off the children's video section of the store.

At toy stores, children look for the toys that are targeted at their age range. Toys, then, should be grouped by age, rather than by other factors. If it is at all manageable, the displays should have a sample toy available so kids can see and feel the toy. Once a train set is assembled, for example, it is a world of action with bridges and tunnels, people, villages, and other accessories.

Toys related to a theme or topic can be grouped together as well. For example, Superman, Batman, or Star Wars licensed action figures and play toys, introduced with the release of the movie, can be grouped together to leverage the excitement the movie has already generated.

The most important real estate in the toy store is near the area where customers enter and exit. A large display seen when entering a store can create a lasting impression. It becomes the comparison point for the products that the children see subsequently. If it's close to the cash register as well, it can become a source of impulse purchases that are picked up when Mom and Dad have taken out the wallet to pay. Accordingly, it is extremely competitive to get into this section of the store.

The changes of seasons offer display and promotion opportunities. During back-to-school, Christmas/Hanukkah, Easter, and presummer seasons, children are in stores en masse. Kid-oriented displays and promotions can draw kids to a specific store over its competitors.

Displays at checkout stands can be an effective means for introducing a product. A small, free sample can help establish a bond with the store and encourage brand loyalty. Collectibles are favorites with children. If kids can collect a series of stickers or stamps in order to get a free gift, it will encourage loyalty to the store. Coupons have not been tested effectively with children, but they appear to hold opportunity for promotional ideas. A discounted product offered through coupons may entice a young buyer.

Kids love contests because they love competition and the possibility of winning. Contests can be arranged by going to the store or through mail-ins. Displays in the store can advertise the contest. Trips and merchandise are popular prizes.

Advanced Shopping: Mall Mania

As they get older, kids gain more independence to go shopping on their own. The primary hangout and shopping place for kids once they gain that independence is the shopping mall. On any given Saturday, shopping malls are mobbed with kids, particularly as they reach their teen years. The mall not only enhances the shopping experience, but it also provides kids with the perfect audience for their purchases. At an age where peer approval is critical, the mall serves its purpose well by providing kids with a sort of support network of other kids.

After watching TV shows and movies, Jamie, aged 11, has a pretty solid grasp of current trends. She discusses the cool products and hot items with her friends. She is not a trendsetter, but she likes to be in style and have the latest products. On Saturday, Jamie and some friends often decide to hang out at the mall.

They scout around and make note of not only the items they like but also the ones their friends seem to like. Jamie and her pals often spend an entire afternoon at the mall, stopping for lunch at a pizzaria or fast-food restaurant. After getting a pretty good idea of what's available and the prices of the items, Jamie may try on a few articles of clothing and maybe even make a few small purchases. The big investments are saved for when she can go shopping with Mom or Dad.

Jamie returns home with a few small purchases plus a good idea of what she would like to purchase next. So how does she eventually make that higher-priced purchase? With an allowance of $3 per week, she doesn't have an abundance of disposable income. She usually spends that on candy or comic books, or sometimes a movie. So she goes to her parents. With most children receiving money as they need it, Jamie knows that if she plays her cards right, she could definitely come out ahead.

Enter Mom and Dad. Younger children and preteens tend to buy big-ticket items with their parents. After scouting out the items they want with their friends, they go shopping with Mom and Dad. They return to the mall, go to a smaller store, or shop at a department store. As early as age 7 or 8, children seem to know what they want.

Parents let their children guide them through the stores. As children get older, the amount of parental advice that they follow decreases. So although a 7-year-old may think that she knows exactly what she wants, she can be swayed or pressured by her parents. But an 11- or 12-year-old knows what she wants and goes for it with gusto, using a range of techniques that we have outlined earlier. Sometimes they can even get Mom and Dad to pay without having to bring them along.

As kids get older, they don't like to be seen by their peers in the company of their parents. So kids devise means of obtaining spending money without bringing their parents along. Some parents hand over their credit cards to their kids, usually with words of caution. This allows teens not only to be able to scout out items with their friends but also to make large purchases.

How One Store Does It: The Gap

How can a store attract young consumers? It's a question that retailers should be concerned with from the first view the shopper has of the store when they enter to how merchandise is displayed and how sales help are trained.

The Gap and its sibling store, GapKids, for example, use what could be called the show-everything technique. The Gap puts stacks of colorful, easy-to-match clothing throughout the store. As a result, kids will very often find something they want and will come away with a purchase—even if it's a plain Gap T-shirt. The Gap is renowned for durable classic clothes, and it has reinforced its quality image with a responsive returns policy.

The Gap is thought of by kids as a sartorial safety net. The store's classic mix of clothes makes it a safe bet for pleasing both parents and peers. The photos of gorgeous models posted in the store in Gap apparel create the impression in kids that they can achieve that look as well. The appearance of Luke Perry, the star of the Fox Network's teen hit "Beverly Hills 90210," reinforced the chain's image as a hip store.

Music and Electronics

Regardless of age, funds, or time commitments, kids always manage to browse in record stores. It is not hard for the stores to attract customers. Once inside, it's easy for the kids to find something they "need." Stores often put brightly colored tags on sale items. Sales are an effective technique for enticing young buyers to make purchases. Even after they make the purchase, they can rationalize that they "only" spent $7.98.

Another stop for many kids is the electronics store. Kids look for large variety and products with lots of features. They are entertained by rows and rows of television sets. And they like being able to examine the gadgetry on answering machines or telephones. (See Table 9.)

Music stores and electronics stores often employ college-aged students. The workers are familiar with what kids want, what parents want, and what the final, weighted compromise will probably be.

Electronics won't necessarily be purchased by a young person. More often they will become a present purchased by a parent or grandparent for a birthday, graduation, or holiday.

Table 9. Types of Electronic Equipment Child Owns or Uses
(by percent)

	Total	Boys	Girls
Television (color)	65.8	66.7	64.8
VCR	59.6	60.8	58.3
Camera	49.4	46.3	52.7
Clock radio	46.6	46.4	46.7
Pocket or hand-held calculator	45.6	47.3	43.8
Portable stereo radio (boom box)	43.8	42.5	45.1
Portable/walk-about stereo with headphones (Walkman)	41.2	41.6	40.7
Compact or console stereo (all-in-one)	22.9	21.2	24.6
Stereo receiver/tuner/amplifier (all-in-one)	19.2	21.1	17.2
Separate stereo components	15.8	16.3	15.3
Camcorder	12.5	11.6	13.4
Compact disc player	12.3	11.8	12.8
None of these	5.9	5.7	6.1

SOURCE: CMR KIDTRENDS REPORT, based on data from The Simmons Kids Study (1991).

Cards 'n Things

After spending some time in stores where they may not be able to afford many items, kids find a haven in card shops. Hallmark stores, for example, supply a range of basic goodies that are within the budgets of young shoppers. It could be a poster, knickknack, or a card for a friend or relative.

Hallmark uses techniques similar to those of The Gap. By displaying all the available items, the store makes it easy for a kid to find something. Even if a young shopper just goes in because a friend needs something, it is rare for him or her to leave without making a purchase.

Big novelty cards hanging from the walls attract attention. Cards with Snoopy, Woodstock, and other characters appealing to youngsters are often at eye level. Anniversary, graduation, and birthday cards are higher up. The layout is similar to a supermarket.

Summing Up

Questions to Consider

1. What kind of store will be best for you to sell your product in?

2. Where is the optimal place in the store for the product to be displayed? Is there a logical grouping for the product? Can it be displayed

in such a way that either a taste or play sample can be offered to give children an idea of what the product is like?

3. Will the placement of the product be accessible to the child? Will children be able to see and touch the product easily?

4. Are there contests or seasonal promotions that you can create to generate more interest in your product on the part of the retailer and the customer?

9
Tuning in TV Advertising

Pop Quiz

1. At what times do kids watch TV in substantial enough numbers to merit advertisers' attention?
   (*a*) Saturday morning, (*b*) weekdays after school, (*c*) prime time, (*d*) any of the above.

2. Are any of the following perfectly OK in a commercial?
   (*a*) urge kids to tell their parents to run out and buy your product, (*b*) tell kids your product will make them more popular, (*c*) remind kids the price is "only" $9.99, (*d*) none of the above, (*e*) some of the above.

3. Which is true?
   (*a*) adults don't remember ads from their childhood, (*b*) if you advertise to kids, you can create a lifelong relationship.

4. Which is true of younger children?
   (*a*) they need a simple, clear story line so they won't get distracted, (*b*) they are so sophisticated and verbal, that you don't need to worry about losing them.

5. Which types of companies have created ads for kids in the past few years?
   (*a*) travel, (*b*) home video, (*c*) cosmetics, (*d*) blue jeans, (*e*) all of the above.

Answers: 1. *d*; 2. *d*; 3. *b*; 4. *a*; 5. *e*.

What Was Your Favorite?

What do I want? I want my Maypo! How many ways does Wonder bread build strong bodies? Twelve, of course. What does Tony the Tiger say about Kellogg's Frosted Flakes? They're Gr-r-reat! Everyone knows... it's Slinky. Rice Krispies go Snap, Crackle, Pop. Silly rabbit, Trix are for, what? Kids, naturally. Wheaties are the Breakfast of Champions—unless you're a child of the 1980s. Then they're what the big boys eat. You deserve a break today (at McDonald's). Just do it.

Make you a little nostalgic? You're not alone. Advertising is part of the culture of growing up in America in the twentieth century. We all remember the ads from when we were kids. Hearing them conjures up memories of sitting by the radio, listening to Westerns and detective stories, or, for the children of the 1950s, camping out in front of the television on Saturday morning with a bowl of cereal watching "Mighty Mouse," "Roy Rogers," or "Bugs Bunny."

That rush of feelings is one of the most powerful pieces of testimony to the power of advertising. A memorable ad not only makes you feel predisposed to have warm feelings toward the product when you're young, but it also stays inside you long into your life, making you want to twist off the top of an Oreo when you're feeling in a playful mood, curl up with a bowl of Campbell's chicken noodle soup when you've got a cold, pull out Clue with your friends on a rainy night, or play with a yo-yo when you're brainstorming for ideas.

Research shows that, despite economic swings, brand remains one of of the key factors in the purchase decisions of some three-quarters of consumers. Over the past few years, as the baby-boom generation—the first generation to grow up with television—has settled down and had kids, we've seen the durability of brand loyalty in the revival of all manner of children's products from the 1950s, 1960s, and 1970s—from big brand name products like Barbie to long-ago hits like Erector sets, Duncan yo-yos, Creepy Crawlers, Troll dolls, Silly Putty, and Slinky.

The Hula Hoop Factor

At the San Francisco-based toy company Kransco Group—makers of Frisbee, Hula Hoop, Slip n' Slide, and Power Wheels—one wag has dubbed the revival phenomenon "the Hula Hoop factor." Every few years, the company has found, sales of Hula Hoops go up, as a new crop of parents comes along and buys them for their kids. In the late 1980s, Hula Hoop marketers saw the biggest jump yet—sales doubled to 2 million units in 1987 and went even higher after that.

Parents figured they'd had so much fun swiveling their hips to keep the hoop in the air, back when they were kids (a mind-boggling 25 million Hula Hoops were sold the first year they were on the market) that their kids would love it, too.

Hula Hoops started showing up as feel-good props in ads ("Feel like 19 again," proclaimed an ad for Kellogg's Product 19 with a middle-aged person using a Hula Hoop). They made the "Tonight Show," Disneyland events, and a halftime show of the Super Bowl. "I've been in marketing 11 years, and it's the most unusual thing I've ever seen," one Kransco marketer said.

Should You Advertise?

Of course, Kransco rushed to its ad agency to film a commercial to keep the Hula Hoop revival going. But should you advertise? It's one of the most important questions you will face, and it's not an easy one to answer.

Advertising is probably the best route for getting your name out and building awareness for your product. It establishes instant credibility: "They have enough money to advertise—they must be a real company!" It's efficient. Appearing instantaneously on television sets in a major city, a region of the country, or across the nation is certainly a simpler and quicker way to introduce yourself to consumers than knocking on every one of your potential customers' door and asking for a few minutes of their time. And, since television sales departments, ad agencies, media buying companies, and market researchers have a fairly sharp understanding of what media children watch and read, it's not particularly hard for marketers of children's products to find their audience.

The downside is that advertising is expensive. A typical national ad campaign to roll out a new product can run well over a million dollars. You need considerable resources, then, to run a national ad campaign.

Nevertheless, you do have some options. You can choose to create a spot-market campaign, which will run only in certain metropolitan areas you're targeting for growth. Also, children's programming is generally less expensive than network prime-time shows. Moreover, with the explosion of children's programming on cable networks like Nickelodeon, syndicated weekday programming, and local spot programs, and with the rise of children's magazines, it's possible to stage a market-by-market or a niche-market campaign to "influential" kids, at a considerably cheaper cost than a full-fledged campaign.

Beware of the Giants

You're going to *have* to be smart if you have a limited budget. Some of the biggest companies in the world are heavy advertisers in the children's market. And, as marketers' understanding of children has grown more sophisticated over the past 20 years, many of those companies have begun to apply the proven strategies of packaged-goods marketing to the children's marketplace—such as advertising all year round to even out the sharp swings of the market (parents, after all, are spending money on their kids all around the year) instead of jamming all of their marketing dollars into the fourth quarter.

The amount of advertising being spent to reach children has grown commensurately. Kellogg, Co., for example, spends more than $25 million a year to promote Frosted Flakes, Corn Flakes, Rice Krispies, and its other brands to kids, according to tracking services. McDonald's has been tracked at $20 million-plus a year for its corporate-image campaigns to kids with Ronald McDonald and his cast of burger-land cohorts, short-term promotions, and Happy Meal offers. Philip Morris spends an equivalent amount behind Kool-Aid, Kraft macaroni and cheese, Cool Whip, and its other brands for kids.

Mattel, which has become one of the strongest marketers of children's products, spends in the neighborhood of $20 million to announce its latest additions to the Barbie line, its strongly successful Disney preschool toy line, and long-standing favorites like Hot Wheels cars. Hasbro budgets a comparable amount to promote its boys' and girls' fantasy action dolls, like G.I. Joe and My Little Pony; its resurgent Nerf product line; and its licensed products, board games, and toddler toys.

Twenty million dollars is a *lot* of money. Many companies' *sales* don't match the sums of money that big players like Kellogg, McDonald's, Mattel, and Hasbro spend on advertising.

But Don't Be Intimidated

Budgets of that size, however, haven't scared off the growing number of companies that have come into the market. And, on its own, it shouldn't put you off if media advertising fits your business objectives. The number of companies that have launched ad campaigns to reach children has been steadily growing.

Children's advertising, in turn, has expanded from traditional products for kids like toys, sweets, and breakfast cereals to sneakers, frozen foods, blue jeans, videos, first-run movies, restaurant chains, toiletries, and even vacation destinations. The National Dairy Board—deferring to the fact that it's easier to entice kids to drink milk through fun, informative commercials, than by encouraging Mom and Dad to *make* them do it—has been running dazzling, animated and live-action commercials. The ads run on children's television and, while drawing on the latest high-tech production technology, get across the basic points that milk builds bones and teeth and is a source of minerals and vitamins.

NIKE has extended its "just do it" campaign theme to commercials that encourage kids to play sports. Levi Strauss, which knows kids play a big role in choosing the clothes they wear, has created a series of ad campaigns that connect the Levi name with kids' lifestyles. ConAgra has created animated characters to tell the product message of its Kid's Cuisine frozen dinners to children. Disney alerts kids to new movies and video releases. Pizza Hut has begun to promote its pizza to kids.

Not advertising, to be sure, can have consequences if the size of your brand warrants it and if children play a major role in the purchase decisions. Children's Market Research was once invited in to do research for a major company on a cheese product. The product seemed to be popular with kids. The company wanted to know what they thought of it.

CMR came back with the recommendation that the company should start an ad campaign to solidify their position with kids. The company chose not to follow the recommendation. They were a fairly slow, conservative organization. "We're doing well enough. Why do we need to do this?" they asked.

Polly-O String Cheese, at the same time, did come in and advertise to kids—and did it with a series of delightful ads, playing off its icon with a live-action, hip, rapping parrot who sang about Polly-O. Polly-O's brand profile among kids took off. The story shows that, before you make the decision to advertise or not to advertise, you have to look not only at your own objectives but also at the competitive context in which your products operate. In addition to building awareness and establishing credibility, advertising can give you a competitive edge—particularly when you're the first one in.

The Numbers Tell the Story

In 1980, $110 million was spent on advertising in children's programming on the three networks, according to *Broadcasting* magazine. By the early 1990s, the figure had jumped past $170 million. New media outlets, like Nickelodeon, pushed the figure higher still. Ad revenues at Nickelodeon soared from $13 million in the mid-1980s to well over $60 million in the 1990s. Fox Broadcasting's new blocks of programming on Saturday morning and weekday afternoons and Disney's after-school programming block added another boost. The estimated total of broadcast advertising by the mid-1990s will be well over $350 million.

Toys, bolstered by video and computer games, remain the biggest advertiser on children's programming, according to a review of children's programming by the Better Business Bureau. Slightly more than 33 percent of all ads to kids are for toys. Cereals, waffles, Pop-tarts, and other breakfast foods rank next. They make up about 23 percent of ads to kids.

Snacks and drinks are next at 18 percent, followed distantly by fast food at 6 percent, and milk and other health foods at 3 percent. Peek into the smaller numbers, however, and you get an idea of the great amount of tinkering and experiments that are going on. Some 2.5 percent of the ads on kids' TV, for instance, were for recreational products. Records, books, and school products were close behind, and they were followed by videos, phones, athletic shoes, toothpaste, household goods, personal-care products, and clothes.

Club Med, Too?

Yes, Club Med, too. Swinging singles aren't forever. The vacation resort began to set aside 10 percent of its $15 million ad budget to encourage kids to take Club Med's "antidote to civilization."

The resort company already had been expanding its offerings to families. It opened its first family village in 1980. By 1992, 6 of Club Med's 16 villages were exclusively for Mom, Dad, and the kids. Families were accounting for 40 percent of the company's revenues. Four of the top five Club Med resorts, in revenues, were family destinations.

However, the biggest motivator for Club Med to start directing part of its message to kids, Club Med president Michael Kubin said, was a research finding by the Roper Organization. "Seventy-three percent of family vacation decisions are influenced by children," he said. "That's a huge number. It means that when 5-year-old Jimmy says he wants to go to Disney World or Club Med, Mom and Dad are listening. The crumb grabbers are determining where the family goes on vacation."

Focus groups by TBWA, Club Med's ad agency, confirmed it. Asked if their kids' wishes on vacations were important, parents in six markets overwhelmingly said yes.

For Club Med, then, the goal was "to make sure we are there, at that pressure point." The resulting commercial showed kids splashing in the ocean, building sand castles, and taking part in Club Med's kid activities—learning trapeze, clowning, and a Caribbean-flavored, hand-clapping musical track.

On the one hand, the commercials reinforced the ads Club Med was running in prime time to appeal to grown-ups. They used many of the same images to make the case that parents could escape from the stress of their jobs and not have to worry about their kids' being bored, by coming to Club Med. On the other hand, kids were a backdoor way to reach parents in homes were Club Med was not a top-of-mind choice for a vacation of any sort.

"When you're talking to a kid who is 4, 5, or 6 years old, you're basically talking to a blank slate," says Kubin. If Club Med convinced them it was "a fun place to be," they'd argue the resort's case to Mom and Dad.

Television: The Traditional Choice

There are many options to choose from if you want to reach children. We'll cover print advertising in the next chapter, but, first we want to talk about television. Television is the medium that advertisers usually think of first when they want to reach kids.

The simple explanation is that television is a big part of kids' lives. Kids watch a lot of television. On average, according to most estimates, they watch 3.5 hours a day. Of course, many households watch a lot less. Many households have a firm rule that kids can watch only one hour of TV a day, but some households watch a lot more. And the level of interest that kids have when they're in the room with the television on, as parents will readily attest, varies wildly. With those provisos, it's still safe to say that the television is one of kids' favorite forms of entertainment.

We know that kids tend to be visual. Television sates that need. Although we're used to having TV portrayed as the vast wasteland, television is also one of the most influential educators that children have. Kids see places and things they never otherwise could—from the moon, to cockpits of space ships on missions around the earth, far-off cities, deserts and jungles, architectural wonders like the pyramids of Egypt, and the habitats of exotic animals.

Television teaches children the nuances of the society they themselves are part of—language, dress and interaction among people, values, and the career and lifestyle choices children will make as they grow up. It also entertains them with cartoons, music, and other fun stuff.

We've noted before that the work of childhood is deciding what kids want to be. They want to know what everyone else does and likes so they can decide what choices they should make. Kids bring that curiosity to advertising. They look to advertising to tell them what's new in toys, snacks, and other stuff; to be entertained, and to find out what other kids are doing. Kids study commercials as intently as they watch programs. Some kids have told us that they like the commercials *more*.

Results Now

Kids act on what they watch, too. According to CMR KIDTRENDS REPORT, a whopping 81 percent of kids exercise "some" to "a lot" of influence over the brand of sneakers they get. Sixty-four percent exert influence over the brand of cola that goes into the refrigerator.

Moreover, they remember what they see. Kids Media Watch asked 1000 kids to list their favorite commercials. For 7- to 12-year-olds, Pepsi, NIKE, Coke, McDonald's, and the Energizer bunny topped the list. Nintendo, Teenage Mutant Ninja Turtles, Disney products, Reebok, and the National Dairy Board followed.

They get the message. "I like McDonald's commercials because of the food, the music, and that they play together," an 8-year-old said. "They're funny. They make me feel good."

"I like the action," a 10-year-old boy said of Teenage Mutant Ninja Turtle ads.

You don't have to be a number one brand to benefit from advertising. In 1988, 7-Up broke ranks from soft-drink convention and created a series of ads just for kids. Leo Burnett & Co., the company's ad agency, created an animated character, Spot, based on the red dot from the side panel of the 7-Up can. In the commercials, Spot comes to life as a hip, humorous animated character, who spreads chaos and fun from the refrigerator across the house. Kids responded. Sales of 7-Up enjoyed double-digit increases.

Marketers of Butterfinger, the chocolate-covered candy bar with the peanut-butter center, adopted Bart Simpson as their spokesperson in an animated campaign in 1989. The spot they created showed Bart in a lunchroom at school explaining his version of the four food groups to a friend: "the sandwich group," "the cow group" (milk), "the jungle group" (fruit) and, most importantly, the Butterfinger group. The campaign hit the market just as the Simpsons phenomenon was taking off. Sales of Butterfinger jumped 13 percent in one year. The campaign went on to win the American Marketing Association's Effie Award for marketing effectiveness.

According to a survey of 40,000 college students conducted by Decision Center Inc. of New York and MarketSource of Cranbury, New

Jersey, 62 percent of college students buy the brand they grew up on. But you don't need research to tell you this. Look in your own medicine cabinet, or open your kitchen cabinet. Chances are that many of the brands you grew up on are still there—General Mills' and Kellogg's cereals, Campbell's soup, Arm & Hammer baking soda, Crest or Colgate toothpaste, Nabisco cookies and crackers, Quaker oatmeal. Arm & Hammer's recent success in expanding its franchise brand into baking soda toothpaste was made possible by the trust and loyalty that it has built up for generations with its baking soda.

Who Do You Want to Reach?

Before you create an ad campaign, you need to decide who you want to reach. In most cases, it will be the same audience you designed your product for. It's good to set down on paper what you know about the audience.

The document should cover the basic questions about your target market—age, sex, purchasing behaviors, past associations with the product, lifestyle fit of the product, solutions or benefits the product offers, and how it will be bought (by kids on their own? with Mom and/or Dad? as a present?). It should also address the competitive environment: Who is the competition? What are the relative market shares? What are their strengths and weaknesses? What do they say in their advertising, and where do they run their ads?

This statement will be a starting point for deciding what you want to accomplish in your ad and what programs you will choose to run the commercial on.

A Note About Ad Agencies

In some companies, such documents are done by corporate marketing staff; in others, they're done by the ad agency. This split probably reflects changes in the advertising profession during the past decade. Traditionally, companies looked to ad agencies as "partners" who are brought in on products from conception and stayed for the duration. Today, though, many companies have taken advertising in-house. Others have broken advertising up into its different components of market research, marketing consulting, creative development, and media buying and contracted out to specialists the responsibilities for the different jobs.

The line of reasoning is that divvying up the work saves money, especially if you have someone on board who knows enough about the field to coordinate everything. You are the best judge of what you should do. Our only caution is not to overestimate your abilities or the amount of time you have free to be your own ad agency.

No matter which route you take, there are some basic characteristics you should look for in the people you work with. The most obvious are trust and rapport. Experience in advertising to children is also important. Some ad agencies have built up an expertise through years in working on children's products. Griffin Bacall in New York City is one such agency.

Like the children's products companies, the ad agencies that have the most experience in working on children's products tend to be in New York City (in close proximity to such major players as Hasbro, Nabisco, and General Foods), Chicago (which is close to General Mills and Kellogg), and Los Angeles (Mattel).

You'll realize in a moment that there are a lot of differences between addressing children and addressing grown-ups. They run from what works with kids, to what's forbidden (there are clear guidelines set by the networks and by the Better Business Bureau on what you can and cannot say to children in advertisements) to different media buying rate structures for children's programming. Experience counts.

This Can Be Fun

As companies have learned more about kids, they've gotten better at talking to them. And they've found that making ads that are pitched to kids is fun. Marketers have gotten more adventurous. Whereas ads for kids in the 1950s were wooden, stilted, and decidedly simpleminded, they now are some of the most creative on television—the place where new technologies in animation and production hit first.

"Kids used to be thought of as a backwater because of regulations," says Tim Price, who, as group creative director of Foote, Cone & Belding, has created many of Levi's memorable commercials for children. "But it's not." Price credits that in large part to the grown-ups who make the ads coming to respect the market: "Kids are very smart," he says. "They're so sophisticated, it's sometimes numbing. Once you get into your mind that they're smart, you're years and years ahead."

The first piece of advice from advertising people we have talked to is to "take down the top," "let down your hair," "chill out," or—however you prefer to say it—shake off your inhibitions and preconceptions, relax, and be willing to have some fun. As it is with going out and interviewing kids, as we outlined in chapter 3 on focus groups, this is your chance to put yourself into the mind of a kid and learn to think like one.

The Formula: Tell a Story

Fairy tales have endured for hundreds of years for a very basic reason. They tell a compelling story in a straightforward way, with a clear narrative and, quite often, a moral to sum up the lesson of the tale. It's a good role model for copywriters to aspire to.

Many children's ads follow a basic narrative story line. A character, such as Bart Simpson, gets into a scrape, or, as in the case of Kellogg's ever-helpful Tony the Tiger, arrives on the scene to help out a child. The product is offered either as the solution to the problem the story has presented or as the reward that is earned at the end of the story. The storytelling device brings the child in and keeps him or her involved as the commercial unfolds.

Keep It Simple

Remember all those wonderful things you put in the strategy document at the outset? They looked great. They were great. But you're never going to cover absolutely everything about the product—all its points, benefits, and features—in 15, 30, or 60 seconds, the standard lengths for television commercials. You have to prioritize.

What do you really want the child to remember after he or she has seen the commercial? Your product's name, of course. Beyond that, you have to be ruthless in sorting out the few, basic points you want to make. And you have to make sure that what you put in the commercial—from the characters you use to the images and words you create—all support those few basic points.

Lois Welch, associate director of strategic planning and research at the ad agency DDB Needham in Chicago and the holder of a Ph.D. in child psychology, often reminds people of the time her 7-year-old son took her to see *Return of the Jedi*, the futuristic, action-packed finale of the *Star Wars* trilogy.

"Mo-om, you've got to see the best part," the child implored her. Finally, the "best part" arrived. The movie's heroes were locked in a massive battle against the bad guys. Laser guns were zapping everywhere. And her son tugged on her arm and pointed. "There! Look!" But he wasn't pointing to the battle. He was entranced, instead, by a tiny frog in the corner of the screen that had the hiccups.

"Adults have an ability to take in lots of information and pick out the main point," Welch says. "A child is very apt to get distracted and pick out what's of interest to him, instead of your main point."

At DDB, that's been distilled into a directive to apply to all children's ads: "Keep out the frogs." That is, be mindful that you haven't put something in the commercial to distract from the point that you want to make. If you're not sure kids are getting the message, set up a research project to ask them. Considering the amount of money that is at stake in an advertising campaign, it is always advisable to test your ad before you put it on the air.

Limit Your Arguments

A television commercial to a grown-up may have four or five appeals: "YoungSelf! It removes wrinkles! It makes you feel younger! You'll be more popular! You'll have more fun! And it's cheaper than Brand X! And available at your neighborhood drug store!"

Children's ads, by contrast, typically have two to three appeals. Fun and happiness is the most common theme, according to the Children's Advertising Review Unit (CARU) of the Better Business Bureau. The theme appears in 26 percent of ads, including 71 percent of fast-food commercials. Two other themes, tastes good and smells good, and product performance are next at about 18 percent each.

Child researcher James McNeal found similar results in his research on kids. Appeals to fun and sensory gratification are common in ads. Affiliation, the sense of being part of a group, comes next. After that, however, it drops off to nurturance, achievement, pain avoidance, deference, and autonomy. Kids' needs, as expressed in ads, are far different from those of grown-ups. Among adults, affiliation is the number one appeal. "Adults consider play, well, a little childish," McNeal says. When you create your ad, you must identify the most appropriate appeals for your product.

Know Your Target's Age

By the time kids are 12 or 13 years old, they can sift through stimuli and pick out the most important idea. Six-year-olds, on the other hand, need a slower pace and more direction. We've noted in considerable detail the physical and emotional changes and social advances kids make as they grow up.

Don't overestimate your target, though. We're used to reading how sophisticated today's kids are. But, underneath the whiz-bang, computer-literate, microwave-handy exterior, kids are still children. "Kids have learned to cope with new technologies for generations," Lois Welch notes, "but they're no more able to understand the theory of relativity than kids 50 years ago."

Use Older Models

Kids have a seemingly limitless repertoire of insults, but none stings as much as being called a baby. This was brought home to Children's Market Research when during the 1970s a company that makes baby food asked it to conduct focus groups for an ad campaign the company was considering that would pitch baby foods to older kids. The kids blanched. Baby food?! How could we put that in our lunch boxes?

Kids may have some nostalgia for their baby pictures, but they basically only have one direction: forward. Their lives are focused on figuring out how to do the things that older kids are doing. If you want an 8-year-old's full attention, talk to him or her with a 12-year-old.

Make It Fun, Make It Bright, Make It Rock

On Super Bowl Sunday, 1991, PepsiCo, Inc., launched a new ad campaign for Diet Pepsi. By the following Monday, kids in school yards across the country were mimicking the commercial: "Uh-huh! You got the right one, baby, uh-huh!" went on to become a tremendously popular campaign.

Little Caesar's comic slogans "meatsa meatsa" and "pizza pizza" made viewers double up with laughter—just as McDonald's did years before with tongue-twisting jingles that ticked off, helter-skelter, the chain's entire menu and the ingredients in a Big Mac.

Kids love to be entertained, and they crave new experiences, from the silky feeling of a snake's skin to the reflected rainbows of prisms. They study ads with the same intentness, and they watch them over and over and over again. They like repetition. They develop favorite commercials. They sing along with the jingles. It's no surprise that many creative directors we talk to believe that it pays to "reward" children, particularly slightly older ones, with little details that they will notice for the first time on a second or third viewing. Attention to detail keeps kids tuning in. "If a 10-year-old can get everything from your ad the first time she sees it, it's over," says one creative director. "They're never going to tune in again. So we try to put some surprises in."

A Procter & Gamble commercial for Sparkle Crest combined live action, stop-motion animation, painted matte backgrounds, miniatures, cel animation, Paintbox animation, rotoscoping, and computer graphics. In the 30-second commercial, from D'arcy Masius Benton & Bowles, Sparkles, the cool, sunglasses-bedecked animated toothpaste character, took two kids on a rocket trip from the bathroom into the night sky, past a gas station (with tubes of Crest instead of gas pumps), past a drive-in movie theater (where a vampire drops his victim to pull out the Crest), over the ocean, where dolphins frolic with dolphinlike swimming tubes of Crest, and, finally, back into their home.

The results, to an unsuspecting grown-up, can be dizzying. Kids' ads, in general, are louder, faster, and more colorful than the common fare on prime time. "The first time a lot of adults see kids' ads today, they go 'Whoa!'" says Julie Palley, director of marketing for youth wear at Levi Strauss. "But 10-year-olds today are used to a lot of action. Each time they see your spot, they should see something they haven't seen before. Otherwise, you're going to lose their attention."

Learn What Kids Care About

It's not easy being a kid, says one copywriter we know. "They get a lot of pressures. They're constantly being told what to do by parents, teachers, coaches, and other authority figures. 'Do this.' 'Do that.' 'Learn this.' 'Learn that.' They're constantly on the receiving end. So, when we do commercials, we try to show them out on their own, in control, and tell them, 'Hey, it's OK.'"

Teen and kid shows that address the issues they care about become social phenomena. "Beverly Hills 90210," for instance, quickly turned into required viewing for adolescents and teens. Its willingness to take on the pressures to succeed, the social stresses of fitting in, and the search for self that is unique to youth were instantly recognizable. Kids called it "our" show.

Kids pride themselves on being different from grown-ups. They're not adults. They're unique. You should acknowledge that you appreciate their interests and concerns. As one boy said in a focus group, "How do adults think they can save the world? They can't even play Nintendo."

Not Cynics

As we noted in Chapter 1, "Children of the 1990s," children tend to try to find the good in things. There are certain universal themes kids identify with—good and bad, right and wrong, friendship, mastery, industry, and self-esteem. Images of families, a tried-and-true element of ads to parents, work well with kids, too (though, from a kid's perspective).

McDonald's traditional pitch of food, family, and fun is right on target, Kids Media Watch has found. Children like the warmth and interaction of the people in the ads and see McDonald's as a friendly and happy place. "They make me feel good," said an 8-year-old girl from St. Louis. "There are kids my age on the commercials," an 8-year-old boy from North Carolina said.

New Is Cool

"We have many rules," says an executive of an ad agency. "One of them is give them something they've never seen before." It could be a new visual technique, a pop-music star who's rocketing up the charts, or a rising sports hero.

The National Dairy Board caught kids' eyes by using new special effects to underscore milk's contribution to building bones and muscle. The ads showed a boy's turning, before the viewers' eyes, from a squirt who gets pushed around by the school bullies into a teenager with a muscular physique, who does not have to take the bullies' guff. The commercial quickly became a favorite of kids.

Sports hold a universal appeal, both to boys and girls. "I like the way Michael Jordan slams the ball in the hoop, the way he can jump real high; he's cool," said a 10-year-old boy.

Tony the Tiger and Co.

There are enough icons in children's advertising to fill a back lot in Hollywood. We mentioned Tony the Tiger. Fruit Loops cereal has Toucan Sam. McDonald's, of course, has Ronald McDonald. Kool-Aid has Pitcherman. LEGO has the LEGO Maniac. Chester the Cheetah, the cool, hip icon for Frito-Lay's Cheetos cheese snacks, was so popular, the company entertained offers to turn him into a Saturday morning cartoon character until children's activists convinced them the cartoon would be taking unfair advantage of kids' interest in the character.

Kids like characters they can identify with. All of the different characters embody a trait (some more than others) that appeals to kids—impishness, good taste, hipness, or charm.

Humans are OK, too, but they're tricky. Child researcher Arlyn Brenner recalls testing an ad campaign that was supposed to star young Olympic champions. "Kids had a hard time identifying with them," she says. "They see them and think, 'I'll never be as good as that.'" The lesson: "Kids like to see role models they can emulate, or aspire to. But it can't be too far afield. Showing the perfect kid may not work."

For decades, LEGO Systems have been part of the experience of growing up. But, in research, the company found that its products, while liked, were not on children's must-have lists.

So it set about repositioning its product as a popular toy among boys 6 to 12 years old. To accomplish that, it created the LEGO Maniac—a boy who thrived on his LEGO space sets, castles, pirates, and cars. "It was a real departure for us," Richard Garvey, LEGO vice president of marketing, wrote in an article in *The Advertiser* magazine (Fall 1991, p. 62). The ads were almost a rock video in nature. In the spots, the Maniac dances to a rock-inspired sound track in a specially made denim jacket adorned with LEGO's trademark.

In a few days, the LEGO executive added, the company's public affairs department was swamped with calls from parents and kids who wanted the company to know that *they* were LEGO maniacs, too. Sales of LEGO products to kids aged 6 and up nearly doubled, becoming the fastest segment of the company's market.

Media Buying

There's one critical element of television advertising we have not yet covered. When do you show your ad? Many ad agency media departments have specialists in the children's market.

It's important to take time to understand kids for several reasons. Children watch specially created children's programming both on the networks on Saturday morning and in syndicated shows, which air primarily on weekday afternoons. But children also watch many prime-time shows and are big fans of many syndicated rerun family sitcoms, such as "Brady Bunch," "Charles in Charge," "Cosby," and "Family Ties." (See Table 10.)

Children watch in heavy numbers in all time slots when they are at home. According to CMR KIDTRENDS REPORT, based on The Simmons Kid Study, Saturday morning still commands vast numbers of

Table 10. TV Viewing Patterns of Children Aged 6 to 14
(by percent)

	Total	Boys	Girls
Early morning (Mon.–Fri., 6 a.m.–9 a.m.)	9.1	10.7	8.6
After school (Mon.–Fri., 3 p.m.–5 p.m.)	21.1	20.5	21.6
After school (Mon.–Fri., 5 p.m.–8 p.m.)	29.2	29.6	28.8
Kids prime time (Mon.–Sat., 8 p.m.–10 p.m. and Sun., 7 p.m.–10 p.m.)	28.0	28.7	27.2
Sat. early morning (6 a.m.–8 a.m.)	5.6	6.7	4.3
Sat. morning (8 a.m.–1 p.m.)	24.1	25.7	22.5
Sat. daytime (1 p.m.–5 p.m.)	10.1	12.2	7.9
Sat. evening (5 p.m.–8 p.m.)	14.9	17.5	12.1
Sun. early morning (6 a.m.–8 a.m.)	3.0	3.1	2.9
Sun. morning (8 a.m.–1 p.m.)	9.3	10.1	8.5
Sun. daytime (1 p.m.–5 p.m.)	9.6	12.3	6.8
Sun. evening (5 p.m.–7 p.m.)	12.1	14.7	9.4

SOURCE: CMR KIDTRENDS REPORT, based on data from The Simmons Kids Study (1991).

children, particularly younger children. But among 6- to 14-year-olds, Saturday morning may not be the time slot with the biggest audience of kids anymore. Research shows a very large viewing audience after school, during 5 p.m. to 8 p.m. Almost 30 percent of kids have the television on during those hours, when Mom and Dad are fixing, serving, and cleaning up from dinner. Prime time ranks next, at 28 percent. Then, Saturday morning from 8 a.m. to 1 p.m. comes in, with just over 24 percent. There are also large numbers of 6- to 14-year-old viewers from 3 p.m. to 5 p.m. on weekday afternoons—slightly more than 21 percent of children tune in then.

Saturday morning is terrific for reaching younger kids. About 33 percent of 6- to 8-year-old boys are tuned in then, as are 26 percent of 6- to 8-year-old girls. But as kids get older, they drift away to sports, socializing, and other Saturday diversions. Only 16 percent of 12- to 14-year-old kids watch TV on Saturday mornings.

Competition from Video Games

Children also have different entertainment choices than adults, such as playing video games. According to electronics industry research, more than one-third of all households with kids have video games. The most popular time to play video games is Sunday afternoons between 3 p.m. and 5 p.m., according to ratings services. If video games were a program, they'd have a 9.5 rating—competitive with many shows! That slot is closely followed by Saturday and weekday early evenings, Sunday early afternoon, and Sunday evening.

Television programming also faces stiff competition from VCRs. According to the same research, Sunday from 3 p.m. to 5 p.m. is also the most popular time for kids to view programs on the VCR. VCRs have a rating of 7.6 in households with kids at that time. That is followed by afternoon and early-evening time slots on Saturdays and Sundays.

Even the best commercial won't create awareness and preference for you if the television set is not turned on. Marketers are well advised, then, to bring their media specialists into discussions early when planning a campaign. Media planning should function hand in hand with creative development.

What About Mom and Dad?

Parents are still the gatekeepers. Many companies create parallel campaigns, one for parents and the other for kids.

In a reader survey in 1990, as we noted earlier, *Parents* magazine found today's parents deeply involved with their kids. Close to half the parents who were interviewed said they spend more time with their kids than their parents spent with them. Two-thirds said they communicate better with their kids than their parents did with them.

In creating a campaign for parents, you'll probably stress different points than you do with kids. You may talk more about the product's durability, value, or educational benefits. Then again, you may address the little kid inside the grown-up's body. That's worked pretty well for Toys R Us, the giant retail toy chain.

The Rules

We've told you what to put into commercials to kids. Now we're going to tell you what you can't put in. You can't tell kids their parents are miserly, unloving old Scrooges if they don't spring for a new toy. You can't tell kids their social status, physical strength, or intelligence will immediately take great leaps if they buy your sugar candies. You can't show a product doing something that cannot be duplicated by the child for whom the product is intended.

The rules have been established by the Children's Advertising Review Unit of the Better Business Bureau. Children's Market Research once was asked to show kids a toy. The commercial had to be reshot because it was not clear to the kids that, to make the toy move, they had to hold it in their hand.

Networks often have additional guidelines for children's products. Ads, for example, must end in a 5-second "island" that shows only the product. Sports heroes, movie stars, and other celebrities cannot appear on Saturday morning ads.

The Children's Advertising Review Unit publishes a slim pamphlet that specifies the basic guidelines for all television ads. They fall into seven basic categories: (1) product presentations and claims, (2) sales pressure, (3) disclosures and disclaimers, (4) comparative claims, (5) endorsements, (6) premiums, and (7) safety.

If you don't obey, it can cost you. An ad agency we know had to reshoot scenes for a commercial because it failed to put a boy on a skateboard in kneepads and a helmet. CARU makes its guidelines readily available. The unit periodically updates the guidelines. Here is a summary of the highlights.

Product Presentations and Claims, Sales Pressure, Endorsements

The basic rule here can be summed up in one sentence: What the child sees is what he or she should get. If the product is red, it must be red in the ad. If the airplane doesn't emit a buzzing sound in real life, it cannot do it in the ad. All of the characteristics shown in the ad—speed, size, durability, or, in the case of food, nutritional benefits—must be in the product that will be on the retailer's shelf.

You cannot urge kids to tell their parents to buy them the product immediately. And you cannot say buying your product will add to a child's or a parent's prestige. You cannot hoodwink kids on price by reminding them your widget costs "only" $9.99.

Endorsements should reflect real-life experiences and beliefs and should not appear within or adjacent to programs in which the endorser appears. No Teenage Mutant Ninja Turtle toy ads, for example, can appear in the "Ninja Turtle" TV show.

Disclosures and Disclaimers, Comparative Claims

If assembly is required, you must say so. If batteries must be purchased separately, you must tell kids that as well. Comparative claims must be supported by factual information. If you show the whole line of products in your toy line, you have to inform your viewers that the items "must be purchased separately."

If your sugar-coated corn puffs cannot stand up on their own, you must tell kids they are "part" of a healthy breakfast. If you're touting the prize the child will get when he or she hops over to your restaurant or picks up your brand of cereal, you cannot highlight the prize—the premium to marketers—more than the product that you have to buy to get the premium.

How you say these things is as important as what you say. Kids have a limited vocabulary. You must use simple, clear language. And you should say it both on the audio track and in print.

The underlying rationale is simple: Children trust what they see and hear.

Safety

Because children imitate what they see, you cannot show them doing things that will put them or others in harm's way. For this reason, ads for vitamins and drugs were banned from children's programming in the 1970s.

If an ad shows a child in a swimming pool operating an appliance or in another setting that could pose a safety risk, a supervising adult should be shown. Products should show children of appropriate ages.

The Good News

Sounds like a lot to remember, but the overwhelming majority of advertisers comply with CARU's guidelines. According to a 1991 survey of 10,330 commercials (the most exhaustive study on the subject), 96 percent of commercials to kids are truthful and accurate. Only 0.6 percent of cereal ads had violations, 1.8 percent of drink and snack commercials, and 2.8 percent of toy commercials. Were it not for the biggest offenders, primarily phone services, the percentage would have been higher still.

Not only will you have to reshoot a commercial if you err, but you will also be embarrassed publicly. You may even lose your customer. CARU hears complaints when companies are suspected of breaking the rules and singles out companies for violations.

Some of the biggest companies in the country have been cited, and some of the offenses have created publicity that has resulted in legal regulations. One commercial showed the Easter bunny eagerly awaiting phone calls from kids—without explaining that kids who called would not be interacting with the Easter bunny at all, but only hearing a tape recording!

A watchdog mentality is pervasive among parents today. Action for Children's Television, a longtime children's rights group, has threatened to petition the Federal Communications Commission (FCC) to revoke the license of television stations that are not sensitive to the needs of children. The American Pediatrics Association has called for an outright ban on advertising food to children. Many editorial writers and governmental officials empathize with parents. Advertisers are guests in the consumer's house. It's to your benefit to be gracious.

Summing Up

Questions to Consider

Before you create a commercial, be sure you can answer these questions:

1. Can you describe exactly who you want to talk to, by age, sex, region, attitudes, and lifestyle?

2. Can you identify the most important benefit your product will offer the viewer? Can you describe it in five words or less? Do the same with the second benefit. If you are arguing more than two benefits, are you absolutely certain the audience will remember them? Have you proven it by testing?

3. Is the message you are sending kids consistent with the one you are giving parents? If not, why not? If you aren't addressing parents, why not?

4. Does your ad tell a story? Is it exciting? What's new about the ad— its look, its sound, its music, its speakers?

5. Are you talking in kids' language and in emotions and ideas they relate to? How do you know?

6. Have you tested your commercial to make sure that it communicates effectively to kids?

7. What television programs will offer you the best environment for reaching the numbers and types of children you want for your campaign?

8. Have you strictly followed the rules for product claims, disclosures, presentation, sales pressure, safety, and the other concerns of the Children's Advertising Review Unit of the Better Business Bureau?

10
The Printed Word
Magazines and Direct Mail

Pop Quiz

1. How many magazines are published for children?
   (*a*) 25, (*b*) 50, (*c*) 85, (*d*) more than 150.
2. Advertising in magazines serves
   (*a*) basically the same marketing purpose as advertising on television, (*b*) a very different purpose.
3. Who is more likely to recall a print advertisement and to have read every word in the ad.
   (*a*) kids, (*b*) grown-ups.
4. How many households does Fox Kids Club's *Totally Kids* magazine, which supports the television network's children's programming, go to?
   (*a*) 200,000, (*b*) 300,000, (*c*) 900,000, (*d*) 3.4 million.
5. By renting certain direct-mail lists, what percentages of households with children is it possible to reach?
   (*a*) more than 75%, (*b*) 50%, (*c*) 35%.

Answers: 1. *d*; 2. *b*; 3. *a*; 4. *d*; 5. *a*.

Kids Are Readers, Too

Kids can watch figure skaters, pro-basketball stars, Olympic athletes, and heroes of the baseball diamond and football field on television. They can read about them in enthusiasts' magazines like *Sports*

Illustrated, Sport, and *USA Today's* "Baseball Weekly." They can study their statistics on trading cards from such companies as Topps, Don Russ, Upper Deck, and Fleer. But there's one magazine where a kid can find out what a sports star's favorite color, ice-cream flavor, and TV show are—and what their "worst day" was.

Sports Illustrated for Kids, published by Time-Warner's *Sports Illustrated,* was created to bring the universal love affair of kids and sports down to the specific needs, interests, and style of 7- to 15-year-olds. And it has been an enormous success, growing to more than 600,000 subscribers in only a few years on the market and achieving a 65 percent awareness among kids.

It is probably the most prominent example of the explosion of interest in children's magazines that coincides with the arrival of the new baby boom. Children's magazines, in turn, are one example of a larger upward trend in use of the printed word. The others are direct mail and such alternative media as in-school posters and cereal boxes. In this chapter, we give you a rundown on the basics—the inner workings of children's magazines, what kids like in print advertisements, and how to procure a list of households with children to create a direct-mail program.

Television tends to get the most attention from marketers, both in media dollars and marketing priorities, but there are compelling benefits for using the printed word. It's educational; a child looks to a favorite magazine to open up new worlds to him or her. It's hands-on; a beloved magazine can become part of a child's treasures that is shown to parents, saved in a special place, and returned to again and again. On average, readers of *Sports Illustrated for Kids* thumb through a single issue of the magazine *seven* times.

And it's special. Kids love mail. LEGO's direct-mail catalog, sent to a select group of customers, is pored through for new products, accessories, and special discounts.

Print advertising is generally done by the same ad agencies that create television commercials for the children's market. Direct mail is typically done through a combination of direct-response specialty agencies, list "brokers" who keep tabs on the hundreds of direct-mail lists that can be rented, and packagers who cut costs by putting together cooperative mailings that pool marketers.

The Magazine Explosion

According to industry estimates, the number of children's magazine titles has almost doubled from 85 in the mid-1980s to 160 today. Some boast circulations that magazines for adults would envy. (See Figure 9.)

Figure 9. Kids have become active collectors of comic books. The phenomenon has helped make the books an investment item, and spurred more advertisers to reach kids by advertising in comic books.

Welsh Publishing Group of New York, which specializes in magazines based on licensed characters, launched *Simpsons Illustrated* magazine, based on the Fox Television Network's offbeat family, with a first-run circulation of 2 million.

Teenage Mutant Ninja Turtles, another Welsh magazine, which mixes features on the Turtles with articles on the rollerblade craze, skateboarding, and other activities of interest to kids, grew to a circulation of 1.2 million. *Barbie* magazine, styled as a fashion magazine for preadolescent girls and offered to girls when they buy a Barbie doll, had built up a circulation of 600,000. *Garfield,* a humor magazine based on the cartoon cat, and the fourth title in Welsh's Kid Power advertising package, had a circulation of 400,000.

Fox Children's Network, the fourth television network's programming slate of Saturday morning and weekday afternoon programs for kids, created a quarterly magazine, *Totally Kids,* as an incentive for kids to join the Fox Kids Club. More than 3.4 million kids have signed up. For its part, Disney, which goes head-to-head with Fox for weekday viewers, has *Disney Adventures* magazine.

The National Geographic Society has spun off *National Geographic World* magazine for young readers. The National Wildlife Federation has created *Ranger Rick* and *Your Big Backyard* for kids. Children's Television Workshop, the producer of "Sesame Street" and other beloved children's programs on public television, publishes *Sesame Street, 3-2-1 Contact,* and *Kid City* magazines. Nintendo Corp. created *Nintendo Power* magazine to introduce kids to new video-game software programs, give pointers on existing games, and foster loyalty among Nintendo's legions of owners. *Beckett's* updates kids on the latest prices of baseball cards, with feature stories on the established players and rising stars in the major leagues.

Magazines serve two marketing purposes. First, like adult magazines, they are "delivery vehicles" for advertisers interested in reaching a particular audience. Second, many children's magazines are marketing vehicles created by companies like Nintendo and organizations like National Wildlife Federation, National Geographic Society, and Consumers Union (which publishes *Zillions*, a *Consumer Reports* for kids) to instill loyalty to a product, social cause, or organization that will last through childhood and, in some cases, well into adulthood.

Whether you should choose to create a magazine or use an existing magazine to deliver your message to children depends upon the nature of your product, how much patience you have—children's magazines are expensive and time-consuming investments—and, of course, how much you have to say.

In the fall of 1992 McDonald's rolled out *McMagazine*, a quarterly magazine produced by Quad/Creative Magazines of Milwaukee. The magazine, distributed in 8600 McDonald's restaurants, was a logical move on two levels. First, it was a concrete example of McDonald's commitment to families. Second, like the playgrounds in many McDonald's restaurants and the toys and activities in McDonald's Happy Meals, it's another way for families to pass the time while they're eating at the restaurant. A test issue drew advertising from Coca-Cola, Mattel, V.F. Apparel, Polaroid, and U.S. Gold's Olympic Gold video game (*MediaWeek*, July 20, 1992).

For Nintendo, creating a magazine was a commonsense business decision. There was no specific vehicle to present new software titles to the universe of Nintendo owners. At $49.99 for a typical package, a software program is an expensive purchase. Without *Nintendo Power*, kids would probably stick with the established titles and shy away from new programs.

Magazines that have been spun off from existing, grown-up titles have an enormous resource to draw on for expertise and personnel in their parent publications. They also have a unique claim to the subject matter that they cover.

For most marketers, the most cost-effective use of magazines is as a tool for advertising their products to the target market. The key questions, then, revolve around advertising.

Benefits of Print

In general, print advertising enables marketers to amplify and expand on the positions they have set out in television advertising. Research by *Disney Adventures,* one of the leading children's magazines, was reported on at a Consumer Kids Conference* and laid out the benefits. The basic benefits are no different than they are for magazine advertising for grown-ups. Kids are "proactive, involved, and attentive" when they read a magazine, said Lynn Lehmkuhl, publisher of *Disney Adventures.*

The first benefit is that both children and parents look upon magazines as educational. It really shouldn't be surprising. Kids associate reading with school; reading at home is an outgrowth of reading at school. "Children expect to learn something from a magazine," Lynn Lehmkuhl said. In Disney's research, kids said much the same thing. "When you're reading, you're getting information," a fourth grader from White Plains said in one focus group. "When I read, my brain keeps stuff in my head, so I can hear it over and over again."

A second benefit is that kids tend to believe what they read in magazines. From school, the printed word has credibility. Marketers, as a result, have an added burden of making sure they live up to the responsibility that power vests them with.

The third benefit for magazines is the control they give kids. Kids can move at their own pace. "They can read an ad for as long as they want," Lehmkuhl says. "And if they want, they can go back to it." We already have mentioned *Sports Illustrated for Kids'* research finding that shows kids read each issue of the magazine seven times. Kids, in turn, can develop their own style of reading and using the magazine.

Since it's a tangible object, if they see a feature or ad they particularly like, they can show it to a parent or friends. Contrast that with television. The commercial is gone in 30 seconds. That is not a big window of opportunity for Mom or Dad to rush out from doing the dishes to see the object in the ad that the child's heart is set on.

*The Consumer Kids Conference, sponsored by The Marketing Institute, held in New York City and Coronado, California, February 24–25, 1992.

Although there's a tendency to compare and contrast television with print advertising, we think the more appropriate stance is to see print advertising and television advertising as complementary, not competitive. Television communicates immediacy, motion, and music. It conveys excitement. But, as every parent knows, it's a passive experience. Disney researched reactions of 120 kids from third through sixth grade in White Plains and Cincinnati to 15 minutes of TV programs and commercials, and two magazines. The results revealed that kids tune in and out of programs, lounging on the floor, gazing around the room, looking up at the ceiling, and looking at the person next to them.

"TV is conducive to doing other things at the same time," Lynn Lehmkuhl said, including, it appears, relaxation. "When I'm watching TV," a fourth grader from Cincinnati told the Disney researchers, "my brain goes on vacation."

What Magazines Attract Kids

One of the first decisions in print advertising is to choose the magazine. Like television programs, magazines are an "environment." The process is slightly different than it is for grown-up advertising. Advertisers for adult products usually create a campaign, then look to place the ads in the magazines whose readers are closest to its target market. In contrast, print advertisements to children are frequently created to fit the content of a magazine. Marketers, for example, might create ads with a sports quiz for a sports magazine and ads with a nature quiz for a nature magazine.

The general starting point is to look for magazines that offer environments that complement the advertised product. *Sports Illustrated for Kids*, for example, is a good environment for trading cards, sporting goods, apparel, games, and foods kids associate with activity—breakfast cereals, snacks, fast food, candies, and beverages that "give you energy."

Barbie, beyond the obvious, is a good environment for cosmetics, apparel, fitness items, and products in general that are associated with being fit, trim, and attractive. It's also a logical place for food and beverages that girls like. A sample issue included ads for Barbie brand makeup and cologne—a line of wash-off lip glosses, peel-off nail gloss, and mildly scented colognes from Kid Care; the Buena Vista *Dance Workout with Barbie* video; Pro Set Beauty and the Beast trading cards, based on the Disney movie; Jacques Moret bodywear; SweeTARTS; a poly-bagged Cool Whip activities book; and, of course, Mattel, for Barbie.

Garfield and *Mad,* as humor magazines, are good places to advertise products that bring a smile, such as new movie or video titles.

Nintendo Power is a logical placement for companies that make video games and accessories for Nintendo video game systems. The magazine also can be a good environment for products and services that kids use before or after they play video games—snacks, food, beverages, and comic books or licensed products based on the characters in Nintendo games (Mario and Luigi and the Teenage Mutant Ninja Turtles, who star in one of the system's popular titles, for example).

The underlying thinking in matching products to magazines is that the child is already predisposed to a certain sort of activity, mind-set, or attitude by the articles and graphics in the magazine. "I'm in the mood for playing basketball," the child might think. "I'll go out and play, and when I come back inside I'll be hungry. I'll want to eat some (fill in the blank)."

Print Advertising: Be Interactive

Just as kids want to be entertained when they watch a commercial on television, they want to have fun when they read an ad in a magazine. But what constitutes fun is slightly different. According to publishers of children's magazines, kids like advertisements that are interactive. They want to be engaged by an ad. Children tend to save magazines; it's part of their natural impulse to be collectors. They return to magazines a half-dozen or more times. So they will pass by an ad multiple times.

As in television campaigns, there's been an explosion of creativity in print advertising to children in the past few years. A sampling of ads that have run in *Sports Illustrated for Kids* shows the range of creativity that ad agencies and marketers have brought to bear to involve kids in their ads. The Gap created ads on a special, heavy-stock paper that featured rare birds that kids could cut out and fold to create a colorful, three-dimensional Scarlet McCaw. The birds' claws formed a ring that kids could slip a pencil into to make a "perch" for the bird.

Several marketers have run insert sheets of stickers. The Gap created a sticker ad with an environmental theme. Kids could punch out stickers that proclaimed, "Save the planet." Starburst candy was featured in another such ad.

Levi Strauss invited kids to write in for posters of the fanciful "species of kids" ads that we covered earlier in Chapter 3.

For a special Olympics issue, Coca-Cola created an ad that featured a maze of how to get to the Olympics. When the kids followed a set of separate instructions to fold the pages of the ad, the maze was revealed to be the Coca-Cola script! Donna Sabino, the research director for the magazine, says that the publication has found that kids come back time and again, and refold such ads, "to make sure they still work."

Nabisco created an interactive maze for a Chips Ahoy ad for Welsh Publishing. *Disney Adventures* has a games and puzzles section. Advertisers have taken the cue to create puzzles and games that complement their products and services. McDonald's has run trading cards in several magazines. General Mills created a series of comic strips starring Apple and Cinnamon, two characters dressed as an apple and a cinnamon stick, respectively, who fight crimes that usually involve a wily bad guy trying to make off with little kids' Apple Cinnamon Cheerios.

It takes some creative thinking, but magazines' research shows that kids reward marketers' effort with enthusiastic responses. *Sports Illustrated for Kids* reported that its kids' are 76 percent more likely than adults to recall magazine ads, and five times more likely to read all the words in an ad.

Kids' Ads Are Different

Magazines have found that kids have a very distinct way of reading ads. One factor marketers have to take into consideration is that kids don't seem to have the appreciation of white space and a clean presentation that grown-ups have. They like clutter. That's why you see so many ads that literally take up every inch of space on the page with cartoons, photos, graphics, puzzles, games, and words. These elements draw kids' attention to the ad and keep their attention. Kids love detail.

A fanciful ad for Gatorade, for example, mixes cartoons and real photos, with fast facts about Gatorade and its star endorser Michael "Be Like Mike" Jordan ("Michael was born in Brooklyn, N.Y." says one, with a fancifully drawn arrow to Brooklyn, on a U.S. map. "Gatorade was born in Gainesville, Fla." says another, with an arrow to that city. "How many points has Michael scored so far?" The answer is "over 12,000!!!"). There is not a single unused spot in the ad. If there's not a picture of Jordan covering the space (there are four shots of the Chicago Bulls star guard in the ad), there are thought balloons, headlines, little cartoons, or splotches of color. "It's an adventure to read it," says Donna Sabino.

Sports Illustrated for Kids' recall research on its ads has found that mixtures of fact and fantasy, such as imposing a cartoon character onto a photograph, are loved by kids. Children also like short blocks of text, as opposed to the frequently long blocks of type in grown-up ads. The kids say long blocks of type remind them of school books—a turnoff. Children love to get nuggets of information that they can use to stump their parents. And they like movement.

It's no surprise, then, that many ads for kids show enormous, cartoon-drawn ocean waves, diving athletes, and odd little facts. "There are 371,292 possible fruit flavor combinations in every bag of SKITTLES." "Can you name the planets that start with *M*?" asks an ad for M&Ms with a rendering of the planets in the solar system, M&M-like *M*s marked on Mercury and Mars.

A second factor marketers have to take into consideration in creating print advertisements for children is the age of the reader, says Geoffery Gropp, vice president for advertising for Welsh Publishing. Ads for younger children must be simpler, from the skill level of the puzzles to the sophistication of the language and design. Connect the dots, for example, is an appropriate game for a 6-year-old. By the time a child is 9 or 10, however, connect the dots is a little passé. The key—as we have said throughout—is to know your market and its capabilities.

It has been said that many kids cannot distinguish between the editorial material and the advertisements in children's magazines and that advertisers have capitalized on that by making their ads look as much like the stories and photos in the magazines as possible. Consumer groups have put several marketers into the harsh glare of the spotlight for allegedly trying to deceive little kids into thinking ads were really comic strips. If that is the case, it's probably not as savvy a strategy as the activists would like us to believe. Kids *should* know an ad when they see one. You want them to know you are trying to sell them your product. However, by the time kids become avid magazine readers—say 8, 9, or 10 years old—the research we have seen indicates that they *do* know the difference between advertising and the editorial product.

Asking a 10-year-old whether the aforementioned Gatorade ad with Michael Jordan is an ad or a story is likely to draw a sarcastic look on the order of "Are you *nuts*?"

Kids Are Curious: Make the Most of It

A third factor marketers of products for children have to keep in mind is that, as we've noted earlier, kids pay enormous attention to detail. One researcher we know once asked a child to point out what he liked about a specific ad. The child responded that it was a good ad—"for an

R-rated ad." The youth had read the distinguishing ® by the company's name that indicates it was trademarked and had concluded that it was the same symbol he'd seen before in movie ads. The researcher was duly impressed at the attention to detail that the child had brought to the ad.

Kids are innately curious. They are not blasé about ads, as grown-ups are. They are information sponges. That makes them receptive to ads; ads teach them what's new. They're probably more curious about the marketers' products than the marketers realize.

With the growing level of curiosity kids have about fitness, we wouldn't be surprised to see food marketers stepping up educational campaigns about what's really inside the products they make. The arrival of new food labels from the U.S. Food and Drug Administration will only increase interest in the subject, as parents and kids discuss relative merits of products at the dining table and in grocery aisles. There seems to be a significant opportunity for marketers to help teach kids how to read labels, understand the concepts, and relate them to their own diets.

And—remembering the looks of awe we have seen on children's faces in tours of factories for products from cars to breakfast cereal—we would not be surprised to see a growing number of campaigns that explain the mechanics of how products are made. How does an ear of corn turn into corn flakes? What makes the Reebok Pump "pump up"? How does the "air" get into NIKE Air sneakers? You have an audience that's innately curious about your product. Why not try to satisfy that curiosity?

One of the most engaging graphics in Levi jeans commercials was an animated sequence that showed two mules pulling in opposite directions on a pair of Levi's. The sequence, a representation of the drawing on the patch of Levi's, taught a generation of wearers that Levi's are a very tough pair of pants.

Be Sensitive to How Kids Think

A cautionary note, as with television, is that you must be careful not to let your message get lost in your creative impulses. This is particularly true for younger children. As NIKE's Tom Phillips said, kids are true and literal consumers.

Magazine researchers have accumulated dozens of anecdotes of slight misunderstandings that turned into major confusion. We noted the ® being confused for a "restricted" movie rating. *Sports Illustrated for Kids'* editors, when the magazine was being conceived, were convinced that kids' insatiable curiosity about the rules of baseball, football, basketball, and other sports made a question-and-answer column on the subject a natural for the magazine. When they took the column "Rules of the Game" to kids, however, they got an unexpected reaction. The kids felt put off. Asked why, the kids said that rules reminded them too much of what their parents and teachers are always telling them to obey. The name of the column was changed to "What's the Call?"

Some magazines conduct their own, ongoing research to help their advertisers learn more about the market and what kids respond to in ads. *Sports Illustrated for Kids*, as we mentioned earlier, interviews 300 kids every other month in shopping malls in various locations across the country.

Along the way, the magazine's researchers say they have learned why heroes are so important to kids. They give kids someone beyond their parents and teachers to use as a role model for making choices on everything from careers to ice cream. One of *Sports Illustrated for Kids'* most popular features, in fact, asks sports stars questions such as what their favorite ice-cream flavor and TV show are. "Kids say they test themselves to see if their favorite things match their heroes," Susan Alexander, the marketing director during the magazine's launch, told a Consumer Kids Conference audience.

What does it mean for you? As you do when you create an ad, you should research the audience to get a solid understanding of what your kids' feelings, attitudes, and perceptions are. What you find will help you not only position your product to a quality that appeals to the market but also get you ideas on what kind of setting, words, and images you will want to use in your ad.

Fox Creates *Totally Kids*

"Kids love getting their own mail," says Bert Gould, vice president of the Fox Children's Network. Gould knows. He runs the Fox Kids Club, which has more than 4.5 *million* members. We'll talk more about corporate clubs in our next chapter on premiums and promotions. For now, let's cover one of the key selling points for kids to sign up for the Fox Kids Club: *Totally Kids*, a colorful, features-packed magazine Fox sends out four times a year to its members.

Fox conceived the magazine as a marketing tool to reinforce the children's programming on its weekday afternoon and weekend morning schedule. "It's very costly," says Gould. The magazine has been the primary part of the $3 million to $5 million investment Fox has spent to build the club.

Kids, who don't pay to get the magazine, love it. A testament to that fact is that "Kids Talk," a regular feature in the magazine, regularly brings in mountains of mail in response to a specific question.

"What part of the world would you like to explore and why?" asked one recent issue. "I would like to explore the south part of the world, such as the continent of Antarctica because I want to see a live penguin," one child from Gresham, Oregon, responded. "I would like to explore Russia because of what has been going on recently," a boy in Lafayette, Indiana, replied.

Each issue of *Totally Kids* is customized with the station number, call letters, and address of the appropriate local affiliate—a key component of Fox's strategy to use the magazine to promote awareness of its network of affiliate stations. That adds up to 130 different versions. The strategy appears to be working: WNYW in New York, the largest chapter, has 201,642 members; KITN, Minneapolis, has 134,711; WTTE, Columbus, has 126,583; and WXIX, Cincinnati, 123,767.

Totally Kids has some general-interest articles. A recent issue, for example, had a six-step program for starting a vegetable or flower garden and a map of the United States for vacationing kids, with bits of information on each state. But most of the articles are related to Fox programming. A feature on the plants, animals, and terrain of Tasmania was keyed to the Tasmanian devil, the star of one of Fox's animated TV shows. A two-page board game was based on the cartoon Beetlejuice. The celebrity featured in a one-page question-and-answer interview was Adam Jefferies, star of the Fox TV series "True Colors."

Fox has used its mailing list to learn more about its market. Its research, for example, has shown that 98 percent of Fox Kids Club members, who average 8.35 years old, go to the movies at least once a month and 54 percent go twice or more. More than 90 percent like to read books, and 56 percent read comic books. The research can be a selling tool to bring in advertising.

Fox has attracted national advertising as well. Kraft General Foods sponsored an advertorial on nutrition. The U.S. Postal Service sponsored a story on stamp collecting. Warner promoted *Batman Returns* in the magazine, and Disney and CBS/Fox have promoted new videos with advertising. The individual stations are free to sell local advertising on their pages as well.

Fox has learned that kids offer a special set of problems in direct marketing. It's found, for example, that kids are enthusiastic joiners. The network encourages kids to sign up for the Fox Kids Club during programs and at local events like the circus. As result, 30,000 new members a week sign up—but up to 10,000 are usually duplication. "Kids sometimes sign up five, six, seven, eight times," Gould says. "They love to sign up."

Direct Mail and Kids

Direct response for kids is not exactly new. Since the 1940s, children have dutifully clipped the tops off cereal boxes to get everything from Flash Gordon decoder rings, to spy kits and baseball accessories. The difference today is that the companies keep the names and addresses of the kids who send in the coupons and use them to build databases to develop an ongoing relationship. The benefit of direct marketing is that you can target your best customers—the people who really want to hear from you— and avoid wastage of advertising to persons who are not prospects.

LEGO's glossy, 40-page catalog that it sends to select customers enables families to choose from about 200 LEGO toys, ranging from preschool Duplo building blocks, to more complex sets in LEGO's Town, Pirates, Castle, Space, Trains, and Technic series. The shop-at-home catalog lets parents put a rush order on items, to make sure they arrive for holidays. And, as an added bonus, the company does not charge for regular shipping costs. "They make it so convenient," says one mother who uses the service to stock up on birthday gifts for her kids' friends. "They have great customer service—some of the best I've ever encountered." For the mother, the shop-at-home service not only offered an easy way to shop, but it also reinforced LEGO's position as a company that cares about its customers.

There are two ways to build a direct-marketing database. The first is to use your own list of customers. This can be done from warranty cards, coupon redemptions, telephone or mail inquiries, catalog sales like LEGO's, or membership clubs. The second method for building a database is to rent a list of names.

If you choose to use the second method, you set out the parameters of the type of household you want to target. For example, you might target couples under 35, with children under 5 years old, with household incomes of more than $30,000 a year. You pay the owner of the list each time you use it. If a person to whom you send an offer returns your coupon to you, then the person becomes part of your list. List brokers serve as an intermediary to help you find the best list for your needs.

Disposable diaper manufacturers and other baby- and toddler-care companies put coupons into mailings that go out to new families. Photo studios like those of Sears and J.C. Penney send out invitations to new parents to bring their babies in for photos.

Building a List

At the 1992 Consumer Kids conference, Jerry Heisler, the director, special products, in the corporate development group of Metromail Corp., a direct-marketing consulting firm, outlined the available options in lists of households with children. They begin, he noted, before a baby is even born, with lists compiled from birthing classes, maternity shops, coupon offers from offices of obstetricians/gynecologists, and other sources. The names go into the Young Family Index, a list of 3.6 million households that offers about 85 percent "coverage" of all births in the country.

You can buy lists of established families, high school students, college students—in all, there are hundreds of different lists of families and young people. Usually marketers interested in reaching households with young children send the mail to the family. Parents tend to open children's mail anyway, and offerings of lists specifically of children are less plentiful.

Marketers, for example, can rent the list of 411,000 subscribers to *Sports Illustrated for Kids*, for $70 per 1000 names or $31,000 for the entire list, Heisler noted. Like many companies who rent their lists, he added, the magazine puts some restrictions on how it can be used. For example, the company forbade telemarketers from using the list, because it did not wish to have its subscribers telephoned. (Many parents consider telemarketing an invasion of privacy.) Also, the magazine prohibits its list being used for questionnaires, surveys, or political or religious offers, and it does not rent to competing sports magazines.

Some lists, such as *Parenting* magazine's subscriber list, can be sliced and diced in different ways, Heisler noted. The magazine offers lists of subscribers from the past month, subscribers from the past quarter, and its 587,000 current subscribers, Heisler said. The magazine's lists illustrate the different kinds of demographic groups available in lists. *Parenting* subscribers tend to be, on the average, 30 years old, college educated, with a median income of $35,000—"a real nice audience for many of the programs direct marketers have in mind," Heisler says.

One of the keys, said Heisler, is to look for a large list. That way, you can test a direct-mail solicitation within the group and increase the list in successive mailings. Children's Television Workshop, for example, offers a universe of 3.7 million active families who are former subscribers to its magazines. They can be purchased at $45 per 1000.

What Do You Say in Direct Mail?

Direct mail can be used in a variety of ways. It's generally considered less effective than television or print advertising for creating awareness—even if you're sending a glossy, photo-filled brochure or catalog rather than a plain, standard letter. In the consumer's mind, mail is generally considered a medium of transaction. That is, it's a place where you make purchase decisions.

Again, consider the environment. Consumers are used to getting bills, invitations, and similar items in the mail that require a response. Catalogs, the primary marketing material consumers get in the mail, may be graphically appealing, but the point of sending them out is to persuade consumers to call a phone number and place an order.

If you have created a database of existing customers, the consumers on it are already familiar with your name. They will, in turn, be more likely to open a letter from you when it comes in the mail. They can be expected to be receptive. For LEGO, creating a catalog was a strategy to make sure that all the consumers who wanted it could have access to the hundreds of different items the company makes. Many stores simply don't have room for them all.

Marketers of children's products use direct mail to encourage trial. This can be done by sending out a sample of a product or by mailing coupons for discounts on the purchase of the product in stores. To a lesser degree, marketers also use direct mail to inform consumers of product updates and new accessories.

Making It Cost-Efficient

The downside of direct mail is that it is very expensive. Sending out a mailing can easily cost $1 per household. Jerry Heisler said a mailing can be done for $300 to $400 per 1000 households. Even at that, it is very expensive if you mail to 100,000 or more households, particularly if you don't hit the right households.

One check on wasting money is to match your list against those from Metromail, R.R. Donnelley, Polk, or another of the major database marketing companies. The U.S. post office, in addition, licenses about 20 direct marketers to sell change-of-address information that consumers file with the post office when they move to a new home—the NCOA, or National Change of Address list. Young families are one of the most mobile demographic groups in the country for the simple reason that having children leads many people to buy larger houses. The NCOA is updated monthly.

"What if you have a list but don't know if there are children on it?" Heisler asks. No problem. A marketer who has compiled a database for other purposes can glean from it the households with children by running it through Donnelley's, Metromail's, or Polk's lists of households with children. The big database companies can also enhance an existing list—telling you, for example, zip-code determined psychographic information about the attitudes and behaviors that can be predicted from where your customers live; the types of cars they own; or the occupations, hobbies, interests, and income from warranty cards they have filled out for products. Sears ran its list through databases to find out which of its catalog households had young children. The resulting names were sent a catalog of back-to-school clothing.

Cooperative Mailings

In addition to focusing on your direct-mail list as much as possible, a second method for cutting costs is to send out your direct-mail offer in a cooperative mailing. Teaming up with other marketers defrays the costs of doing it all yourself. Direct-marketing specialty companies package cooperative mailings to bring together noncompeting companies that want to reach a similar audience.

America's Growing Families, for example, packaged by Larry Tucker, Inc., reaches 17 million households with children up to 11 years old—a household penetration of around 75 percent. Young Parents, another list, goes out to 5 million households with kids under 2 years old. The packager provides the mailing list, postage, and outer envelope. The marketer provides the insert. The packages typically cost about $35 per 1000 households, plus the cost of the insert—a far smaller sum than sending it out yourself. The programs have proven popular with packaged-goods marketers for sending coupons.

Other companies have packaged cooperative programs that get distributed in schools, summer camps, and other venues. Some publishers and catalog companies make space available for marketers to send out direct-mail solicitation in their packages, as well.

Custom Magazines

Direct marketing and magazine publishing can work hand in hand in custom publishing. Custom publishing has become increasingly popular in the grown-up world. Many of the major publishing houses have opened divisions devoted to it. The idea basically entails harnessing the magazine's publishing resources to create a special magazine that fits the interests and needs of a marketer's audience.

Welsh Publishing, for example, created a shrink-wrapped magazine for General Mills cereals—the first example of shrink-wrapping a magazine onto a cereal. The topic of the magazine was careers. The "Career Adventure Series" began on Honey Nut Cheerios and then was extended to other General Mills cereals. Welsh has also created a comic book for Kraft General Foods Jell-O. The comic book followed the exploits of Jell-O Man, the superhero spokesman of the product's commercials.

Summing Up

1. There has been an explosion in children's magazine titles. Kids have become an avid audience for magazines and read both the editorials and the advertisements very closely.

2. Marketers who have a substantial audience, a loyal market, and a product that may not get adequate explanation through other channels—such as new video-game software titles—sometimes start their own magazines or license the brand name to a third-party publisher for a magazine. Most marketers should seek out magazines with an environment that will complement the advertisement.

3. Kids like print ads to entertain and involve them. Many marketers create puzzles and games. The marketer should remember not to let the brand name and product message get lost in the business and bustle of the ad.

4. Direct mail offers an opportunity for marketers to address their best customers. Direct-mail lists, representing the households that will receive the material, can be developed through warranty cards, coupons, and other interactive devices or can be purchased through a list broker.

5. To save money in direct marketing, many marketers turn to direct-marketing cooperatives, which bring together noncompeting companies targeting similar audiences. The marketers provide the insert material; the packager provides the envelope and mailing list and sends out the materials to the households.

11
Extending the Excitement
Premiums and Promotions

Pop Quiz (True or False)

1. The most popular participatory programs in the United States for kids aged 6 through 14 are the YMCA and YWCA.
2. Fifteen percent of kids aged 6 to 14 belong to a religious club or choir.
3. Barbie raised $500,000 to further the cause of world peace.
4. More than 200 companies have marketed their products through schools.
5. If promotions were good enough for us when we were kids, they're good enough for kids today.

Answers: 1. *true*; 2. *true*; 3. *true*; 4. *true*; 5. *false*.

Stickers on My Sneaker?!

A soft-drink marketer once asked Children's Market Research to show groups of 7- to 10-year-old boys and girls its brainstorm for cashing in on the boom in sticker collecting. The idea was stickers for kids to decorate their sneakers. To baby boomers who have fond memories of spending their childhood afternoons drawing logos of their favorite sports teams and rock bands and the names of their boyfriends and girlfriends on their canvas-topped sneakers with Magic Markers, it might seem like a logical enough idea. Many of the toys, foods, and hobbies of kids in 1950s, 1960s, and 1970s have made comebacks as baby boomers have indulged their children with the same things they loved from their own childhoods; Slinkies and Cheerios are two examples.

Graffiti-covered sneakers, it turned out, was not going to be one of them. To the new generation, plastering stickers on their Air Jordans and cross trainers wasn't a kicky, individualistic style statement. It was defacement. The kids turned up their noses at the idea of doing anything that would dilute the brand image of the NIKE or Reebok name. To many of them, it was an investment decision. At $50 to $130 a pair retail, the sneakers were, after all, the most prized and expensive items in many of the kids' wardrobes. Would Mom and Dad want to put a great, big sticker smack on the fender of their BMW?

The soft-drink company, after looking at the research, ended up deciding that asking kids to put stickers on Air Jordans would not fly.

There's a lesson in here. What worked in the past won't necessarily work today. It's a lesson that is particularly applicable to premiums, events, and promotions—the category of marketing programs that runs the gamut from contests and sweepstakes, to track meets, box-top and label mail-ins, and the "surprise inside" box of Cracker Jack or cornflakes.

What Premiums, Events, and Promotions Do

The goal of premiums, events, and promotions is to boost interest in your product by tying it to a rising star, a popular event, or a trend in the popular culture (hence the marketing shorthand *tie-in*). The program can stimulate trial of your product by the target market, reinforce brand loyalty, and create an air of excitement around your product. If you tie into the right athlete, star, movie, or event at the right time—for example, Michael Jordan, *E.T.*, or *Terminator II*—you can get a ground swell for the product. When a child gets a premium of a Batman toy with a Happy Meal from McDonald's, his or her regard for McDonald's rises. If a child gets to meet an Olympic champion at a special event, the brand that sponsored the program shares the halo of warm feelings.

When the consumer thinks of the promotion, premium, or event, he or she will think of the product. But the marketing discipline is trickier than it looks. To work, there has to be a commonsense fit between the product and the person, event, or trend that it's tying into. The program has to be something that kids will want to be part of—or it will backfire, making your company look hopelessly out of it.

Generally speaking, the program has to be something that parents will approve of. Premiums and promotions are the most sensitive front of marketing to kids. They've been the root of the loudest and angriest protests from parents.

"When you market to children, an immediate red flag goes up," says Stacey Bender, who has created event-marketing programs at Ogilvy & Mather and Ruder · Finn and who became president of Neale-May, Bender & Partners.* "People say, 'Wait a minute: Kool-Aid and MY children?!'"

The most heated debates have been over marketing in schools. Whittle Communications' Channel One, the advertiser-supported daily current-events television program to high school students, has been challenged in court and been the subject of running debates in newspaper editorial pages and school board meetings. But the debate runs much deeper than Channel One.

Consumers Union has come out against all marketing in schools. "Irresponsible" and "exploitation" are the words the consumer advocacy group has used to describe in-school marketing.

There are no easy solutions. On an ethical level, you as a marketer must decide what is appropriate. On an objective level, you must decide what settings and what types of programs will serve as logical extensions of your brand's positioning. And, on both a business and community level, you must be willing to make a commitment to be responsible.

"You really have to become part of children's lives," said Bender. "You have to work with children in the places they're involved in, primarily schools, parks, and recreation departments. And you need to give them something that's of value to them."

In this chapter, we try to guide you through the options in premium, promotion, and event marketing programs. We show you examples of what other companies have done, and we try to sort out some of the thorny issues that have arisen over this type of marketing to children.

McDonald's Happy Meal

Probably no company in America is as well known among children as McDonald's. Every day, 8 percent of all kids aged 2 to 7 visit 1 of McDonald's 8500 stores. That's a total of 1.2 million kids. In surveys, more than three-quarters of fast-food consumers identify McDonald's as the fast-food restaurant kids enjoy most. (See Tables 11 and 12.)

*The Consumer Kids Conference, sponsored by The Marketing Institute, New York City, Coronado, California, February 24–25, 1992.

Table 11. Reasons Why Child's Favorite Restaurant
Is His/Her Favorite
(by percent)

	Total	Boys	Girls
Best foods	55.0	54.4	55.6
Best toys/prizes	23.7	23.8	23.6
Best meal packs	19.7	19.8	19.7
Have the most fun	16.0	14.3	17.9
Best playgrounds	14.8	14.6	15.0
Child's friends go	12.2	11.6	12.8
Best birthday parties	6.2	6.3	6.0
Other reason	15.9	17.2	14.5

SOURCE: CMR KIDTRENDS REPORT, based on data from The Simmons
Kids Study (1991).

A large part of McDonald's success is due to the Happy Meal. The
Happy Meal was invented in Kansas City in 1977 by the local
McDonald's ad agency. McDonald's extended the concept to the
national level in 1979. Today, McDonald's rotates Happy Meal promotions every 4 weeks, 52 weeks a year.

On the face of it, a Happy Meal is a simple thing. It consists of a
cheeseburger, hamburger, or Chicken McNuggets, with a small order of
fries and a small drink, plus a toy, in a four-color box or bag decorated
with games, puzzles, and jokes. But to McDonald's officials, it is the
height of synergy. The result is a wild success. In one four-week period
in 1983, McDonald's became the biggest auto dealership in the world
when it gave away 45 million die-cast metal Mattel Hot Wheels cars.

The typical Happy Meal promotion is preceded by "a great deal of
careful planning by an awful lot of people," said McDonald's Don
Packard.* Generally, preparations begin one year before the event. The
company looks for tie-ins that will position the restaurant as being "on
top of what is hot for kids." The toy and packaging carry a single theme
that is extended in translucent menu-board signs, counter displays,
cutouts, and advertising. Different toys often are rotated throughout the
promotion to encourage kids to collect them all.

One of the most successful Happy Meal promotions linked
McDonald's with Nintendo just as the video-game company was releas-
ing *Super Mario Bros. 3*, the latest generation of its hit video game, in the
summer of 1990. McDonald's created four toys based on Mario, the star

*Consumer Kids Conference, Chicago, 1991.

Table 12. Restaurants Child Has Visited or Eaten in During the
Last 30 Days
(by percent)

	Boys			Girls		
	6–8	9–11	12–14	6–8	9–11	12–14
McDonald's	70.0	67.2	65.9	75.0	68.0	74.8
Burger King	39.8	41.5	44.1	43.2	44.0	45.3
Pizza Hut	41.5	42.0	40.7	38.6	43.2	48.9
Kentucky Fried Chicken	26.7	26.8	29.8	23.1	27.1	31.6
Taco Bell	26.1	21.6	25.3	27.7	29.0	29.0
Hardee's	17.5	21.6	21.4	16.9	19.6	26.0
Wendy's	15.8	20.1	18.5	15.6	20.3	19.6
Domino's Pizza	15.5	15.8	23.3	12.0	17.1	25.2
Little Caesar's	13.1	19.6	20.2	11.8	14.6	17.1
Dairy Queen	13.1	15.8	15.2	13.8	18.7	16.6
Arby's	10.9	17.0	11.4	11.5	18.1	12.2
Red Lobster	5.2	10.2	13.3	7.7	12.7	12.9
Ponderosa	8.6	10.7	10.6	7.1	11.3	11.1
Dunkin' Donuts	11.1	7.4	11.9	9.0	10.6	8.1
Sizzler	7.0	10.0	9.6	8.7	10.2	7.0
Jack-in-the-Box	9.2	5.7	9.3	7.8	8.1	7.4
Churches Fried Chicken	7.8	7.2	9.5	7.7	5.4	6.5
Popeye's Famous Fried Chicken	8.3	7.1	7.9	4.4	8.2	8.5
International House of Pancakes	6.6	4.5	6.3	3.5	5.5	9.4
A & W	6.1	3.3	4.9	3.4	7.7	5.2
White Castle	4.2	5.4	6.3	4.5	5.5	4.9
Godfather's Pizza	3.6	4.2	6.3	3.4	6.3	7.4
Olive Garden	3.5	3.5	6.9	4.4	5.7	6.5
Roy Rogers	6.0	2.6	5.8	3.2	6.9	5.8
El Pollo Loco	6.6	3.0	5.7	4.7	3.0	3.2
Ground Round	3.8	4.4	5.0	3.1	3.8	3.3
Arthur Treacher	3.4	2.8	4.0	3.2	3.8	2.9
Gino's	2.3	3.1	3.4	2.8	4.3	2.0
Other restaurants	35.6	36.3	41.8	28.1	35.6	40.1

SOURCE: CMR KIDTRENDS REPORT, based on data from The Simmons Kids Study (1991).

of the game; his brother, Luigi; and two of their archnemeses, a Goomba
and a Kupa Paratrooper.

To extend the video theme, McDonald's used computer-generated
images for the Happy Meal box, in-store signage, and ads. As a further
incentive, it packaged a discount for a subscription to *Nintendo Power*,
the Nintendo fan magazine. "It was a lot of fun," Packard says, "and it
was the most successful Happy Meal program ever to that time."

Kids Are Joiners

Findings of CMR KIDTRENDS REPORT, based on The Simmons Kids Study, show that kids are enthusiastic joiners. And parents, eager to expose their kids to new experiences, endorse and encourage their kids' trying new things. Just ask your neighbor who's spent the weekend schlepping kids to birthday parties, baseball practices, soccer games, Sunday school, Girl Scouts, and music lessons. Many parents will welcome you into their homes if you become a part of this process.

Most kids participate in clubs. YMCA, YWCA, and their parallel Young Men's and Young Women's Hebrew Associations, are the most popular; almost 45 percent of girls and almost 40 percent of boys of the 2500 kids surveyed belong to them, according to the CMR KIDTRENDS REPORT, based on The Simmons Kids Study. (See Table 13.)

Sports, scouts, and religious groups come next. A little more than 17 percent of boys play Little League baseball. (Girls still are outnumbered on the baseball diamond; only 4 percent play.) Sixteen percent of boys belong to Cub Scouts or Boy Scouts, and almost 16 percent of girls belong to Girl Scouts or Brownies. Close to 15 percent of kids are in a religious group such as a choir—a level of religious involvement that is higher than is generally recognized on Madison Avenue.

A little more than 13 percent participate in other organized sports, such as soccer, swimming, or basketball. More than 13 percent of girls and almost 11 percent of boys take part in school clubs. Almost 6 percent of girls and 4 percent of boys belong to 4-H, heartland America's beloved animal-raising, homemaking, and agriculture club.

Corporate clubs have strong followings as well. Fox Children's Network's Fox Kids Club attracted almost 8 percent of girls and almost 6 percent of boys in the survey. More than 5 percent of the girls and almost 5 percent of the boys belong to one or more book clubs. Burger King Kids Club got more than 4 percent of girls and more than 3 percent of boys. (See Table 13.)

Starting your own kids' club can be a time-consuming and expensive process. We talk a little more about that later on. But many of the existing children's organizations accept and welcome corporate support.

Fleischman's Yeast, for example, sponsored a national calendar sale for 4-H. The corporate support helped the farm and crafts organization raise funds. For Fleischman's, 4-H was a smart fit. The market that supports 4-H—generally, small towns in farming communities in the country's heartland—is one of the strongest markets for home baking and, thus, for yeast.

Many communities' youth sports sign-ups are sponsored by national marketers. The corporate support provides money for the organizations

Table 13. Memberships/Clubs Child Belongs To

(by percent)

	Total	Boys	Girls
YMCA/YWCA or YMHA/YWHA	42.2	39.6	44.9
Religious groups (such as choir)	14.6	13.1	16.2
Organized sports (excluding baseball)	13.3	16.9	9.6
Little League baseball	10.8	17.2	4.0
School clubs	10.9	8.7	13.2
Advertiser/corporate clubs (such as Kraft's Cheese and Macaroni Club)	6.8	8.0	5.6
Fox Kids Club	6.6	5.5	7.6
Book club	5.0	4.8	5.2
4-H Club	4.9	4.0	5.8
Girl Scouts	4.2	—	8.6
Boy Scouts	4.0	7.6	—
Burger King Kids Club	3.7	3.1	4.3
Brownies	3.6	—	7.3
Cub Scouts	3.0	5.9	—
McDonald's Kids Club	2.5	2.9	2.2
Baseball-card club	2.2	2.9	1.4
Fan club	1.6	0.9	2.3
Other scouts	1.1	1.1	1.1
Local theater group	1.0	0.8	1.1
Record club	1.0	1.0	0.9
Campfire Girls	0.8	—	1.7
Explorers	0.4	0.4	0.5
Other memberships	15.0	14.2	15.8

SOURCE: CMR KIDTRENDS REPORT, based on data from The Simmons Kids Study (1991).

to spread the words through big signs, public-service announcements, and fliers. If you become a corporate big brother to a youth organization, you get your name on signs and brochures. More importantly, you can earn good will among a very important market.

Make the Promotion an Extension of Your Product

By this time in the development of your product and marketing program, you know what your product's positioning is. You know what benefit it offers. You can tick off its primary features, in order of importance. You know who the market is and what the market is like. You can probably describe the household of your prototypical customer, down to what kinds of television programs are watched and what kind of clothes are worn.

When you create your promotion, you'll draw on all of that information. The setting and substance of your promotion should be a logical extension of your positioning. A promotion linking candy and dentists would not be a logical extension. Dentists fill cavities that candy can create, and kids usually don't think of going to the dentist as fun.

Baseball-card giveaways at major league baseball games, on the other hand, are a natural. Nutritional campaigns by dairy-industry groups, fruit-industry groups, vegetable-industry groups, or meat-industry groups make sense as well. The dentist's office is a logical place for toothpaste, toothbrushes, or sugarless gum.

Cracker Jack recently gave away miniature versions of Topps baseball cards as its "surprise inside." It was a logical fit. Kids eat Cracker Jack at baseball games. Baseball-card collecting, meanwhile, has become enormously popular. It was a fun combination. Some airlines program children's storybook tapes or sing-along selections on in-flight headsets.

Athletics have become a popular extension for products whose image is linked to energy. Hershey, for example, sponsors track-and-field meets. Keebler puts on one of the biggest prep track events in the country. Candy and sports aren't quite as tight an association as baseball and Cracker Jack or as baseball and baseball cards. Both Hershey and Keebler, however, have positioned themselves over the years as companies that have an interest in families. Sponsoring a prep track meet, then, is an extension of the companies' interest in families.

Make It Fun

The point—to paraphrase Cyndi Lauper's anthem from the 1980s—is kids want to have fun. And that's your first step—make it fun. Kids love to root around in cereal boxes for gimcracks. They enjoy playing with the Happy Meal toys, such as Ronald McDonald cars, while they eat their Chicken McNuggets and french fries. They enjoy mastering mazes and puzzles. They take great pride in being able to collect box tops and labels and to mail them off for a special prize.(See Figure 10.)

Quaker Oats' Life cereal made a splash, for example, by licensing Where's Waldo—the best-selling book character who kids must spot in a detail-filled scene—and putting a find-Waldo game on the box.

Children tell CMR researchers that getting a prize along with a bowl of cereal is like getting a free present.

Figure 10. Tying in with an upcoming movie, television show, or event is a favored route for promotions. Promotion agency Strottman International of Irvine, California, linked Denny's Restaurants to Hanna-Barbera's "Jetsons" for a series of activity books. "The Jetsons" are controlled by Turner Broadcasting.

Figuring out what's fun just takes a little imagination. Find an idea. Then research it, study it, and talk to kids. Many companies, surprisingly, embark on premiums and promotions without researching them. These programs can cost millions of dollars. They should not be left to chance.

Find What's Hot

Kids are always looking for something new. The next step, then, is to get ahead of the market and find out what is going to be hot. Major marketers like McDonald's are in constant contact with Hollywood movie studios to find out what movies will be coming out in the months ahead that will be appropriate for them to tie into for a Happy Meal promotion.

What's hot for your product depends on who you are trying to reach and what you want to say. It can be a professional sporting event, a musical tour, the championship competition of a youth organization, even the beginning of the school year. It can be a popular board game. Pizza Hut created a sports edition of the board game Pictionary, at its apex; VF Corp's Lee jeans brand created a hip-pocket edition of the game.

The fast-food chain Hardee's got one of its biggest monthly sales increases in history when it gave away figurines of the California Raisins with Hardee's breakfasts. The giveaway was timed to coincide with the height of the popularity of the pudgy, clay-animated, Motown-styled singing raisins of the California Raisin Advisory Board's advertising campaign.

Where In The World Is Carmen Sandiego, Broderbund's highly successful computer software geography game in which kids become detectives in pursuit of globe-trotting crooks, has been leveraged by companies that want to promote an all-family image. Holiday Inn, for example, created a summer-vacation contest linked to Carmen that gave out family vacations and copies of the game to winners. Kids liked it because they like the game. Since it's educational, parents generally look on it more highly than video games. The contest probably didn't on its own convince families to stay at Holiday Inn, but it reinforced the decision to stay there by creating goodwill.

The cable television network Nickelodeon created a $20 million promotional campaign to kick off its first Saturday night schedule of original programming. Sega of America, Pizza Hut, and Kraft Handi Snacks were among the sponsors. The centerpiece of the Slime Time Sweepstakes—the name leveraged Nickelodeon's popular "Double Dare" game show—was a call-in matching game.

Plan, Plan, Plan

Planning ahead is key. Most promotion agencies start work on a program 12 to 18 months ahead of the event.

Promotion planning for the U.S. basketball team's entry in the 1992 summer Olympics began in the fall of 1991, almost one year ahead of the event. With the decision by the Olympic governing bodies to allow professional athletes for the first time to compete in the games, marketers knew there would be a ground swell of interest in the team. For 20 years, sports fans had been chafing to send "the best" basketball players to the games.

As the biggest National Basketball Association stars—Michael Jordan, Magic Johnson, Larry Bird—began signing on for the Dream Team, marketers began laying their own plans. In early summer, the campaigns began breaking. Kellogg put a promotion on cereal boxes offering a Dream Team jacket featuring five team members for two box tops and $4.99. McDonald's created a series of commemorative drinking cups featuring different members of the team. Skybox came out with a series of Dream Team basketball cards. Nine other marketers created their own programs.

The outpouring of enthusiasm turned out to be even larger than expected. The basketball games became "the" Olympic event to watch. Media estimators said that, because of the high level of viewing, the sponsors made back a large chunk of their sponsorship fees from the free air time their signs in the stadium got in the pre-Olympic warm-up games.

Achieving that kind of success isn't easy, and it can be expensive. Sponsorships of the Olympic Dream Team cost an estimated $5 to $10 million to cover the basic sponsorship fee and the ensuing promotion and advertising campaigns. And it takes a good eye. The release of a major movie—*Batman, Star Wars, Robin Hood, Little Mermaid, Beauty and the Beast*—brings out cross-promotions in droves.

Many marketers prefer to use the old reliables. New colors and product lines from crayons have turned up in cereal boxes. Duracell gave away *Great Pumpkin* storybooks, based on the Peanuts comic strip, at Halloween. Hardee's has given away miniature versions of classic Little Golden Books.

The Barbie World Summit

In 1989, when Barbie celebrated her 30th anniversary, the free publicity and special events surrounding the milestone pushed Barbie sales up 30 percent in one year. The event was so successful, Mattel's senior management asked the doll's marketers to come up with another special event for 1990.

At the time, kids seemed to be taking a greater interest in world peace, the environment, and other social issues. So Barbie's marketers decided to create an event that would "empower kids to do something about making the world a better place," said Pat Wyatt, senior marketing director of the girls toys division of Mattel, who described the program at the 1992 Consumer Kids conference in Coronado, California.

The result was the Barbie Children's Summit. The event would bring together girls from 27 countries for a summit meeting in New York City at Thanksgiving to discuss important issues. The event would be topped off with the children's riding in Mattel's float in the Macy's Thanksgiving Day parade.

The program, as Mattel designed it, was bigger than a one-day event. Months in advance of the event, it began with the selection of the children to attend the event. In partnership with *Scholastic* magazine, Mattel created and distributed lesson plans for teachers on social issues like peace, the environment, and hunger. In addition to discussing the issues, the program encouraged children to draw pictures that would respond to the following phrase: "The world would be a better place if..." From the entries, Mattel chose the kids who would go to the summit.

Meanwhile, in a publicity and advertising campaign, Mattel declared that November would be Barbie Children's Summit Month. The company said that for every purchase of a Barbie during the month, it would make a donation to a cause that the children at the summit would vote on to receive the money. "There's never been a better time to buy a Barbie," the commercial said.

Mattel raised $500,000. Sales for the month of November rose 10 percent over sales for the same month the prior year, which had in itself been a record for Barbie. A special in-store display, including voting boxes for children to voice their concern on the issues of the day, won Barbie feature displays in retail stores. And Mattel got a rush of publicity from newspapers and the electronic media.

The events climaxed with the summit. Kids came from as far away as Germany, India, and Israel. United Nations teachers helped interpret. Shari Belafonte helped the children produce a record. The children engaged in a lively discussion of the issues, before deciding that world peace was the one they cared most about. Mattel contributed the $500,000 accordingly to the Carter Center in Atlanta, Georgia, started by former President Carter, to promote elections, voting rights, and world peace. The program met its objectives, but that turned out to be only one of the benefits. Seeing the children was "truly inspiring," Pat Wyatt said.

Kool-Aid Summer Fun

Functionality also means giving the consumer something he or she otherwise might do without. Kraft General Foods (KGF) found one such opportunity in the inner city in the 1980s. Kool-Aid Summer Fun enabled kids in four cities to swim for free all summer long at municipal swimming pools. At the same time, it raised money for financially strapped parks and recreation departments.

Here's how it worked. The marketer offered to pay the 25-cent admission at the swimming pool for every child 6 to 14 years old who presented a Kool-Aid proof of purchase. In addition, KGF would make a 10-cent contribution to the city's parks and recreation department.

More than 120,000 labels were redeemed. More than $50,000 was donated to the parks departments. KGF got 10,000 letters from kids thanking the company for the best summers of their lives. TV news shows from the local six o'clock news up through "P.M. Magazine" and "Good Morning, America" ran features on the program. More than 4.5 million people heard about it.

Kool-Aid sales increased 14 percent.

"Everybody benefited" who worked on the program, said Stacey Bender. "The children, because they were able to swim. The parks departments, because they were able to encourage kids to come to the pool and make a certain amount of money. And Kool-Aid, because it was a very logical fit for Kool-Aid's positioning as a summer soft drink."

To heighten interest, KGF brought in an Acapulco cliff-diving champion who had risen from the barrios of East Los Angeles to do media interviews and meet with kids to promote the program. The choice not only was someone who could generate excitement, but he also was a role model.

KGF also sponsored a "kids triathlon." And it invited kids to create their own Kool-Aid stands—supplied with free product—as a fundraiser for community centers. Supermarkets put up posters to advertise the promotion. The program ran for five years.

Make It Educational

A promotion also can offer the marketer an opportunity to educate children. As we noted earlier, a promotion is a sensitive subject. Some educators viewed the showing of commercials on the Channel One in-school television program as selling off students' time as if it were a commodity. But marketing does not have to be controversial. Done sensitively—putting education over explicit selling—a program can benefit kids. Apple Computer and IBM have long won plaudits for their programs offering personal computers to schools. A well-conceived program also can be an outward sign that the concern for the quality of education that chief executives often talk about is backed by a positive commitment to help, which goes a long way toward building brand equity. More than 250 companies have created programs for schools.

Whether or not a program becomes controversial is a function, we think, of two factors. The first factor is whether advertising or the educational function is more prominent. Many companies have downplayed their presence by keeping their name to a minimum. For example, some companies don't run ads in the sponsored magazines they have created. Instead, they run their corporate logo at the beginning or end of the issue. Being low-key doesn't mean you won't get noticed by your audience. With kids' reading every word in the magazine, as we noted in our chapter on print advertising, they'll remember you.

The second factor is how appropriate your product is to the school. One editor we know turned apopletic after his kindergartner came home from school one afternoon with a sample bag of brand name fruit leather she'd been given in a corporate-sponsored lesson on "healthy eating"—a loose fit, considering the sugary content of the snack, even by the most generous standards.

Is your product part of the adult world that kids will be learning about in school? Is it from a foreign country that they will study? Is it a tool, such as a computer or calculator, that they will be using in school? If you can answer any of these questions affirmatively, it's not hard to move from there to a subject to tie into.

Pizza Hut, for example, has attracted 600,000 classes and 16 million students to a long-running program promoting reading. The program, dubbed Book It, set reading goals for students. Kids who reached the goals got free personal-sized pizzas. If the entire class reached its reading goal, the class got a pizza party with sodas.

Scholastic magazine has created partnerships with marketers on products from Motts juices to the Discover Card credit card, Lee jeans, and AT&T. The partnerships have resulted in special editions of *Scholastic* on subjects like the Constitution, reading, the environment, and communications.

Procter & Gamble's special issue on the environment was extended into take-home materials and wall charts for the classroom. The marketers got "positive name recognition with the students," without having to "hit [them] over the head" to buy a product, a *Scholastic* executive noted.*

Consumer Age, October 21, 1991.

Kraft General Foods has also created promotions to introduce kids to computers and provide physical education equipment for schools. The Post cereals "Catch onto Computers" promotion, conceived when many schools were starting to latch onto the computer phenomenon, staged tutorials in 22 cities to introduce kids for one hour to personal computers. The program also offered free computers to schools, through proof-of-purchase redemptions. More than 40,000 schools got free computers.

The Milwaukee Conference on Corporate Involvement in Schools set out an eight-point set of principles for marketers. The guidelines were signed by superintendents of schools from half a dozen of the largest states and by leading educational groups, such as the national Parent-Teacher Association (PTA). Here is a sampling. We print it in the interest of your knowing what educators want from you.

> (1) Corporate involvement shall not *require* students to observe, listen to, or read advertising. (2) Selling or providing access to a captive audience in the classroom for commercial purposes is exploitation and a violation of the public trust.... (4) Corporate involvement must support the goals and objectives of the schools. Curriculum and instruction are within the purview of educators. (5) Programs of corporate involvement must be structured to meet an identified education need, not a commercial motive.... (8) Sponsor recognition and corporate logos should be for identification rather than commercial purposes.

Keebler Promotes Self-Esteem

Such promotions require a long-term perspective. Goodwill may not show up immediately on the net profit line of the next quarterly report. The results accrue over time. Tom Garvin, at the time president and chief executive officer of Keebler, looks at such corporate citizenship as integral to Keebler's business.

"We want people to think of us as a 'quality' company," says Garvin. "It's certainly in keeping with that image for us to be a responsible company."

Keebler has tackled some of society's knottiest issues in its corporate goodwill programs. In the mid-1980s, when the drug epidemic was at its worst, Keebler formed a partnership with the President's Drug Awareness Campaign and the national Parent-Teachers Association to create a novel program to get at one of the root causes of drug abuse: low self-esteem. Keebler directed the program at parents. "Children see themselves through their parents' eyes," a brochure for the program explained.

The program had two elements. The first was a video, called *Mirrors*, which showed how parents contribute to low self-esteem by not spending time with their children, ignoring their accomplishments, criticizing their shortcomings, and inhibiting them from trying new things. The video went on to offer concrete steps parents can take to make kids feel good about themselves. To create the video, Keebler contracted Bonneville Communications of Salt Lake City, the ad agency that has gained notoriety for its high production values and for its family-oriented public-service announcements it has created for the Church of Jesus Christ of Latter-Day Saints.

The second element of the program included brochures and discussion guides to extend the issues the video raised. The brochures, which were meant to be taken home, were packed with self-help advice ("Explain your values, but explain why," offered one. "Listen intently when [your children] have a story to tell. [It] helps them realize that their thoughts and ideas are important to you." Another advised, "Set firm limits. Young people need to know what is expected of them." Additional advice included, "Remember that your children often hear you, even when they're paying attention to something else.")

The company sent out the materials to PTAs across the country and set up special nights when parents could see the video and could share their own problems and suggestions with other parents.

Although many companies have steered clear of the Environmental Protection Agency because of the volatility of debate on pollution, Keebler has worked with the agency to honor students who have created grass roots recycling programs, clean-up campaigns, and environmental awareness programs. Keebler's contribution included corporate grants and an honorary dinner in Washington, D.C.

Keebler decided not to create TV commercials or print campaigns to tout its good citizenship. Its self-promotion has generally been limited to having its name, or its logo of Ernie the Elf, appear in the credits of the programs. The company believes that if the program does its work, consumers will notice the Keebler name. "We think we're gaining long-term customers," Tom Garvin says. Plus, he adds, "we really do want to make a difference."

Make It Collectible

Kids are natural-born collectors. It's part of growing up. Collecting teaches children to organize, it empowers them, and it opens the door to new worlds. For example, baseball-card collecting, in its contemporary form, opens up the world of baseball to children and, with the boom in values of rare cards, teaches them some of the basics of investing.

Collectibles, then, have become one of the most popular forms of promotions. Cracker Jack won fans by producing miniature baseball cards. McDonald's Happy Meal promotions often are based on collecting. When a new movie comes out, McDonald's buys the right to produce figurines of the characters. Every time a child buys a Happy Meal, he or she gets a new character.

Stamps and stickers are popular collectibles as well. The U.S. Postal Service has been partner to several promotions. Kids like them because they can collect stamps. The Postal Service likes them because they encourage kids to write letters.

Stamps can also be collected for redemption, like the old S&H Green Stamps. Camp Hyatt, Hyatt Hotel's kids club, for example, issues every child a "passport" upon signing up. Every time a child stays at the hotel, the passport is stamped. As kids pile up stamps, they qualify for prizes like a watch or backpack.

It might even be possible to teach kids to collect coupons. Mattel, targeting primarily grown-ups, has borrowed the packaged-goods marketing tool of coupons to sell toys. It doesn't seem like a great stretch to expand to kids.

Inside One Club

Over the past decade, Amurol Products of Naperville, Illinois, has been one of the most successful new-product companies in the gum and candy market. The subsidiary of William H. Wrigley Co. introduced Bubble Tape, a 6-foot-long coiled "roll" of bubble gum in a circular box, one of the four top-selling brands of bubble gum. It has launched all kinds of curious new packages—bubble gum sticks in tiny models of school lockers, powdered bubble gum in miniature plastic jugs, neon pink and green bubble gum in toothpastelike tubes on plastic ropes that kids wear on their neck. Amurol's sales have grown threefold in four years.

The company gets its ideas from popular culture. It does "a lot" of traditional quantitative and qualitative research, says Gary Schuetz, the company's vice president of marketing. But its secret weapon is The Candy Tasters Club.

The Candy Tasters Club is made up of 2000 kids from the Chicago suburbs. Several times a year—"no more than four," Schuetz says—members of the club come in for 10 minutes or so, in small groups, contribute their comments on product ideas the company is considering, advertising strategies, and competitors' products. In appreciation, the company gives them a goodie bag of products.

The club has taken on a life of its own. Kids hear about it from friends, and then they call, write, and visit to sign up. "They like the idea that they can tell their friends they were part of the development process when a new product shows up in the store," says Schuetz. The actual value is supplemental to the company's other research. But the goodwill it creates is significant, and it serves the corporate mission of trying to learn everything there is to learn about kids.

"Part of our responsibility is to get into the life and mind of kids and see what's hot and what's cool," says Schuetz.

Candy is an intensely competitive business. Girls aged 11 to 14 are the biggest bubble-gum chewers there are. They are also one of the most fad-driven segments of the kids' market. Amurol introduces 12 new products a year. Eight last as long as two years, and, if the company is lucky, four will go on beyond that.

Pros and Cons of Clubs

From the statistics at the beginning of this chapter, it's easy to see that clubs are popular. Kids enjoy being in touch with other kids with the same interests. A club is, in a sense, another form of a peer group.

Clubs can also encourage children's participation in their families' purchase decisions. Camp Hyatt, for example, promotes family vacations at Hyatt Hotels. Delta Air Lines' Delta Fantastic Fliers' Club, with 700,000 members, encourages families to fly Delta. Members get a quarterly magazine. The club even has a mascot, a friendly lion named Dusty the Delta Air Lion.

Some clubs are extensions of products. Some are ends in themselves. Getting started is not hard. It just takes a mailing list. You may have one from your own warranty files or purchase receipts. If you don't have one internally, you can buy one that will fit the basic profile of your market from a list broker.

There are two challenges in clubs. The first is getting noticed. The explosion in the number of clubs means that you have to have a particularly appealing idea that is bigger than just being a loyal consumer of your product.

All kinds of companies have started kids clubs. We've noted the TV and fast-food clubs. Barbie's loyal following has a club through Mattel. LEGO encourages collectors of its construction-block sets to explore their creativity and trade ideas through a LEGO club. Those clubs are based on children's products.

The second challenge of clubs is maintaining them. Running a club is expensive. Some marketers we talked to have committed more than $500,000 in starting their clubs. A club is a commitment. You can't easily back out. You've created an expectation in your market's mind that they will be receiving mail from you on an ongoing basis. Disappointing a child—and the child's parent—will backfire on you in the market. Ill feelings can linger long after a program disappears from your marketing budget. In our research, we talked to many parents who have expressed disappointment at a corporate club's not living up to their expectations. A partnership with a child is like any kind of partnership—it means long-term commitment.

The third challenge is offering something of substance. If the mail you send a child is nothing more than a sales pitch for your products and coupons for buying them, both the child and the parent will be disappointed—and, quite likely, angry. What began as an effort to create long-term loyalties can backfire in long-term animosity.

You don't have to start your own club to benefit from a kids' club. Trans World Airlines, for example, approached Burger King to create a joint promotion with the Burger King Kids Club. The airline created articles about how airlines are designed and operated for the club's newsletter. Included in the package was a special discount for kids flying anywhere in the continental United States with a paying parent. The program generated millions of dollars in bookings for the airline.

The Opportunity in Stores

There's probably a broader opportunity in stores than is currently being tapped. As research in previous chapters has shown, kids are intensely interested in shopping and go on a variety of grocery shopping trips.

Supermarkets are doing some in-store food sampling for kids, but there is opportunity for more. Some stores let kids take their own shopping carts and practice shopping next to Mom. Others send newsletters to kids.

There appears to be opportunity for sampling of other goods and services in toy stores, department stores, and on and on.

Make It Accountable

Before starting off on a promotion or premium program, set clear goals for what you want to accomplish. They can be addressed in several ways. If sales data are accessible, you can define a percentage increase in sales you want to achieve during the promotion period. You can contract research to determine how much consumer awareness of your brand has grown and how well known the promotion is. Through research, you can determine whether the qualities associated with your brand have changed.

If there is a strong public relations component, you can track how many newspaper articles and radio and television stories the promotion generates.

It's important to set clear targets. If you spend money, you should be accountable for it.

Summing Up

Questions to Consider

Before you undertake your promotion, answer these questions:

1. Who exactly do you want to reach, and what is the message you want to send?

2. How will your idea deliver that message?

3. What are you doing to make it fun for kids?

4. How is your idea functional? What purpose will it serve for kids? How does it fit into their lives and the popular culture?

5. Is it educational? How can you maximize that? Are there ways it can serve a need in the community? Is there a public-service component?

6. Does your promotion involve collectibles?

7. Can you extend it into an ongoing relationship? Do you have the ingredients for a club? What would such a club accomplish, and how would it do that?

8. Is there a partner in the form of another company, a community group, school, or government who can help you achieve your goals?

9. How will you measure the success of the program?

12
Nintendo Case Study

The Best of Both World

Pop Quiz

1. Who is Mario?
   (*a*) the hero of Nintendo's best-selling video-game series, (*b*) a Brooklyn, New York, plumber who can run, swim, fly through the air, and turn into a raccoon, (*c*) the brainchild of a Japanese video-game designer, who first used him in Donkey Kong in 1981, (*d*) all of the above.

2. What are the two most popular times for playing video games?
   (*a*) weekdays after school from 3 to 5 p.m. and Saturday morning from 9 to 11 a.m., (*b*) Sunday afternoon from 3 to 5 p.m. and Saturday evening from 5 to 8 p.m., (*c*) Saturday morning from 9 to 11 a.m. and weekday evenings from 5 to 8 p.m.

3. What did Nintendo do to get the attention of an apathetic market?
   (*a*) bought a lot of TV time, (*b*) let word of mouth build demand, (*c*) decided to stage its first test market in the most populous city in the country, New York.

4. Which best describes Nintendo at various times in the United States?
   (*a*) top-selling toy, (*b*) number one Saturday morning cartoon, (*c*) number one in circulation of a boys magazine, (*d*) all of the above.

5. How much of its sales does Nintendo draw from toy stores?
   (*a*) less than 38%, (*b*) 68%, (*c*) 78%, (*d*) 88%.

Answers: 1. *d*; 2. *b*; 3. *c*; 4. *d*; 5. *a*.

Zapping Koopas!

"The Mushroom Kingdom has been a peaceful place, thanks to the brave deeds of Mario and Luigi." So begins the story of *Super Mario Bros. 3*, the third installment of the Nintendo video-game series. The video-game stars are Mario and Luigi, the comical, happy-go-lucky Brooklyn plumbers in floppy caps and coveralls who rise from their Everyman status to become the unlikeliest of heroes.

Once again, they are being called to the rescue. Although all is well in the Mushroom Kingdom, the Mushroom World is anything but placid. The evil Bowser—king of the Koopas, a clan of evil turtles with the Midaslike ability to destroy Mario and Luigi with a mere touch—has sent his seven kids "to make mischief as they please."

The Koopa kids have stolen the magic wands from the seven countries of the Mushroom World and turned the poor old kings of the lands into lowly beasts. It's up to Mario and Luigi to catch up with the Koopa kids, restore the poor kings—one at a time—to their human form, save the princess and—whew!—bring peace and happiness back to the Mushroom World.

Along the way, Mario and Luigi can run, jump, swim, sprout raccoon tail and ears (which enables them to fly through the air), turn into statues; and whap, kick, or jump up and down on their enemies—among other things.

The tricks come in handy because Mario and Luigi have plenty of enemies. They range from Goombas (a flying creature), to Chain Chomps (a cannon ball with a menacing set of jaws), Thwomps (concrete blocklike creatures that try to fall down on top of Mario), Venus Fire Traps (fireball-spitting flowers), boomerang-wielding turtles, and, of course, the Koopas (a family of beasts that are part reptile, part animal—and "just love being mean!").

Along the way, the resourceful brothers can get help from coins (collect 100, and one gets another life), a star (which renders Mario invincible), a leaf (which turns Mario into a raccoon), a mushroom (another route to an extra life), a super mushroom (which transforms Mario into Super Mario), and a "fire flower" (which enables Mario to throw fireballs). The latter is generally uncovered by ramming a wall of bricks or popping open special blocks marked with musical notes, a question mark, or the letter *p*.

More often than not, the bad guys win, and Mario and Luigi plummet off the screen with a droll, musical, computer-generated Bronx cheer. That, in turn, only serves to make the kids who play the game even *more* determined to make it past "the third country," "the fifth country" or wherever else they expired, and, someday, maybe even conquer Bowser.

Tales of Nintendo lovers' playing into the night, through the week-ends, or, in most cases, until Mom or Dad steps in and turns off the machine are legendary. More importantly, for our purposes, is the less-told story of Nintendo Co.'s strategy and persistence in making the unobtrusive but pricy ($79, plus upwards of $49 per wafer-thin, plastic software game cartridge) tan-and-gray rectangular plastic box a fixture in one-third of America's 85 million households *in just five years.*

By 1992 Nintendo had developed a family of products ranging from the basic Nintendo Entertainment System, Game Boy (a portable, hand-held video-game system), and the next-generation, more powerful Super Nintendo Entertainment system.

Roughly $1 out of every $5 spent on toys in the United States as of 1992 was being spent on video games. Video games have become a multibillion-dollar industry.

Nintendo became so successful, it created an opportunity for compe-tition. Sega of America, after stumbling early on, got a one-year jump on Nintendo by introducing the more powerful 16-bit next generation of video-game systems. Heading into the Christmas of 1992, Sega Genesis and Super Nintendo—the competing 16-bit system from Nintendo—were running neck and neck in the high end of the video-game market. The two brands had become the Coke and Pepsi of the toy business.

What Nintendo Accomplished

Nintendo of America, Inc., had the ingenuity to figure out how to com-bine the sheer excitement and gimmickry of the toy business with the careful attention to detail of classic packaged-goods marketing. It gen-erated the immediacy and responsiveness normally associated with restaurants, department stores, Hollywood, and other retail-driven companies. The strategy enabled the company to avoid the boom-and-bust cycle that destroys many new toy companies. It also has earned Nintendo the respect of its industry. "They're packaged-goods kind of people," says one ad agency executive admiringly. "They've got very savvy management."

The goal of Nintendo has been to combine "the discipline of packaged goods with the entrepreneurial *right now* experience of restaurants," says Peter Main, the company's vice president of marketing and the architect of the strategy. "I think Nintendo is a very interesting hybrid of those two systems."

The net result single-handedly resuscitated a toy category that every-one else had given up on, and that toy stores, consumer electronics retailers, and mass merchandisers had openly resisted after being badly burned both psychologically and financially when the first generation of video games crashed and burned in the mid-1980s.

The company has opened up a debate around dinner tables, in public-interest groups, and in academic circles on how much video-game playing—if any—is enough, and whether the time lost to homework, outdoor play, and other traditional childhood activities is compensated by the claims that video games can improve hand-eye coordination.

Nintendo, moreover, has refashioned the toy industry, driving toy manufacturers virtually out of the business of making high-end toys for boys that would compete with Nintendo. Many of them, instead, put their research and development staffs to work to create hardware and software accessories for Nintendo. In addition, Nintendo changed how kids use media—shifting millions of kids out of television viewing into video games—and quickened the integration of technology into a new generation of households.

With the backing of the people of Seattle, Nintendo of America had become enmeshed enough in American culture for its controlling family to lead a bicultural Japanese-American acquisition of the Seattle Mariners baseball team. This development marked the true marriage of "America's pastime" with the favorite indoor pastime of a generation of young Americans and helped create a new bridge between Japan and America.

Even without baseball, Nintendo has earned itself a place alongside the status elite of marketers to children—Disney, McDonald's, Fisher-Price, Mattel. Like those companies, Nintendo has come to have a strong enough brand equity that its name on a product virtually assures its success. "The name sells the product," says one toy-industry analyst. "They're part of the fabric of the toy business, like Barbie."

What Marketers Can Learn from Nintendo

For marketers, Nintendo is worth studying for three reasons. First, its success shows the value of crossbreeding in marketing—that is, taking the strategies of one product or service category and transferring them to another one. Second, Nintendo's track record proves the value of listening to your consumer, starting from the time the consumer enters the purchase cycle to answering questions that arise after the consumer buys the product. Third, Nintendo shows the value of persistence.

Minoru Arakawa, the president of Nintendo of America, recalls being all but bodily ejected from the offices of merchandise buyers when he first started making sales calls to try to interest retailers in what would become the megahit of the 1980s. Arakawa persisted because he believed in his product. "We believed that people were not tired of good, entertaining games," he says. "People were tired of mediocre, average games."

To convince the market, Nintendo undertook the unusual step of creating "probably the highest-profile test market ever taken," in the words of vice president of marketing Peter Main. The company went into New York, at Christmastime, and sold out its product. That got the attention of the industry. Since then, there has been no turning back.

The Marketer Behind the Brand

The marketer behind Nintendo's success is Peter Main, a Canadian with an affable smile and a conservative style—particularly so for the eccentric, self-indulgent worlds of the toy and consumer electronics industries— who had come no closer to the toy business than buying presents for his two kids before becoming the senior marketer for Nintendo in 1986.

Peter Main, like Sharon Fordham at Nabisco, is a product of his environment. The strategies and systems he has put into place at Nintendo come from his own personal experience at some of the marketing world's biggest names—Colgate and General Foods, where he rose through the ranks to run a 3500-person division—and his own experience as an entrepreneur.

"Peter's background is not toys or electronic products," says Minoru Arakawa. "But I believe common sense is more important than experience in toys and electronic products. Peter has really good common sense as a marketing person. He has a good management style, and he has a good reputation among the dealers, and also the advertising, the public-relations company, and the people working in the company."

Main was born in Kitchner, Ontario, a town just outside Toronto, into a family that itself was on the cutting edge of technology for its time. Main's father was an executive in the consumer electronics industry, who went into radio and television stations, eventually becoming the chairman of the board of Central Ontario Television. Peter Main went to business school at the University of Western Ontario.

He started his career at Colgate-Palmolive as brand assistant on "the house of Ajax" in the 1960s. He went on to manage dental creams, shampoos, and other personal-care products, eventually becoming a group product manager for new products.

In 1969 he moved to General Foods, as a new business planning manager. He stayed there for nine years. When General Foods acquired Canterbury Foods, a Canadian restaurant concern, Main was sent to assist with the acquisition. He ran White Spot, a 3500-employee chain of 150 Canadian sit-down family restaurants that were part of the group. General Foods saw Canterbury as a vehicle for expanding its Burger Chef fast-food operation into Canada. Unfortunately, the economics weren't there. Canterbury was sold, and Main stayed to manage it. Restless, he moved to another company to run their restaurant business. Then he dabbled in entrepreneurship, investing in a photo-finishing business.

Main met Arakawa in the 1970s in Vancouver. They were neighbors. At the time, Arakawa was a civil engineer, who had earned his bachelor's and master's degrees at Kyoto University in Japan, gone on to graduate school at MIT, and remained in North America, working on office buildings, condominiums, and other projects.

When Arakawa told Main he was giving up civil engineering to join his father-in-law's business, a Japanese arcade-game concern called Nintendo, Main was surprised. "It was a nonentity," Main says. To Arakawa, however, the new American outpost was a challenge. "I have always liked challenge," says Arakawa. "Whether it was the entertainment business or civil engineering does not matter."

The two kept in touch. Arakawa brought Main down to Seattle to consult occasionally. Finally, Arakawa invited him to come down to stay, promising that "we are going to do some exciting things." In 1986 Main accepted his former neighbor's invitation.

The success of Toyota, Honda, Nissan, and Mazda—Japan's big car companies—have created the impression that Japanese companies have had an easy time coming into the United States and dominating markets. In fact, many Japanese companies have not done well. Japan and the United States have very different marketplaces. Japan is a small, centralized country, while the United States is sprawling and diffuse. Japan's retail environment is composed largely of mom-and-pop stores. Manufacturers in the United States must come to terms with gigantic mass merchants, discount chains, and vast department stores.

The innovations in computer hardware and software have come generally from U.S. companies, like Apple, Microsoft, IBM, Lotus, and Sun Microsystems. Likewise, the gold standard in entertainment "software"—from Hollywood movies to rock 'n' roll records—is American. For Nintendo to succeed, then, it would have to combine its Japanese strengths in video-game hardware and game design with American marketing know-how.

The partnership of Arakawa and Main is a microcosm of the Japanese-American blend that Nintendo of America became. Arakawa provided the knowledge of the product, the instinct for what the games should accomplish, and the tone for the company. Main built relationships with the trade, set the marketing strategy, and helped the Japanese understand the nuances of the U.S. marketplace.

Fighting Against History

The first task for Nintendo was to learn from the mistakes of the companies that had gone before it. The first generation of video games had one of the wildest roller coaster rides in modern business. It began in the mid-1970s in pinball arcades and college bars with the introduction of a few rudimentary games, the most famous of which was Pong, a sort of table tennis in which two competitors would bat an electronic ball back and forth across a video screen with two flat electronic "paddles."

By the early 1980s, the early games had given birth to a primitive home video-game system that attached to television screens. The system brought the first generation of games home and added additional games based on other sports, like auto racing and baseball, and outerspace adventures. Interest quickly escalated. The companies, many of them ad hoc affairs run by video-game designers with little or no expertise in running inventories or marketing programs, wholeheartedly responded by shoveling out more and more titles. Quality control rapidly evaporated, and as quickly as the industry had soared, it crashed.

Sales that had rocketed from nothing to $3 billion then plummeted within two years to less than $100 million. *Video games* became a punch line synonymous with one-shot phenomena, excessiveness, and self-indulgent business practices.

Nintendo had technology on its side. The system it was developing for the U.S. marketplace, when Main arrived, had 8 kilobytes of memory—roughly twice that of the existing video games—which enabled software makers to write more complex programs with better animation and more sophisticated games. Nintendo also had the benefit of two years' experience in the Japanese market—where consumers were going nuts over its products—on its side.

Still, the prospects before it were daunting. Nintendo's first research on American consumers showed that Americans harbored disappointment—and even resentment—over the first generation of the product. Video games were lousy value. "Taken at face value, the research said, 'Don't do it,'" Main says.

The brainstorm of test marketing the product in New York helped distance Nintendo a little from the debacle. The company moved 25 staff members, lock, stock, and barrel, to canvass the metropolitan area, pushing the product. It added the double-barrel of a sizable ad campaign. In the spring of 1986, the company followed up with additional test markets in Los Angeles and San Francisco. It advertised less but got similar results. By the official introduction at the summer Consumer Electronics Show in Chicago, the wall of resistance by retailers was beginning to crumble.

"We were learning to be a consumer-driven business," says Main.

Defining Your Company and Product

One of the biggest tasks Nintendo set for itself was to define and implement a kind of relationship with retailers that the toy industry had never seen before. The first step was defining what and where it wanted to be. The company's executives did not want consumers to think of it as a toy company. Letting that happen would severely limit the market, which they saw as much larger than children.

"We call ourselves an electronic entertainment product producer," Arakawa says. "Toys are only for children. Our product is not only for children but for adults, too."

The definition drove the distribution strategy. "To position ourselves as a total family medium, our distribution had to be balanced between toys, mass merchants, consumer electronics stores, and specialty channels such as catalogs," says Main. At first, mass merchants like Wal-Mart, K mart, and Target; and consumer electronics chains were standoffish. About two-thirds of Nintendo's sales came through toy stores. But, the first year's success got others interested. Today less than one-third of the company's sales are through what are traditionally known as toy stores. Mass merchants are equally important, with electronics stores and department stores not altogether far behind.

Controlling the Pipeline

Getting the product into the store, however, was only half of the challenge. The second half was *managing* it. It was here that Nintendo broke with tradition in the toy industry and broke new ground. The toy industry has always had a reputation as a boom-and-bust business. Fads like Hula Hoops, Pet Rocks, Beatle wigs, trolls, and Cabbage Patch dolls have tended to reinforce that image. But the fickleness of kids is only part of the problem. The other half is the willingness of companies to play along, stuffing the pipeline with product and eating the costs when the fad dies.

Nintendo was determined not to fall into that trap. It was here that Main's restaurant background paid off. Restaurants are a fiercely competitive business. The benefit of the business is that a marketer knows right away whether something is working or not. If it's working, people line up to order it; if it's not working, they ignore it. Marketing's success or failure is rung up every day at the cash register.

"It's a wonderful change from having to wait two months for Neilsen data to see how an idea conceived nine months ago is working," says Main.

The Retail Influence

Instead of looking at itself as a supplier to the retailer, Nintendo recast itself as a partner. The company made a point of finding out from the retailer on a regular basis whether a product was selling. Instead of relying solely on orders from retailers, which are continually subject to the inflated expectations of the natural desire to want a hit, Nintendo carefully tried to calibrate its production and shipments to the actual sales it got at the cash register.

"We tried to produce products and ship products [based on] live consumer demand and not the vagaries of responding to retailer perceptions," Main says.

Main cited one year in which there was particularly feverish demand. The company shipped 33 million video-game cartridges. That was fewer than it really wanted to send. Based on cash register sales, Nintendo had projected it could sell 43 million games. Selling 43 million, of course, would have saturated consumer demand. The company's goal was to keep the market just a little hungry for product. The ideal was to come in just barely under demand, say, 40 million cartridges.

Nintendo had had orders from retailers for a whopping 110 million cartridges, more than triple the number it sold and more than double any reasonable estimate of the total demand for the product. If the company shipped the number of products retailers had asked for, "it would have been an absolute calamity in the first quarter," Main says.

The company would have had to have an absolute fire sale to get the product off the shelf, which no doubt would infuriate customers who had bought at full price at the height of the Christmas buying season. Alternatively, it would have been stuck with leaving the product on retailers' shelves, which would have meant virtually shutting down production in Japan and, ultimately, irritating the trade, who never like to have a product gather dust. Either alternative would have surely taken the hot-product glow off of Nintendo.

At first, retailers balked at Nintendo's strategy. They didn't want to share cash register sales reports, and they accused the company of meddling in their business. Eventually, they came around. The company gets reports on a regular, weekly basis from more than half of the outlets it sells in.

To give it a second source of data, the company equipped its field sales staff with hand-held, portable computers to tote up inventories in stores and send back reports on what's selling and what's not. The sales force is responsible for checking into stores every two weeks. Every Monday, the Nintendo management team sifts through the sales reports.

The Chip Controversy

The other step Nintendo took to control the quality and quantity of product in the marketplace was the most controversial. The company created a "lockout" chip that software cartridges would have to contain for the game to run on the Nintendo video-game hardware. Nintendo used the chip to license the right to produce software for its machines.

Critics complained that the company had created a monopoly. Some also noted that controlling the supply of the chip let Nintendo artificially undershoot demand, to create a consumer frenzy to find popular software. Nintendo, for its part, maintained that the shortfall was exacerbated by a chronic shortage of the lockout chips.

The Entertainment Influence

Working at Nintendo is "like working at an entertainment company," says Bill White, the company's advertising manager. "We're title driven. It's a software strategy. We believe in a very direct pull philosophy. It's very retail in nature. We're able to see the results of our work. And we react very quickly—to keep the pressure on, or turn it off, and move onto the next software title."

The strategy determined Nintendo's advertising strategy. The company spends more than $100 million a year on advertising. Virtually all of the sum is thrown behind the titles that Nintendo believes will generate enthusiasm for the Nintendo name. Even when Nintendo has launched new generations of hardware—such as Game Boy and the Super Nintendo 16-bit hardware system—it puts a major share of its marketing dollars into the software games that will run on the system.

The Packaged-Goods Influence

Nintendo rewards retailers for supplying it with data by turning its information and strategies into programs to help retailers sell more product. Nintendo takes a traditional, packaged-goods approach. In line with that approach, the company created an in-store boutique, called The World of Nintendo, to highlight new products and encourage year-round traffic in stores. The concept quickly was adopted in 5000 stores.

A second result of embracing packaged-goods marketing is cross-merchandising. In Chapter 11, in the discussion of premiums and promotions, we outlined the McDonald's Happy Meals promotion that heralded the arrival of Nintendo's *Super Mario Bros. 3*. Nintendo also has created cross-promotions with Nabisco, for Oreo Cookies and Chips Ahoy, and with Pepsi-Cola. "We have similar targets," a Pepsi executive says. "Young people enjoy video games. They're also attracted to drinking Pepsi. And Nintendo's a hot company and industry innovator. We like to think of ourselves as the same."

A third outgrowth of its packaged-goods approach is its aggressive licensing program. It spun off two animated television shows. The first was "Captain N the Game Master," which became the number one show on Saturday mornings. The second was a cartoon based on Mario; it became one of the leading weekday afternoon shows. And Ralston-Purina cereal, Nintendo brand, captured a 1.4% market share.

Keeping Up with the Consumer

As much as Nintendo kept up with its retailers and licensees, it kept up even more with its customers. The company established a dedicated phone line, staffed by 80 "game counselors," to handle queries from Nintendo players who had been stumped by a game. The counselors soon got 50,000 phone calls a week.

The service lessened the frustration of Nintendo's audience, and it also provided the company with yet another source of information about the market. The calls were a gauge of how quickly—if at all—new games were being accepted, what kinds of games the market was interested in, and what problems users had with Nintendo. At the end of the week, the company toted up how many calls it got; what games calls came in on; the nature of the calls; and whether the callers were boys or girls, kids or grown-ups. Then the results were put in a report for the marketing staff.

Meanwhile, from warranty cards the company built up a mailing list that exceeded 4 million names. It analyzed the households with PRIZM and other research tools.

Perhaps the most powerful link with its customers was *Nintendo Power*, the company's 1.5 million-circulation, 120-page magazine. The magazine previewed and analyzed new games, and it offered secrets and tricks to help users out on current games—and lots of color graphics. "It was a pretty lethal marketing tool for building loyalty," a Nintendo ad agency executive admits.

Between the sales records, warranty cards, phone calls to game counselors, and the magazine, the company built up a storehouse of knowledge that it could redeploy in its marketing. "By talking with [customers] we can easily get what they are looking for and what they don't like," says Arakawa.

The Game Is the Game

The heart of the company, however, remained the product. "The moniker you hear repeatedly is the name of the game is the game," says Main. "Fun, excitement, and challenge have to be in every game." Executives boiled that down to a three-point positioning: high value, fun experience.

The company has been so successful with the strategy that it has even created a dent in the image of television's hold over children. On Sunday afternoon, between 3 and 5 p.m., the most popular time slot for video games, 9.6 percent of televisions in households with kids are tuned into video games—not regular programming. That's followed closely by Saturday evening from 5 to 8 p.m., Monday through Friday from 5 to 8 p.m., Sunday afternoon from noon to 3 p.m., and Sunday evening from 5 to 8 p.m.

The magazine, in-store displays, and advertising encouraged existing players to move on from basic games to more challenging software. Meanwhile, the company created new programs to expand the market. Game Boy, the portable system, has had dedicated ad campaigns to target adults. One campaign begun on Father's Day 1992 laid out the case that Dad could get a lot more fun out of a Game Boy than a new lawn mower. Earlier TV campaigns positioned Game Boy as a fun way to wile away time waiting in such mundane adult pursuits as waiting for a plane to take off. According to internal company reports, more than 30 percent of the market for Nintendo products is older than teenagers.

The core market, however, remains 8- to 15-year-old boys. To some extent, Nintendo is fighting biology. Below age 7, fine motor skills are not developed enough to let kids be very successful at playing video games.

The company looks to a variety of sources to maintain a supply of product that will excite kids. Software comes both from Japan and from a lengthy list of licensees in the United States.

New Product Challenges

If there has been a complaint that has arisen from Nintendo's followers, it is that the company's conservative, packaged-goods management style has let competitors move faster and take more chances with technology. With Game Boy, Nintendo did not suffer any repercussions. Video-game reviewers said competitive products, such as Sega's Game Gear and Atari's Lynx, were technically superior. But Nintendo's name assured that Game Boy would go to the top of the lists of best-selling toys. A superior software catalog—led by Tetris, a mind teaser created by a Russian designer and bundled into Game Boy—cemented Game Boy's popularity.

With the second-generation, 16-bit hardware systems, however, Nintendo faced a stiffer challenge. Anxious to protect its basic Nintendo Entertainment System and work out all the kinks before coming to market, Nintendo took a cautious approach. Sega, which could not break Nintendo's hold on basic systems, poured its energies into its Genesis 16-bit system.

Sega got into the market a season earlier. Getting an early jump plus having Sonic the Hedgehog, the Mariolike hero of its most popular software program, enabled Sega to generate the enthusiasm necessary to get a toehold in the market. Sega also had the ingenuity to make its 16-bit system compatible with its old system, so kids could play their games on both. When Super Nintendo came to market, it didn't have "backward compatibility," a point that riled parents who had shelled out for the earlier system and who now had to shell out for the new system plus games for it.

Still, Nintendo caught up quickly—a tribute to the Nintendo brand name. Within a year, it had surpassed Sega Genesis on best-seller lists.

Moving into Christmas 1992, the Super Nintendo and Sega Genesis systems were in a classic, head-to-head battle for supremacy. In the end, that might not be all bad. Like Coke and Pepsi's long-running battle in the cola market, a Super Nintendo-Sega Genesis rivalry could build awareness, interest, and enthusiasm for both systems, and develop a market for the products better than one company could on its own.

To be sure, Nintendo and Sega dominate the lists of best-selling toys. Of the 20 toys on *Toy and Hobby World*'s Toy Hit Parade in mid-1992, 11 products were Nintendo or Sega video-game hardware, software, or accessories. At the top of the list, the number one top-selling toy in the country was the Super Nintendo Entertainment System. Number two was Sega Genesis. Number three was the Nintendo Entertainment System. And Number five—after Barbie—was Nintendo Game Boy.

An argument could be made that the competition at the high end of the market was boosting enough interest in video games to keep a fire on sales for all levels of the business. Some families had acquired Super Nintendo *and* Sega Genesis *and* the basic Nintendo system *and* a portable Nintendo Game Boy or Sega Game Gear. Family members would switch back and forth between systems to play their favorite games.

Nintendo knows it cannot afford to rest. "We're like all companies in the entertainment business," one executive notes. "We can't be selling yesterday's blockbuster."

"It all depends on the software," Minoru Arakawa said some time ago. "If we can create software that is fresh and exciting, people will recognize it and continue to buy our product."

Summing Up

1. Every child in America knows that Nintendo has become a success by creating video games that deliver on their promise of challenge, excitement, and fun. The company has become a case study for marketing by drawing on the experience of its marketers to bring the careful planning of packaged-goods marketing and the responsiveness of retailing to manage the wild swings of spectacular success and disastrous collapse of consumer electronics.

2. Nintendo matched production and shipments to actual demand, based on cash register sales, instead of relying on orders. It also created numerous links to its consumers to understand its market, ranging from free 800 numbers, to an enthusiasts' magazine, and a heavy component of market research.

13
Nabisco Case Study

A Miniature Phenomenon

The Problem with Graham Crackers

For generations, the first solid food many parents have given to their children has been graham crackers. They're sweet. They're crispy enough to bring a smile to a baby's face but soft enough for biting with baby teeth. And, of course, they have a pleasing taste. For Nabisco Foods, Co.—the maker of Nabisco Honey Maid honey grahams and cinnamon grahams, the leading brand of graham crackers—it all added up to a dependable business, year in and year out.

But Nabisco knew it could do better. For all their benefits, grahams had a basic problem. "Grahams are eaten very much like a cookie," says Sharon Fordham, senior director of new business for the division of RJR Nabisco, Inc., that is based in Parsippany, New Jersey. "But the form—compared to a cookie—is inconvenient."

Consumers buy Nabisco grahams in perforated, $2^1/_2$- by 5-inch rectangles. The cracker can be cracked along the perforations into four child-sized pieces. But the task takes some manual dexterity. The alternative of giving a whole cracker to a toddler inevitably results in a trail of crumbs throughout the house.

And there was another problem with the traditional graham. For kids brought up on the colorful, electronic graphics and kinetic energy of Nintendo, MTV, Disney videos, and Saturday morning TV, the plain, rectangular graham was pretty pedestrian. Fine for an eight-month-old. But, as soon as children could call the shots at snack time—be they 4, 5, 6, or 7 years old—the graham was left in the dust, especially with the multitudinous varieties of rocket-, car-, fish-, and animal-shaped, yellow, green, and orange fruit snacks. It was pretty simple. "Kids wanted racier, 'funner' snacks," Fordham says. "We had to make a graham that had a snackable form and was a fun, unique shape that kids would like."

The Solution: The Teddy Graham

In four paragraphs, that was the genesis of Teddy Grahams, Nabisco's line of teddy bear-shaped, $1^1/_4$-inch tall miniature graham cookies. (See Figure 11.) The product is one of the most successful new-cookie introductions of all time. In its first two years, the four-flavor line (honey, cinnamon, vanilla, and chocolate) generated $300 million in sales—the equivalent of 32 billion of the tiny bears (or, if you prefer, 100 million pounds of teddies). It won a stack of awards, including the American Marketing Association's Edison "light-bulb" award for new product of the year.

According to the CMR KIDTRENDS REPORT, based on The Simmons Kids Study, 27 percent of children in America between the ages of 6 and 14 have eaten a Teddy Graham in the last seven days. By that measure, Teddy Grahams are the third most popular cookie of American children, trailing only its Nabisco stablemates Oreo and Chips Ahoy.

Figure 11. Teddy Grahams snack cookies repackaged graham crackers into a fun and convenient new shape, in four flavors (vanilla not shown). The box showed off the attributes of the bears, in a colorful format. (Courtesy of Nabisco Foods.)

Moreover, the Teddy Graham ignited an explosion of miniature cookies from Nabisco—including Mini Chips Ahoy, Mini Nutter Butters, mini Oreos, and miniature Saltine, Triscuit, and Cheddar Wedges crackers—generating new revenue streams for the venerable cookie and cracker company. The burst of activity was the biggest and most innovative period of new-product introductions for Nabisco since the 19-year period between 1898 and 1917 when the company introduced Uneeda Biscuits (the company's first nationally distributed product), Fig Newtons, Saltine crackers, Barnum & Bailey's Animal Crackers, Lorna Doone shortbread, and the Oreo sandwich cookie.

Nabisco sells more than $5 billion a year worth of cookies, crackers, nuts, and other food products. But even small companies can learn from their experience. Nabisco's philosophy is basic common sense. "Senior management of this company has a high interest in building the value of the company," says one Nabisco executive. "One of the best ways to do that is through successful internally generated growth. That is generally new products."

Why Teddy Grahams Were a Clever Idea

The notion of creating a "snackable," fun evolution of the graham cracker was a clever idea. Teddy Grahams even have play value, that mythical quality normally associated with toys. Nabisco regularly gets letters from Teddy Graham consumers who say they act out stories with the cookies before popping them into their mouths. Teddy Grahams have been the featured snack at teddy bear picnics by both grown-ups and kids. A Nabisco executive recalls hearing from one fan who reported that she had discovered you could form a circle with ten Teddy Grahams and have them all hold hands.

Moreover, Teddy Grahams made good business sense. A lot of new products fail because they range too far afield from what a company does well. A maker of salad dressing might fail if it came out with microwaveable frozen dinners. The same might hold true for a vegetable processor that takes a stab at making entrées.

Teddy Grahams leveraged Nabisco's core business of cookies and crackers. It took ingredients that Nabisco was already familiar with and, basically, redesigned them into a new form. It was basic "gap" analysis: looking for gaps in the company's product lines and the demographic groups it serves, and devising products that will fill them.

Because of the "added value" of the bite-sized, three-dimensional bear shape, Nabisco could charge $1.99 for a 10-ounce box of Teddy

Grahams, compared with $2.99 for a 16-ounce box of regular grahams. That brought significantly higher margins. The process and outcome of the Teddy Graham makes it a role model for new products for children.

The Woman Behind the Bear

Teddy Grahams originated in the Nabisco new-product team, run out of Sharon Fordham's office in Nabisco's modernistic, suburban office park on a former golf course in Parsippany, New Jersey. Fordham is a likable, hard-working MBA graduate of the Wharton School of Business and, earlier, a graduate of Rutgers University and Franklin High School in Somerset, New Jersey. She keeps all the workaday symbols of the corporate world in her office—appointment schedules, stacks of memos, reports, industry awards, and golfing memorabilia.

There are also hints of the imagination and humor that peek through in the round belly button and chubby arms of Teddy Grahams. These are sorts of things that marketers everywhere use to integrate their own past experiences into their present issues to create new-product ideas.

Take the Magic 8-Ball—a kitschy reminder of postwar suburban America—that was sitting prominently on Fordham's desk during a recent visit. It's a common artifact from the childhood of most baby boomers, of which Fordham is one. The shiny black orb, shaped like an oversized billiard ball, was the 1950s answer to the Ouija Board. You asked a question, shook the ball, turned it over, and an answer would float into view in a tiny porthole on the bottom of the ball.

It's an appropriate *chatchka*, for Fordham herself is very much a product of the 1950s, that era when dazzling new products for kids could be found seemingly every week in the nation's supermarkets. Going to the supermarkets and looking up and down the aisle for products were among Fordham's favorite childhood experiences.

"The grocery store was just the most incredibly interesting place to me," she says. "I used to meet my mother there every Thursday after school. There were always so many new things coming out. Every aisle you went down, you saw something different."

She can still rattle off the favorite new products from her childhood: Fizzies, the bright-colored pills that turned a glass of water into a carbonated, colorful drink; Pez, the little clown-headed or Santa-topped plastic containers that popped out a candy when you lifted up its head, Quik, Hershey's Instant, and other milk flavorings.

"To this day," says Fordham, "I want to be in the store *each week* because there are so many new things coming out, not only in our category but also in other categories, that could have applications for us at Nabisco."

There are two lessons for marketers here. First, it can be enormously beneficial to draw on your own personal experience for new-product ideas. You will still need to put them to the test of market research, but they're a good starting point. Second, it's extremely important to get out of your office and see what's happening in the stores. Your own personal trips to the grocery store, department stores, shopping malls, even the hardware store, can turn up the germ of an idea.

The Competitive Context

Nabisco is the favorite brand of cookie among kids aged 6 to 14, according to CMR KIDTRENDS REPORT, based on The Simmons Kids Study. A whopping 77 percent of kids name Nabisco as their favorite brand—17 percentage points ahead of Keebler, the number two brand, and 49 percentage points ahead of Sunshine, the number three brand.

Nabisco's two top-rated cookies are Oreos and Chips Ahoy: 49 percent of kids had eaten an Oreo in the past seven days, and 39 percent had eaten a Chips Ahoy. Teddy Grahams, as we noted earlier, were third, at 27 percent, tied with Keebler's E.L. Fudge sandwich cookie. Next were Keebler's Rainbow Chips Deluxe at 26 percent, Chewy Chips Ahoy at 22 percent, and Keebler's Magic Middles and Nabisco Fig Newtons at 21 percent.

Nabisco hasn't kept its dominant position by resting on its laurels. The key to the company's new-product development is the ability to read the competitive environment and respond accordingly. In the early 1980s, for example, Procter & Gamble and Frito-Lay launched soft-baked cookies—the former under the Duncan Hines name and the latter under Grandma's brand. Both companies were trying to break into the cookie market.

Nabisco had to defend its turf. The result came to be known as the soft cookie wars. Nabisco came out with a soft version of Chips Ahoy, went toe-to-toe on deep-discount coupons, and successfully blunted its two rivals.

In the process, Nabisco sharpened its new-product skills. The company's 1987 merger with RJ Reynolds—creating RJR Nabisco—heightened the search for new revenue streams for the company. Nabisco came out with Fudge Covered Oreos, an indulgent line extension of its best-selling cookie; American Classics, a Pepperidge Farm-style line of crackers for more sophisticated, grown-up tastes; and Quackers, a cheese cracker shaped like little ducks. But the biggest idea was probably Ritz Bits, a bite-sized version of Nabisco's round, buttery Ritz cracker, intended to make Ritz a "snackable" treat to gobble down like peanuts in front of the TV.

Fordham was in the front lines of both the soft-cookie wars and Ritz Bits, first as product manager on Chips Ahoy and then as director of Nabisco's cracker business. In 1987 senior management asked Fordham to head a new venture by Nabisco that set up an independent team of about a dozen marketers in an entrepreneurial group to conceive new product ideas outside the current Nabisco product line and bring them to market. The goal was to identify "strategic areas of interest" in demographic or consumer trends and to develop products that would play to those trends.

Successful new products don't only generate revenues. They also solidify your shelf space in the store. "There's only so much real estate in a store," Sharon Fordham notes. "Every time you come up with something new, it's going to cost somebody something." If you develop a track record of success, chances are the other guy will be the loser.

Why a Bear?

We opened this chapter with the basic problem that Teddy Grahams were conceived to solve. Graham crackers were a little unwieldy and a little boring. Nabisco wanted to shrink them down to a bite-sized cookie that packed some pizzazz and would be considered a healthy alternative for sugar-conscious parents.

So why a bear?

The decision wasn't a snap call. Instead, it was the end result of a long, methodical search. "We looked at almost every animate and inanimate object you could imagine," says Fordham. The search led to two forms—one of which was a teddy bear and the other, for competitive purposes, Nabisco won't reveal.

The new team took both shapes to quantitative testing with children, to see which one kids would like best. Companies don't always choose the one that tests highest; in those cases, the research can indicate that the gut choice of the marketer will require advertising to build awareness for the name among consumers.

In the case of Teddy Grahams, no such effort was needed. The bears scored quite a bit higher than the other option in comparative scores and got impressive scores on its own.

It's easy to understand bears' appeal. Virtually every child (and many adults) has a teddy bear he or she can snuggle. From the original teddy bear—a stuffed animal manufactured on the heels of a famous story about Teddy Roosevelt's sparing a young bear's life—through A. A. Milne's *Winnie the Pooh* stories, through "The Teddy Bear Picnic," Smokey the Bear, and the Care Bears, the animal has had a special place in the popular culture. Moreover, teddy bears have been trendy of late. Upscale teddy bears, with price tags of more than $100, have popped up in department stores. Like stamps, baseball cards, lunch boxes, and dolls, teddy bears have become collectibles.

Their popularity brought Nabisco some unexpected dividends. Because teddy bears are so well known, designers can evoke the idea *bear* with just a few lines of drawing. Embossing the image of a bear in cookie dough, then, was much easier than many other animals would have been.

The Demographic Match

Teddy Grahams made a lot of sense demographically to Nabisco as well. There are two populations the company finds particularly compelling. The first is the aging population, with its increasing interest in cutting back on fat, cholesterol, and salt and eating more healthy foods. The second group is kids.

But kids, themselves, were to be only part of the target. The other group Nabisco was aiming at with Teddy Grahams was parents. If Teddy Grahams' combination of bite-sized shape and entertaining design appealed to kids, its ingredient attributes—lightly sweet, low fat, and low cholesterol—would appeal to moms.

Nabisco's research showed a surprising degree of concern by parents over their kids' diet. It is often assumed that parents think kids can eat whatever they want, because they're too young to be worried about their health. That's not the case. A survey of mothers by Nabisco found that the most popular snack in lunch boxes is fruit, at 80 percent. Overall, it turns out that parents have a multiplicity of concerns about health issues; getting their kids off to a good, basic start; plus an inability and unwillingness to deny their kids their beloved treats.

The Parental Compromise

Most parents compromise, Nabisco found. To be sure, 60 percent of mothers surveyed by the company said that both nutrition and their kids' interests influenced their food choices. When it comes down to brass tacks, 50 percent said the child's request was more important. It's just too hard to say no to kids.

Parents' goal, it seems, is to find foods that their kids will love and that will be good for them, too. Fully 60 percent of the foods that get packed into kids' lunch boxes are agreed upon by both the parent and the child; 24 percent are chosen on the basis of the child's interests alone; and products that were included solely for their nutritional value got in only 16 percent of the time. This stands to reason because 45 percent of the parents said their kids don't like most of the snacks that are good for them.

Parents haven't given up hope, however. As much as 91 percent said they are interested in giving their kids healthier snacks; 83 percent said they look for snacks that are low in fat and taste good; and 55 percent read nutritional labels on their kids' snacks most of the time.

The idea of Teddy Grahams, then, was to provide a snack that kids would think of as good tasting and fun, and that parents would think of as good, too. The product's health pitch of being low in sodium and saturated fats and containing no cholesterol appealed to parents.

CMR KIDTRENDS REPORT, based on The Simmons Kids Study generally corroborates Nabisco's findings: it's kids' wishes that prevail. Sixty-three percent of kids say they have "some" to "a lot" of influence over the cookies their parents bring into the house.

The lesson is that a product that appeals to both the child and the parent has a good chance for success. Nabisco's research revealed that there was a lot at stake. As many as 58 percent of the moms said they pack lunch for their kids every day; 28 percent do it almost every day; and 11 percent do it two to three times a week.

What Makes a Good New-Product Person?

What makes a good new-product person? Marketing folklore is full of tales of offbeat executives and absentminded professors. Nabisco's experience proves otherwise. "The concept of the wild-eyed, flaming creative type is really not appropriate by and large," Fordham says. "We need someone who can run a business."

New-product people normally come from marketing. Sometimes they come from the financial staff. Generally, Nabisco looks for good, solid business managers who have had experience running businesses. New products are no place to learn how to run a brand. The staff needs to have the technical skills and financial know-how to run a business. They also need to have the intelligence, energy, and entrepreneurial flair to recognize a good idea. They need to have good communication skills, to sell the idea to the other members of the new product team, to management, and finally, to the sales force. "You need to be able to run some pretty long obstacle courses to launch a product," Fordham says.

Getting the Right Design

The other personality trait that you need as a new-product person is passion. The importance came through loud and clear when Nabisco's new-business team took up the matter of exactly what its teddy bear-shaped cookie should look like. "It was an amazing process," Fordham says. "The arguments coming out of the conference rooms—if a normal person had passed by then, he would have thought we were crazy." The snout! The snout has to be higher! The belly button! The belly button should be larger! The ears! The ears need to be rounder!

In the end, Nabisco wound up with a very simple design. A round head, punctuated by two semi-circular shaped ears, two hole punches for eyes, and a circular muzzle containing a smaller circle for the nose and a smile for the face. The bear has a slight paunch, communicated with a slight bulge at the bottom of the torso, and two stubby legs, with three toes on each foot.

The bears come in three poses—the better to facilitate play between different bears en route to the mouth. In one pose, the bear has its right arm extended upward in a wave. In the second, the bear has its hand over its mouth. (Is it popping something into its mouth, or caught in a blush? The consumer decides.) In the third, the bear is happily rubbing its tummy.

"I can't tell you how many sketches and images we went through trying to evolve the image of the bear," Sharon Fordham says. There was no pointless how-many-angels-can-you-fit-on-the-head-of-a-pin discussion. "Presentation, in the end, is every bit as important as the actual eating quality of the cookie."

In all, a single bear has about 15 lines—making it a relatively uncomplicated form for the production line to stamp out and bake without losing the shape.

Production Challenges

The importance of attention to detail was borne out on the production line. Mass production of cookies is no simple thing. Once a cookie's design is set, it is "debossed"—that is, dug out in metal—to go on a rotary mold. Once the ingredients for the cookie dough are mixed, the dough is pressed flat on the production line. The rotary mold rolls over the sheet of cookie dough and punches out the cookies.

Hundreds of cookies are stamped out at a time, about 10 to 20 across. The cookies are then baked, spilled into boxes, sealed, and shipped.

Nabisco keeps close tabs on the costs of new products as they go through the development process. A preliminary costing is done before the physical project is begun, with a financial overview of the general area of interest (e.g., less-sweet graham cookie) into which the product falls and its profit potential. Management must be comfortable with the potential in the area of interest before moving ahead.

The new-product team then starts to identify specific product ideas that have strong consumer interest, and the product development phase begins. The project director gives specific margin requirements to R&D. From then on, periodic costings are done every couple months as more is learned about how the product will be done. At certain points, the manager is responsible for analyzing the economic impact of doing a project one way versus another. Capital costs are also assessed, as the kind of equipment the product will need begins to become clear.

In the end, the budget calculations are almost as important as the idea itself in a new product's success. "Ultimately," says Fordham, "the easiest thing for a marketer to do—and it happens all the time, even with good costing—is to wind up making a product you really can't afford to sell.

"Consumers want it. Everybody wants it. But they don't want it for the 50-cent premium that you have to slap on it to be able to make the product work. You can do lots of 'magic' things. You can downsize the product to keep the price point down. But consumers are not easily fooled, and you don't want to be fooling them, because ultimately they're not going to come back to the product."

What are the lessons for marketers? Create a product that is brilliant, but make it practical. Make sure the idea will mesh with your production capabilities. Keep track of costs along the way. Make sure you can bring the product to market at a price that consumers will be willing to pay.

The Launch Program

A final wave of consumer research showed that Nabisco was on the right track. Between 88 and 93 percent of kids polled said they would buy the product, the range depending on the flavor. The challenge, then, was getting the word out to consumers at large. Packaging carried part of the load of educating consumers about the arrival of the miniature cookie. The boxes showed the little teddy bear cookies "bursting" through the packaging graphics.

Nabisco unleashed 200 million coupons, in newspapers and on the packages themselves. In supermarkets, it set up three-dimensional displays, in the shape of bears, that held 156 boxes of Teddy Grahams.

The third leg of the rollout was a $10 million-plus television ad campaign. Nabisco ad agency FCB/Leber Katz & Partners, following in the tradition of children's ads, created three personalities to represent the product.

Teddy, Eddy, and Freddy—three life-sized, theme-park-like bears in glittering costumes—are rock 'n' roll teddy bears who belt out rock songs to adoring kids. The choice of songs showed Nabisco's nods to parents' influence in product purchases. First up were adaptations of Elvis Presley's golden oldie, "Let Me Be Your Teddy Bear" (restyled to "Let Me Be Your Teddy Grahams") and, in the follow-up campaign, another 1950s anthem, "Rock 'n' Roll Is Here to Stay" (converted to "Teddy Grahams Are Here to Stay").

Nabisco advertised heavily on Saturday morning and weekday afternoon children's programs. But—in another sign of recognition of Mom and Dad's role—it also bought time on prime-time programming for children, when parents would likely be watching with their kids.

Keeping the Edge

Teddy Grahams became an instant hit, as our sales figures at the outset of the chapter reflect. First-year sales totaled close to $150 million—more than double the figure packaged-foods marketers consider a success for a new product. But Nabisco's marketers knew that they couldn't rest long on their laurels. To be sure, other bakers were soon out with miniature animal- and dinosaur-shaped cookies of their own. How could Teddy Grahams keep their edge? The answer was more new products. The reasoning was simple, says Nabisco spokesperson Ann Smith. "Success breeds success."

After the line had been on the market for about 18 months, Nabisco added a fourth flavor, vanilla. The company also came out with the Teddy Grahams Variety Pack, six individually wrapped 3/4-ounce bags of chocolate, vanilla, honey, and cinnamon Teddy Grahams for packing into lunch boxes, selling at $1.99 per pack. Nabisco also came out with a Teddy Grahams cereal, Breakfast Bears. Like Teddy Grahams, the cereal was formulated with both parents and kids in mind. They contained less than half the sugar of most of the top-10 kids' cereals; were low in sodium, cholesterol, and saturated fats; and were fortified with eight vitamins and minerals.

Meanwhile, financial developments at Nabisco's parent company had put more emphasis on developing new-product successes. In 1989 RJR Nabisco was acquired by the investment firm of Kohlberg, Kravis, Roberts in history's biggest leveraged buyout. The debt burden forced the divisions simultaneously to cut costs, improve efficiency, and generate more revenue. Nabisco stepped up R&D.

The World's Smallest Sandwich Cookie

A considerably more ambitious line extension was in the works: a miniature sandwich cookie based on the Teddy Graham cookies. From a marketing standpoint, the product made sense. Teddy Grahams were perceived by parents as a fairly wholesome snack alternative. A Teddy Graham sandwich cookie would offer its consumers a slightly more indulgent treat than regular Teddy Grahams, in the same way that fudge-covered Oreos were aimed at Oreo lovers who were in the mood for a more indulgent treat.

But there were big problems. The first was design. The easiest solution would have been to create a cookie with two fronts. Cookie lovers don't notice it generally, but sandwich cookies basically have two fronts. Both sides of an Oreo are identical.

To Nabisco's new-product team, one of the best things about Teddy Grahams were their "play value." Kids liked to get involved in the product. They would expect a Teddy Graham sandwich cookie to have a front side *and* a back side. The idea of a back side was unique. "Nobody had done that in the industry," says Fordham.

But the larger problem was manufacturing the cookie. Making a sandwich cookie is tricky. Once a cookie is baked, it must be mechanically flipped over, for the icing to be squirted onto the interior face. The cookie then must be aligned for the top wafer to be slipped into place to make the sandwich. For good reason, no one had ever made a sandwich cookie less than $1\frac{1}{4}$ inches in diameter—almost *twice* the size of a Teddy Graham. It requires precision and timing, or you get a mess on your hands.

Consumers gave Nabisco the motivation to push ahead. The company took the concept to focus groups—complete with designs that showed the projected back sides of the little bears, with tiny rear ends and tiny tails. "They said they liked it *a lot*," Fordham says. The research also showed that kids—probably not surprisingly—responded enthusiastically to a little added sweetness, a Nabisco spokesperson says.

For the flavors, the company chose what research showed to be kids' favorites: One Teddy Graham sandwich cookie would be vanilla with chocolate crème. The second would be chocolate with vanilla crème. The third would be cinnamon with vanilla crème.

As expected, aligning the little cookies on the production line turned out to be, for want of a better word, a bear. Before the kinks were worked out, the assembly line was knee-deep in icing and bear wafers, literally. Because the cookie was to have both a front and a back, it needed two production lines—one for the fronts, the other for the backs. "It was very tough," Fordham admits. "It took us a long time. Months. That was really the biggest trick in the product."

The technical specifics of how the company worked out the difficulties turned out to become a competitive advantage. Not long after the finished product hit the market, Nabisco came out with a miniature version of its beloved Oreo, plus a mini version of its Nutter Butter peanut-butter sandwich cookie.

Bearwiches Come to Market

Teddy Grahams Bearwich graham sandwiches, as the resulting product came to be called, got their introductory test market in the fourth quarter of 1990 in Boston, New York, and Philadelphia. The product was priced at $2.29 for a 10-ounce box, slightly higher than regular Teddy Grahams. Bearwiches were a smash. They became the number two sandwich cookie in the test markets, trailing only Oreo. The product was rolled out to the rest of the Northeast and into the Midwest in the first quarter of 1991, and, soon after, reached national distribution.

Teddy, Eddy, and Freddy made a return appearance to launch the product. Once again, the commercial, which showed them serving Bearwiches at the Bearwich's Sandwich Shoppe, drew on golden oldie music. This time, the choice was "I Like It Like That."

Nabisco supported the launch with 200 million-plus coupons. And, in a PR twist playing on the sandwich theme, the company persuaded Manhattan's famous Stage Deli to create a special sandwich, the Bearwich's Platter, featuring a grilled American cheese, bologna, and tomato sandwich, accompanied by the Bearwich sandwich cookies.

At the press event to kick off the line, the Stage's owner admitted that his college-aged daughter was one of Teddy Grahams' biggest fans. Nabisco executives noted an equally impressive finding from focus groups. Consumers had discovered that if you stood a Bearwich on its feet (it stood up), the better it was for playing! Bearwiches developed their own following.

To distinguish it from Teddy Grahams, Nabisco encouraged the brand to have its own personality. In 1992 the company shortened the cookie's name to T.G. Bearwich and created a separate campaign that replaced Teddy, Eddy, and Freddy with cool graphics and hip adolescent images.

Incorporating the Knowledge

Not only did Nabisco generate a new revenue stream with Teddy Grahams and its progeny, but also it learned a lot about cookie technology and about kids. We noted that the miniature sandwiching techniques that enabled Nabisco to produce Bearwiches helped the company turn out the mini Oreo and mini Nutter Butter.

In all, the company has more than a dozen miniature cookies and crackers now—running the gamut from Ritz Bits and Ritz Bits cheese- and peanut-butter sandwich crackers, to miniature Triscuits, Saltines, Cheddar Wedges, and Chips Ahoy cookies. Nabisco has found that adults like miniature products, too. Whereas for kids a primary benefit is convenience, for adults—like kids—there's a strong element of fun.

The concept of fun and play has been creeping increasingly into Nabisco cookies. In Christmas 1990 the company introduced its first seasonal cookie, a white fudge-covered Oreo. Nabisco was inspired in part by M&M Mars's successes with seasonally colored Christmas, Easter, Halloween, and other holiday M&M's candies. It was also aware that in busy, two-income households, the plain white fudge surface of the holiday Oreo was a perfect surface for parents to let kids decorate the cookies with their own designs.

"My sense is most consumers probably wouldn't go to the trouble to make the product, given the time constraints of society today, if they could just go out and buy it," says Fordham, who had, probably not coincidentally, given her nephew a gumball machine filled with M&M's the Christmas before. "It's a lot easier just to buy a product and take it out."

At Christmas 1991 Nabisco took the play value of Christmas cookies one step further and introduced Made 'em Myself, a ready-to-decorate vanilla cookie. Each cookie came with a stenciled holiday design, including a snowman, a reindeer, or a star, and two tubes of holiday frosting (one red, one green) for the child to decorate the cookie with.

Kids didn't have to use the prepackaged design. If they wanted to get creative, they could flip the cookie to its blank side, and draw their own design. The only thing limiting them was their imagination. Considering the burst of ideas that has followed Teddy Grahams, the same probably could be said of Nabisco.

Summing Up

1. Use the things that excite you in your field—the tastes, the shapes, the play elements, whatever—to be starting points for new products.

2. Make regular visits to the store to get your imagination going. You may find ideas, even in categories beyond your own, that you will be able to translate into a new product. Use your daily experience—like going to the grocery store, the mini mart, even the hardware store—as field research.

3. List the products in your product line. Compare your list with the demographic segments of the population. Are there demographic groups that you are underserving that could offer new-product opportunities?

4. Take your existing components or ingredients and repackage them into a new, more appealing form.

5. Bring the product to market at a price that your consumers will be willing to pay. Research the market to find out what price consumers think would be reasonable.

14
KidTrends

Eight Trends for the Nineties

"Video games are the wave of the future."
CHILDREN'S MARKET RESEARCH, INC., 1984

*"It won't be long before we see the return of
the skateboard."*
CHILDREN'S MARKET RESEARCH, INC., 1985

Previous Predictions

There was no crystal ball involved in these predictions. Rather, they
were informed projections, based on research with children, teens, and
parents.

1984: The Video-Game Explosion

Atari had reached its peak and was on the decline. Children appeared
to have lost their interest in home video games. They had been able to
master the games and had grown bored with what once was a fascinating mechanism. At the same time, however, video arcades were still
booming all across the country.

Why? The answer was *advanced technology.* Kids of all ages would
plunk down their allowances in quarters in arcades so that they could
play these advanced, challenging, and exciting games—which put their
primitive, 4-bit home video-game systems to shame.

Within a few years, Nintendo, the maker of some of the most popular arcade games, had swept into the home video-game market with the next generation of 8-bit computer technology. Their games were involving and challenging. Their marketing, which we outlined in Chapter 12, was ingenious. The company avoided the pitfalls of poor quality that proved to be the undoing of the first generation of video games, while it proved to be expert at nuts-and-bolts issues like managing inventory.

How did Children's Market Research foresee the revival of the home video-game industry? The answers are observation and research. CMR had interviewed children and had seen how much video games excited them. From their show of enthusiasm, it became apparent that they would be more than happy to return to their control pads to play an advanced version of their old Ataris.

1985: Skateboards Zoom

In the 1940s and 1950s, skateboards were a piece of wood taken from crates attached to rollerskate wheels. In the 1970s, skateboards became more popular, as polyurethane wheels enabled riders to go faster and do more stunts. But skateboards remained a relatively low-profile pastime.

In the 1980s Children's Market Research began to pick up on the enthusiasm of kids for surfing. It seemed to be apparent that there was significant potential for skateboarding, which was an offshoot of surfing. Like surfing, skateboarding began in southern California.

CMR predicted the trend would push out from southern California and spread coast to coast. In form and speed, skateboards were a natural extension of the surfing craze. Yet, to many people, skateboarding seemed outdated.

Skateboard companies developed polished wooden skateboards with lavish designs. They embellished the skateboards with designs that would appeal to kids, like the skull-and-crossbones imagery from pirate lore and science fiction images. The resulting skateboards, which sold from $40 to upwards of $300, became status symbols for adolescent boys. The kids with the most expensive boards were considered the coolest.

What's Happening with Kids Today?

Kids are more savvy about their world and more aware of the environment, social issues, and problems confronting their families than their parents' generation was. Many of them are growing up with a keen awareness of drugs, racial problems, pollution, AIDS, teenage pregnancy, and other grim realities. Many of them are actively seeking coping mechanisms to deal with their own internal struggles, as well as trying to understand and adjust to a world that holds many uncertainties. While they are active consumers of products and services, they are quick to detect a false note in advertising messages.

They are also a generation that is more aware and tuned-in to the world around them and the responsibilities of adult life. They generally do not expect they will get high-paying jobs and "the good life" without working toward these goals at an early age. Education is important to them, and getting good grades is of concern to them as well as to their families. They are more aware, independent, and reality-oriented than any generation has been in many years.

These changing attitudes and behaviors are leading to new behaviors in the marketplace. So what are kids buying? What do they want? What are the trends of today and tomorrow?

Trend 1: Save Planet Earth

"Nobody is doing anything about pollution. It'll be up to kids to do something," says Mark, a 13-year-old from St. Paul, Minnesota.

That message has already begun to sink in on marketers of products for children in families. The biggest milestone came early in the 1990s, when McDonald's—in a major announcement that followed months of negotiations with environmentalists—declared that it was retiring Styrofoam packaging in favor of paper.

Styrofoam had been the center of one of the most public tug-of-wars over the environment. As the largest fast-food chain in the United States, McDonald's was the target of some of the most heated criticism. Its reliance on Styrofoam containers to keep its hamburgers and fish sandwiches warm became a symbol of the throwaway culture drowning in its own garbage.

Making amends wasn't just a nice PR gesture for McDonald's. It had built its reputation on being a family restaurant. The young adults, high school and college students, and youngsters who were the core of the movement to save the earth were also McDonald's core market. Some cities were banning Styrofoam. With a growing number of fast-food chains, pizzerias, Chinese and Italian restaurants, and sit-down family restaurants already competing for McDonald's market, being depicted as an environmental bad guy was something McDonald's did not need.

Since the problems of diminishing ozone, urban air pollution, overfilled landfills, the shrinking tropical rain forests, fouled waterways, and endangered species will not be resolved in the next 10 years—to be sure, the odds are higher that they will get worse—it can be expected that the generation of kids growing up today will continue to be very concerned about the environment in the coming years.

Their interest in responsible environmental habits is being reinforced at school. Recycling bins, environmental clubs, and classroom lessons on environmentalism are commonplace in schools. Meanwhile, TV programs from "Sesame Street" to the network cartoons have taken up the issue. At home, many parents are bundling newspapers and separating cans and bottles for recycling.

A new wave of tougher municipal recycling ordinances will put even more momentum behind the recycling movement. In many homes, kids are actively involved in recycling. As more cities move to *require* households to recycle glass, cans, newspapers, junk mail, cardboard, and plastic jugs, the numbers of young people involved in recycling will grow.

Kids appear to have integrated the message already. Many mothers report their children put pressure on them to recycle, save water, and conserve energy. "When I throw a can in the garbage," says one Chicago mother, "Jamie, my 7-year-old son, pulls it out and gives me a lecture." "My 6-year-old comes over and turns off the water when I'm washing dishes," says a mom in St. Louis. "She tells me to use the basin."

There will be more opportunities for products that encourage a responsible attitude toward Mother Earth. There obviously will be ways for marketers to include kids in composting and other activities, as there have been to bring kids into recycling. The Body Shop's use of recyclable containers has become a trendsetter for other companies. Books like *50 Simple Things You Can Do to Save the Earth, Save Our Planet,* and *The Green Lifestyle Handbook* will continue to be popular. The Nature Company retail chain's variety of outdoor activity products and its promotion of endangered species has spawned a number of competitors.

On a secondary level, kids take note of the use of recycled materials in products and packaging. Kellogg's inclusion of a notice on the lid of its cereal boxes that the package was made with recycled material is one of the first things kids notice when they open the box. More companies will promote their use of recycled paper and cardboard. Some environmentalists are pushing legislation that would require companies to disclose the percentage of recycled materials in the product. That would certainly put companies on the line.

Kids are well aware that their actions and opinions are important. "We have a very big blue bin in our garage," says Judy, an 11-year-old from Allentown, Pennsylvania. "My mom tries to help. But I guess it's hard to teach an old dog new tricks."

Trend 2: Education—A Means to an End

From local school board elections, to state legislatures, Congress, and the White House, education is moving to the center of the political agenda. It is a reflection of what is happening in households on Main Street, U.S.A. Well aware that their children are growing up in a world that will be harder than the world they grew up in, parents are concerned about the quality of education their children are getting. They are demanding more of public schools.

Many parents, convinced that public schools lack the financial resources, educational innovation, and discipline to give their children a quality education, are pulling their kids out and putting them in private schools, private academies, and parochial schools. Many parents of public- and private-school students are supplementing the education their kids get at school with private tutoring; arts and crafts classes; musical and athletic activities; and special equipment that includes personal computers, flash cards, educational dolls, and board games. How-to books for parents who want to help their kids are booming.

Books are the obvious beneficiary. Sales of children's books have boomed in the past 10 years. That, in turn, has led to an explosion in new titles and the revival of many long-neglected children's classics. Some of the most beautiful and creative production in publishing today—illustrations, type styles, paper, covers—are in children's books.

Reading books, however, takes time. With most parents juggling careers outside the home with their responsibilities to their children, there has been growing demand for products that teach kids and at the same time fit into parents' already-tight schedules. Just as the 1980s saw the rise of convenience foods for the microwave, the 1990s are witnessing the birth of a generation of "convenience educational toys." V-Tech, one of the manufacturers responding to the demand, has invented the Electronic Learning Aids line of high-tech educational products for children. The products teach young students to match shapes and colors. Older kids can learn subjects such as basic math, spelling, simple algebra, and geography.

Texas Instruments and Playskool also have introduced a number of products aimed at both entertaining and educating young boys and girls. Personal-computer products will grow at a steady clip as well. Personal-computer hardware sales grew a mind-boggling, inflation-adjusted rate of 85 percent between 1989 and 1991, according to government figures. Both Apple Computer, which pioneered the home and school market, and the myriad companies creating IBM-compatible computers have benefited.

While many of the computers are brought into the home for parents to bring work home from the office or to start a business at home, kids get time on the computer as well. We have already mentioned in other chapters the popularity of Broderbund's *Where In the World Is Carmen Sandiego* personal-computer game. There will be a growing market for programs that help kids prepare reports and learn subjects from astronomy to zoology.

On a lower-tech level, some marketers are encouraging parents to buy audiotapes and videotapes that promote learning. One such company is Hooked-on-Phonics, which has spent millions of dollars advertising its cassette tapes that are supposed to help both kids and grown-ups learn how to read.

Educational products, however, won't be a "can't-miss" market. As parents digest the first generation of products, there will be a growing public discussion of what works and what doesn't. Educational scholars will weigh in with their opinions. In addition, new generations of hardware and software will threaten the products currently on the market. Current evidence shows that parents are willing to invest in products from books, to arts and crafts, to technology if they believe it will make their children better students.

Trend 3: Family Life Is Alive and Well, but Different

When did the Cleavers turn into a dual-income household? How did Harriet Nelson turn into Murphy Brown? Sociologists will be grappling with those questions for years to come. For marketers, however, it's enough to know that the simple days of 1950s with a working dad and a stay-at-home mom are over. And kids, on the front lines of the changes, will be leading the redefinition of what *family* in the 1990s will mean.

Home and family are greatly valued by today's kids, according to CMR KIDTRENDS REPORT, based on The Simmons Kids Study. The study found that 67 percent of children rate *family* as the most important thing in their lives. Children are independent, but they like to come home to Mom. Although kids are materialistic and value possessions, they appreciate the security of family life.

At the same time, there are indications that—in contrast to the open-ended, cafeteria-style definition of family that has prevailed in the 1980s, with single-mother households, single-father households, divorced mom/divorced dad combinations, and grandparent/grandchild combinations—today's generation of kids is taking a more conservative turn. Many children in focus groups appear to long for a return to the nondivorced, two-parent nuclear family households they see in TV reruns.

In a study by *Seventeen* magazine, 93 percent of the girls aged 14 to 21 who were polled said they would like to get married, and 92 percent said they want to have two or more children. Although teenage girls want to work and have careers, they seem to give priority to marriage and family and are willing to make trade-offs, rather than have it all.

The signs seem to be pointing to another social shift, and, this time it appears to be toward the idea of compromise. Many young girls whom Children's Market Research has interviewed have said they believe they can combine career with motherhood without sacrificing traditional family values. They are not sure entirely how they will accomplish this. But, having grown up with the reality of divorced parents, remarried parents, and never-married parents, many children have had to be resilient and flexible.

It is going to be essential for marketers to keep up with them. It is important for marketers to portray accurately both the families that children are growing up in and the families that adolescents and teens hope to create for themselves when they grow up and become parents. With two-income households and single-parent households, kids will continue to have both increased responsibilities and independence at an earlier age than previous generations. As a result, kids will continue to play an integral and vocal role in the family.

Trend 4: Health and Nutrition

The idea of a well-balanced diet is being stressed more both inside and outside the classroom. Parents are concerned that kids get a good start on having a long and healthy life. Companies are beginning to respond to this health consciousness.

Several categories of food and drink already are enjoying the benefits of the change in attitudes. The most notable shifts have been in beverages. Children have been one of the driving forces in the growth in juice sales. That has led to an explosion in brands and in flavor combinations. It has also led to a new generation of carbonated beverages from companies like Perrier, Tropicana, and Snapple that straddle the juice and soft-drink markets.

The basic question for marketers to answer is: What do kids want? The short answer is that *they want food that tastes good*. Moms can buy shopping carts full of healthy snacks. But if they don't taste good to kids, they won't eat them. Education has increased kids' awareness of what constitutes a healthy diet, but the taste test will continue to be pre-eminent. According to CMR's SNACK AND PREPARED FOOD REPORT, based on The Simmons Kids Study, children still prefer junk food to healthy food. Cookies, salty snacks, ice cream and frozen novelties, snack cakes, and snack pies top the list of kids' favorite snacks.

Cheese, bite-sized fruit snacks, yogurt, granola bars, and fruit cups are also liked, but to a lesser extent. For marketers who want kids to eat healthier, then, the challenge will be to improve the taste of their products.

Healthy snacks, barring the discovery of some as yet unknown magical ingredient, probably never will taste as good as sugar-, fat-, or salt-loaded junk food. The advisable course for marketers of healthier foods, then, will probably be to seek a middle ground to appeal to children and parents. The Frosted Mini-Wheats commercial that offers the product as a solution for a mother who says she wants her child to eat something nutritious and for her child who longs for something delicious is one example.

In addition, it would not be surprising to see marketers of healthy products strike a posture similar to the marketing strategy that has worked in the adult market: "You can't eat sugary, high-fat, salty snacks all the time, because it's bad for your teeth, it's bad for your heart, and it makes you chubby. So, why not substitute our low-sugar, low-fat snack every other day?" Marketers have found that suggesting moderation or a product as a substitute is an effective strategy for children. The strategy answers the child's question of when and how they should use the product.

Trend 5: Looking Good

To some, it may look like the age of vanity. To others it's the decade of fitness. Whatever the title, young people want to look good. And looking good means looking fit and toned. The evolution of beauty has blended fitness and exercise with the traditional notions of appearance. The message is being carried by teen magazines like *Seventeen* and *Glamour* and by television programs that have created a new generation of teen idols.

The redefinition of beauty has occurred hand in hand with the proliferation of health clubs, home gym equipment, exercise clothing, health and fitness magazines, and food supplements. Consumers spend $1.773 billion on home gym equipment, which is three times as much as it was in 1980.

Female celebrities exemplify the new image of body beautiful, body strong. Thin is in, but not too thin. Girls want to be fit but not muscular. The more they read magazines, watch TV, and go to movies, the more they are flooded with images of beautiful women who seem to have it all. Madonna, the pop star cum actress, is a heroine for many young women, despite her promiscuous sexual habits. They see her as sexy, toned, seductive, talented, and, most of all, in control. The last note strikes a chord; many adolescent girls say they want to be in control of their lives.

For teenage boys, meanwhile, working out has become more than an infrequent after-school activity. Teenagers appear to be setting the pace. Dave, a 16-year-old high school sophomore, gets up each morning at six o'clock, in order to work out for 45 minutes before school. He then works out for another 45 minutes after school three days a week. His routine is strict and organized. He tries to play down junk foods in his diet. Instead, he has become a fan of high-protein, high-carbohydrate foods and food supplements. He keeps up with new dietary tips in health, muscle, and fitness magazines.

Girls are responsive. Fifteen-year-old Jennifer says "guys with muscles are superhot." Preteens can't be expected to take up muscle-building and fitness with the rigor of teens. In fact, some of the things teens do could be dangerous for 8-year-olds. Teens will accept the work in working out because they can look forward to the fruits of their efforts. Younger kids are more interested in immediate gratification, and the most immediate gratification is that they want their workouts to be fun. But teens will be an inspirational model for younger kids. Kids can be expected to dabble in exercise equipment, clothing, and accessories. And some fitness activities—as the use of Rollerblades have done—will migrate down to younger enthusiasts.

Trend 6: Sports—Let the Games Begin

Sports have become a popular leisure activity for kids of all ages, both boys and girls. Kids are becoming players and spectators. They are willing to spend money either to be a sports star, to be like a sports star, or to see a sports star.

Boys always have been athletes. They have been brought up on sports and for generations many happy memories have been made by dads playing ball with their sons. Girls, meanwhile, have become increasingly active in participatory sports and become more enthusiastic followers of sports.

Baseball has remained the most popular sport. Kids not only buy baseball equipment, they are enthusiastic collectors of licensed team apparel. The expansion of major league baseball to the Florida Marlins and Colorado Rockies, for example, made Marlins and Rockies caps and jerseys a hot commodity. The popularity of baseball cards, meanwhile, has spawned numerous new card lines.

Basketball, meanwhile, is making a run at baseball as the most popular sport among kids. Largely, this has been the result of marketing by the National Basketball Association. Basketball seems to have the most popular stars. Michael Jordan's feats on the court, combined with his associations as spokesperson for NIKE, Wheaties, Gatorade, and McDonald's—among others—has made the high-flying guard a household name. The 1992 Olympic Dream Team of NBA stars only furthered the sport's popularity.

Football, however, has not been elbowed aside. The Super Bowl is watched heavily by kids as well as grown-ups. And, since it's an easy game to play at school (all you need is a football and some friends), it continues to be a popular participatory sport.

Sports stars have become similar to the rock stars of the 1970s. The Dream Team, to be sure, was called America's Beatles when they went to Barcelona. Sports are one of the few things that reach a broad market. Popular music has fragmented into niche markets, based on tastes—like rap, heavy metal, country, "college-station" rock, pop.

As a result, sports stars will continue to be in demand as spokespersons. Kids will continue to be enthusiastic consumers of promotion and advertising campaigns that tie into sports. And parents, always interested in getting their kids outside, will willingly buy tennis lessons, soccer cleats, baseball mits, game tickets, and other symbols of the athletic lifestyle.

Trend 7: Money, Brands, and Possessions

"Money doesn't grow on trees." Kids have heard this bit of wisdom, it seems, since time began. But parents, however reluctant they may be, more often than not give in to the desires of their children. And children, for their part, gravitate to brands.

A 6-year-old boy walks in The Athletes Foot and demands a pair of NIKE high-tops. At the same time, a 12-year-old girl walks into her favorite clothing store and picks out a pair of Guess jeans that she just must have. In spite of her mother's insistence that she can buy a similar pair for half the price, the girl refuses to compromise. And she gets her way.

A 14-year-old boy struts into The Wiz and asks to see a portable CD player by Aiwa. It has all the features he wants and is bound to last him through high school and into college. It costs a lot, but he convinces his parents that they are paying for quality, not just a name.

NIKE. Reebok Pumps. Sony. Rollerblades. Kellogg's. Kids see brand names not just as a status symbol, but as a sign of reliability and quality. When manufacturers establish significant name recognition, they are able to charge higher prices, without losing too many customers.

This has created a dilemma for families. CMR research has shown many parents will trade down or put off spending for themselves in order to get their kids what they want. But high prices have also forced parents and kids, together, to be smarter consumers. For instance, a family may decide to buy the Reebok Pumps the child wants, but they will scour the newspapers for a sale to buy them at a cheaper price. Or, failing that, they may decide to pay less on another item.

Unfortunately for today's kids, they formed their attitudes on brands when the economy was in the longest sustained recovery of the postwar era. Incomes were rising, so parents could afford to pay more. The 1990s are shaping up as a decade of diminishing expectations. Consumers have to be willing to make do with less. At some point, that trickles down to kids. Possibly the compromise is to spend heavily on one item and pay less for another. Kids have to choose what they really want. If that is the case, marketers of brand name products for children will be competing not only with products in their own categories but also with products in other segments.

Trend 8: AIDS and Sex Education

Because of the AIDS virus, the age group we have concentrated on in this book—6 to 14-year-olds—is developing into sexual awareness at one of the most troubled times in history. Moreover, the announcement that basketball idol Magic Johnson has the AIDS virus showed that even children who are far from reaching the age where they are curious about sex can still be touched deeply by this tragic social problem.

The announcement appeared to be a turning point. Magic Johnson was a revered sports hero and a celebrity who had crossed over from the basketball court to TV commercials and popular culture. Parents who were worried about their teenagers' tendency to think of themselves as supermen and superwomen who were immune to sexually transmitted diseases were joined by parents who were confused about how to answer young children's questions about what happened to Magic.

Parents are concerned about AIDS but many are afraid to discuss the topic with their children. They are unsure how to broach the subject, and many don't know the answers themselves. Books, television specials, and public-school discussions have stepped in to fill the gap. Many of the high-profile controversies over AIDS intervention in public schools—most notably, condom distribution in high schools—do not directly impact the 6- to 14-year-old market of this book. However, AIDS will have a direct impact on children's education.

Children appear to be aware of the dangers of sex, but they still are flooded with images of promiscuous lifestyles in the media, and they find it confusing. It's still considered cool among high-school students to have sex. Although the publicity AIDS has received may not cause all teenagers to practice safe sex, the more aware kids are, the more they will think about their actions and the consequences so that in the long run there may be an impact on behavior.

* * * *

Fast Forward

As we said at the outset, it doesn't take a crystal ball to determine tomorrow's trends. You can do it today. Here are some of Children's Market Research's predictions for the future.

The New American Family

Analysis. Alternative family lifestyles will continue through the 1990s and into the next century.

- The trend toward dual-income households will continue.

- Women will continue to work full- or part-time. Many working mothers of the future will take advantage of such technology as personal-computer networking, fax machines, and phone technologies to work at home to be closer to their children. Economic necessity, however, will require many of them to rejoin the work force on a full-time basis after their children reach school age.

- Children will continue to play a major role in family life and its functioning. They will assume increased responsibility and independence at earlier ages than previous generations.

- Fathers will continue to be more involved in everyday functioning in the family and will be more than the family breadwinner.

- The everyday functioning of the home, however, will continue to be primarily the responsibility of the mother and/or wife. The burdens of dual roles for women have been somewhat alleviated by the more active role children take in household tasks such as shopping, cleaning, and assisting in the care of younger siblings.

Marketing Implications. We live in a fast-paced, convenience-oriented world. Marketers must respond to this.

- Ordering dinner in and eating out will become more common as cooking full family meals becomes less practical.
- Both the phone and the fax will be used to order in. The variety of foods available will expand.
- Companies will need versatile products to cater to the demands of single-parent homes, dual-income households, and traditional families.
- Family activities, purchases, and functioning in general will include children in the decision-making process. They will continue to be aware consumers, and their increased knowledge of money management—spurred by the economic slide of the early 1990s—will make them able evaluators of products and services.

The Technology of Tomorrow: Home Life

Analysis. Advanced electronic equipment in the home will be a status symbol. Families will no longer simply sit down to watch television or the VCR.

Marketing Implications

- Home entertainment systems, including big-screen TVs, digitally programmable stereo systems, sophisticated VCRs, and other high-tech equipment, will become increasingly commonplace.
- TV viewing will continue to be a primary leisure-time activity, but it will be more interactive.
- Camcorders will be light, easy to operate, and relatively inexpensive. They will become as common as cameras and will be used and owned by children and teens.
- Fax machines will be as commonplace as the microwave.

Education: A Means to an End

Analysis. Education is not merely considered to be part of a full life. It is essential for attaining the lifestyle and careers kids seek.

- In the classroom, this will mean more programs to help children reach their own potential instead of operating according to the prescribed curriculum.

- Educational programs will be more customized. Individualized teaching will be made possible through the use of computers and learning systems, which will allow each student to progress at his or her own rate.

Marketing Implications. The individualized approach to education will offer manufacturers and publishers of books and computer software significant new-product opportunities both in school and at home.

- Textbooks and other learning materials will have to be adapted.

- There will be a need for highly trained learning specialists.

- Teachers will play an active part in the interaction between students and computers.

- Home learning systems will augment the school programs.

- Students will have increasing access to computers and fax machines to keep them in contact with peers and school. Even homework assignments may be transmitted electronically.

Food and Eating Habits

Analysis. Children will continue to be involved in the food-selection process. Nutrition and convenience will be key issues and the focus of much attention.

- Children will be exposed to a broad range of ethnic and regional cuisines, such as Mexican, Middle Eastern, and Cajun food.

- Prepared meals from restaurants and supermarkets will become increasingly popular.

- Nutrition will get increasing attention at home and in schools. Nevertheless, kids will still want foods that taste good.

Marketing Implications. Food manufacturers and advertisers will be addressing a more aware young consumer and will have to develop foods that conform to parents' demands for more nutritious foods.

- Compromise products will offer less salt, fat, and sugar but will still deliver good taste.
- Manufacturers will be under pressure to support health claims. Both young and old consumers will demand truth in advertising. Labels will be closely read.

Fitness and Looking Good

Analysis. Enthusiasm for being fit and looking good will continue. Boys want to look muscular and strong, and girls want to be toned and slim.

- Schools will be asked to put more emphasis on physical fitness and will take advantage of new exercise plans and equipment.
- Athletic programs involving both boys and girls will be encouraged in the community.

Marketing Implications

- Athletic and fitness equipment will continue to be a strong industry for use both in school and at home.
- Children will want the latest clothing and accessories, including videos, in order to keep up with an activity.

Environmental Concerns

Analysis. Children are keenly aware of the devastating effects that pollution has on their health. Concerns over environmental issues are more than a social cause. These concerns tap into kids' basic survival instincts.

Marketing Implications

- Manufacturers, of necessity, will be forced to comply with environmental preservation activities. Companies will be boycotted by a more active youth, demanding that companies not destroy their environment.
- Children will lead the environmental movement and will be a catalyst for change. Both directly and indirectly, they will help mold their families' attitudes and behavior.

Money and Money Management

Analysis. Children will continue to be brand and quality conscious and, as they make more purchases, more savvy consumers. Although they will not spend indiscriminately, they will still be interested in brand names.

- Money management will become a part of school curricula.
- Practical economics will be taught at an earlier age.

Marketing Implications

- Quality and getting the best and the most for a dollar will be a growing concern both for parents and children.
- Advertisers must be aware of children's influence and the effect of their advertising.

* * * *

Know Your KidTrends

- Trends in the children's market are constantly evolving. Keep in touch with your consumer.
- Learn to listen to children, ask questions, and observe kids at work and play.
- Go to where the market is—shopping malls, swimming pools, parks, ball games, state fairs, and rock concerts.
- Read kids' and teenage magazines, and watch their television programs.
- Above all, have fun. You've entered a kid's world. This gives you permission to play—while you run your business.

Index

Action figures, 31, 72, 95
Action for Children's Television, 146
Activity boards, 94
Ad agencies, 134–135
Age, 44
  of magazine readers, 155
  phone surveys and, 63
  of target market, 137–138
  of television advertising models, 138
  toy preferences and, 74
AIDS, 223–224
Alcohol, children's attitudes toward, 14–15
American Doll Collection, 84, 94
American Pediatrics Association, 146
America's Growing Families, 162
Amurol Products, 180
Antioch Publishing, 36
Apple Computer, 176–177, 217–218
Archie Comic Publications, 98
Asian Americans, proportion in
    population, 10
Atari, 196
AT&T, 177
Attention:
  during interviews, 61–62
  during phone surveys, 63

Babar and Celeste fragrances, 79
Baby-bust generation, 8–9
Barbie dolls, 17, 31, 68–70, 86–87, 102, 109,
    129, 174–175
Barbie magazine, 149, 152
Bart Simpson, 133
Baseball cards, 86, 111, 171, 179–180
Batman Returns, 158
Bible, on video, 36
Birthrate, growth of, 6–7
Blacks, proportion in population, 10
Blockbuster Video, 120

Body Shop, 216
Bonneville Communications, 179
Boys:
  consciousness of appearance, 77–79
  fitness and, 221
  gross names and, 107
  toys and, 31, 71–73
  (See also Gender differences)
Brand loyalty, 127
Breakfast foods:
  children's influence on choice of, 10, 32
  packaging of, 111
  prizes with, 171
  television advertising for, 131
Burger Chef, 189
Burger King, 169, 182
Butterfinger, 133

Cabbage Patch Kids, 106
Calculators, 82
Cameras, 81
Candy Tasters Club, 180–181
Canterbury Foods, 189
Card shops, 124
Care Bears, 71–72
Catalogs (see Direct mail advertising)
CBS/Fox, 158
Celebrities, 77, 165, 220–223
  breakfast cereal packaging and, 111
  children's awareness of, 76
  endorsements by, 27–29, 123, 144, 154
  live appearances by, 120
  as spokespeople, 133
Channel One, 166, 176
Children's Advertising Review Unit,
    143–145
Children's Television Workshop, 160
Choices, importance of, 22–23
Circuses, 80

Claims, television advertising and, 144
Clothing:
  boys' interest in, 77–79
  children's influence on choice of, 33
Club(s), 169–170, 180–182
Club Med, 35, 131–132
Coca-Cola, 133, 153–154
Colgate-Palmolive Co., 89
Collectibles, 121, 164–165, 179–180
Color, of packages, 109–110
ColorBlaster, 72
Communication, of children, 43
Comparative claims, television advertising
    and, 144–145
Computer products, 217–218
ConAgra Frozen Foods, Inc., 5–6, 90, 110,
    130
Consumer electronics, 81–82, 89–90
  (See also Video games)
Consumers, children as, 115
Consumers Union, 166
Contests, 121
Continental Baking Co., 91
Convenience stores, 115–117
Converse, 78–79
Cool Whip, 129
Cooperative mailings, 162
Cosmetics, 31–32, 79
Coupons, 121, 161
Cracker Jack, 171, 180
Crayola, 95
Curiosity, 22
Custom publishing, 162–163
Custom research, 58–60

Dakin Inc., 31
Dannon, 91–92
D'Arcy Masius Benton & Bowles, 139
D.C. Comics, 77
Delta Air Lines, 181
Detail, children's attention to, 155–156
"Dick Tracy," 95
Direct mail advertising, 148, 159–162
  content of, 160–161
  cooperative mailings and, 162
  cost of, 161–162
  lists for, 159–160
Discover Card, 177
Discovery Zone, 98
Disney Adventures magazine, 149, 151, 154
Doubleday, 36

Drinks:
  children's influence on choice of, 32
  television advertising for, 131
Dual-income households, 9
DuCair Tsumura, 90
Duncan Hines, 202
Duracell, 174

Easy Bake oven, 72, 106
Echo baby boom, 7
Education, 217–218, 225–226
Educational products, 93–94
Electronics stores, 123–124
Energizer, 133
Entertainment, gender differences in
    preferences for, 79–80
Environment:
  children's concern about, 14, 98,
    215–216, 227
  for focus groups, 46
  natural, observing children in, 53–54
Environmental Protection Agency, 179
Erector Sets, 31, 95
Ethnic diversity, 10–11

Facilities, for focus groups, 46
Family:
  changes in, 9, 114, 218–219, 224–225
  children's focus on, 15
  children's influence on purchases of,
    3–4, 131–132
  rising focus on, 8–9
  size of, 8
  [See also Grandparents; Parent(s)]
F.A.O. Schwartz, 119, 120
FCB/Leber Katz & Partners, 208
Fisher-Price, Inc., 86, 90, 105
Fitness movement, 76–77, 220–221, 227
Fleischmann's Yeast, 169
Focus groups, 38–55
  age and sex of children in, 44
  costs of, 46
  discussion guide for, 49–50
  drawings and, 48
  facilities for, 45, 46
  management report and, 51–52
  of parents, 51
  recruiting for, 46
  results of, 51
  role playing in, 48–49

Focus groups, (*Cont.*):
  suburbs as focus of, 45
  target of, 45–46
  warm-up for, 47
Foote, Cone & Belding, 39–40, 135
Fox Broadcasting, 131, 149
Fox Kids Club, 169
Frisbee, 74–75, 107
Frito-Lay, 140, 202
Fruit Loops, 140

Gap, The, 33, 123, 153
Garbage Pail Kids, 107
Garfield magazine, 149, 153
Gatorade, 32, 154, 222
Gender differences, 44, 65–82
  development of, 67–68, 73–74
  in entertainment preferences, 79–80
  fitness movement and, 76–77
  persistence of, 66–67
  products for boys and for girls and,
    71–73
  in supermarket shopping, 80–81
  in toy preferences, 31–32, 74–75
General Foods, 189
General Mills, 111, 154, 162–163
Ghostbuster ghost zappers, 76
Ghostbusters action figures, 95
G.I. Joe, 31, 103–104, 129
Gillette Co., 89
Ginny Doll, 31
Girls:
  fitness and, 220–221
  toys and, 31–32, 71–73
  (*See also* Gender differences)
Goodby, Berlin & Silverstein, 34
Grandma's, 202
Grandparents, purchases made by, 36–37
Greatest Adventure, The, 36
Griffin Bacall, 135
Grocery stores (*see* Supermarkets)
Gross names, 107
Guns, toy, 31, 92–93
  movement to control, 75–76

Hallmark stores, 124
Hanna-Barbera, 36
Hardee's, 173, 174
Hasbro, Inc., 31, 68, 71–73, 86, 93, 103–105,
  129

Health, 219–220
Heinz, 39
Hello, Kitty, 79
Hershey, 171
Hi-C, 32
Hispanics, proportion in population, 10
Holiday Inn, 173
Hooked-on-Phonics, 218
Hostess Grizzly Chomps, 91
Hot Wheels, 31, 105, 129
"Howard the Duck," 95
Hula Hoop, 95, 127–128
Humor, in focus groups, 50
Hyatt Hotels, 180, 181

IBM, 176–177
Independence, of children, 13–14
*International Directory of Marketing Research
  Companies and Services* ("The Green
  Book"), 46

Jackson, Bo, 27, 28
Johnson, Magic, 223
Jordan, Michael, 27, 76, 154, 222

K mart, 191
Keebler Co., 39, 83–84, 96, 171, 178, 202
Kellogg Co., 77, 111, 129, 174, 216
Kenner, 71, 93, 95, 96
Kersee, Jackie Joyner, 77
Kid City magazine, 150
Kool-Aid, 32, 129, 176
Koosh, 102, 106–107
Kraft General Foods, 129, 158, 163, 173,
  176, 178
Kransco Group, 95, 127, 128

Larami Co., 31, 84, 86, 92–93
  Super Soaker, 31, 76, 84, 86, 92–93, 105
Larry Tucker, Inc., 162
LEGO, 17, 31, 86, 92, 109, 140, 141, 181–182
  direct-mail catalog of, 148, 159, 161
Leo Burnett & Co., 133
Levi Strauss & Co., 33, 39–40, 54, 90, 130,
  153
Lewis Galoob Toys, 31, 96
Licensed products, 95–96, 107–108
Lincoln Logs, 31

List brokers, 159
Listening, importance of, 38–39
Little Caesar's, 138
Little Pet Shop, 72, 96

McDonald's restaurants, 17, 105–106, 129,
 133, 138, 140, 154, 166–168, 173, 174,
 180, 215, 222
 Happy Meals, 105–106, 129, 150,
 166–168, 180
McMagazine, 150
Mad magazine, 107, 153
Magazine advertising, 147–158
 benefits of, 151–152
 children's curiosity and, 155–156
 children's thinking and, 156–157
 choosing magazines for, 152–153
 custom magazines and, 162–163
 differences in ads for children and,
 154–155
 interactive, 153–154
 magazine explosion and, 148–151
Makeup, 31–32, 79
Market-by-market campaign, 128
Matchbox cars, 31, 105
Mattel, Inc., 31, 68–71, 86–87, 105, 109, 129,
 174–175, 180, 181
Media buying, 141–142
Metromail Corp., 159–160
Michelin Tires, 21
Milton Bradley, 95
Milwaukee Conference on Corporate
 Involvement in Schools, 178
Miniaturizing, 96–97
Mirrors, 179
M&M Mars, 155, 211
Money, 227–228
Motts juices, 177
Movies, 79–80
Music stores, 123
My Little Pony, 129

Nabisco, 154, 194, 198–212
Naming products, 100–109
 familiarity and, 107–108
 generating names for, 104–105
 ideas for, 103
 importance of, 101–102
 testing names and, 102–103
 types of names and, 105–107

National Basketball Association, 222
National Change of Address list, 161
National Dairy Board, 130, 133, 140
National Geographic World magazine, 150
Native Americans, proportion in
 population, 10
Needs, filling, 85–86
Nerds, 100–101
Nerf, 68, 93, 95, 102, 107, 129
Nestlé, 101
New products, 4–5
 (*See also* Product development)
Niche-market campaign, 128
Nickelodeon, 23, 86, 130–131, 173
NIKE, Inc., 26–28, 33, 130, 133, 222
Nintendo of America, Inc., 68, 86, 133,
 167–168, 184–197, 213–214
Nintendo Power magazine, 150, 153, 168,
 194
Nutrition, 4–5, 16–17, 219–220, 226–227

Official Commemorative NASCAR race-
 cars set, 68
One-on-one interviews, 52–53

Pacific Islanders, proportion in population,
 10
Packaging, 109–112
 colors and design of, 109–110
 information on, 111–112
Parent(s):
 child-rearing and, 11, 12
 educational attainment of, 9
 focus groups of, 51
 indulgence by, 12–13
 obtaining permission from, 60–61
 premiums and promotions and, 166
 role in purchase decision, 13, 35
 television advertising and, 143
Parent-Teacher Association, 178
Parenting magazine, 160
Parker Brothers, 68
Paulist Press, 36
Peer pressure, 25–26
PepsiCo, Inc., 133, 138, 194
Perry, Luke, 123
Philip Morris, 129
Phone surveys, 63
Pizza, popularity of, 17, 39, 84
Pizza Hut, 130, 173, 177

Pizzarias, 39, 84, 96
Play-Doh, 95, 106
Playskool, 86, 217–218
Pleasant Co., 84, 86, 94
Polaroid Corp., 33–34
Polly-O String Cheese, 130
Post cereals, 178
Premiums/promotions, 119–121, 164–183
    clubs and, 169–170, 180–182
    collectible, 179–180
    educational, 176–178
    as extension of product, 170–171
    function of, 165–166
    goals of, 182–183
    planning, 174
    samples, 120, 121, 161, 182
President's Drug Awareness Campaign, 178
Print advertising, 147–163
    (See also Direct mail advertising; Magazine advertising)
Procter & Gamble, 89, 139, 177, 202
Product development, 83–99
    educational products and, 93–94
    filling needs and, 85–86
    flexibility and, 88–89
    ideas and, 83–85
    "kidsized" products and, 89–90
    licensing and, 95–96, 107–108
    miniaturizing and, 96–97
    old products and, 92–93, 95
    product longevity and, 86–87
    research and, 90–91
    straddle products and, 91–92
    successful, 88
    topical products and, 97–98

Quaker Oats Co., 6, 171
Quantitative research, 56–64
    custom, 58–60
    information provided by, 57–58
    interviewing for, 60–62
    phone surveys in, 63
    reasons for, 56–57
    syndicated, 59
    tabulating results of, 63–64

Ralston Purina, 108
Ranger Rick magazine, 150
Rat Finks, 107

Reebok, 33, 133
Research:
    new product development and, 90–91
    testing names and, 102–103
    (See also Focus groups; Quantitative research)
Responsibility, of children, 16
Restaurants, children's influence on choice of, 33
Rock concerts, 80
"Rocketeer, The," 95
Role playing, focus groups and, 48–49

Safety, television advertising and, 145
Sales, 123
Samples, 120, 121, 161, 182
SC Johnson, 90
Scholastic magazine, 78–79, 174–175, 177
Schwarzenegger, Arnold, 29
Sears, Roebuck and Co., 68, 162
See-through windows, on packages, 109
Sega of America, 68, 173, 186, 196–197
Sesame Street magazine, 150
7-Up, 133
Shoppers, children as, 115–124
Shopping malls:
    children's shopping at, 121–122
    mall interviewing and, 60–61
    as site for focus groups, 45
Simpsons Illustrated magazine, 149
Skateboards, 214
SKITTLES, 155
Skybox, 174
SmithKline Beecham, 88
Social awareness, of children, 9, 14–15
Socialization, gender differences and, 73–74
Software programs, for quantitative research, 61–62
Sony Corp., 90, 109
Speedy-Make Ice Cream Maker, 72
Spending, by children, 3
Spirograph, 72
Sporting events, 80
Sports, 221–222
    sponsoring, 171
    universal appeal of, 140
Sports Illustrated for Kids, 77, 148, 152–154, 156–157, 160
Sports stars (see Celebrities)
Spot-market campaign, 128

"Spy v. Spy" cartoons, 107
Stage Deli, 210
Starting Lineup action figures, 72
Stew Leonard's, 120
Stickers:
  ads containing, 153
  collecting, 164–165, 180
Straddle products, 91–92
Suburbs, as site for focus groups, 45
Supermarkets:
  children's influence over purchases in,
    32, 81
  children's participation in shopping at,
    80, 117–118
  premiums and promotions in, 119–121,
    161, 182
Supernintendo, 68
Syndicated research, 59

T-shirt design product, 72
Target, for focus group, 45–46
Target (store), 191
Target market, for television advertising,
  134, 137–138
Technology, 225
Teenage Mutant Ninja Turtles, 95, 101, 133
Teenage Mutant Ninja Turtles magazine, 149
Telemarketing, 160
Television advertising, 126–146
  age of models in, 138
  competition from video games, 142–143
  cost of, 128, 129–131
  guidelines for, 143–146
  media buying and, 141–142
  number of arguments in, 137
  parents and, 143
  power of, 127
  reasons for, 128
  results of, 133–134
  simplicity and, 136–137
  story line for, 136
  target market and, 134, 137–138
Texas Instruments, 217–218
Thirst quenchers, children's influence on
  choice of, 32
3-2-1 Contact magazine, 150
Tie-ins, 165, 167
Tom's of Maine, 89
Toothpaste, 88–89, 139

Topical products, 97–98
Topps Co., 107
Totally Kids magazine, 149, 157–158
Toy(s):
  age and gender differences in
    preferences for, 71–75
  children's influence on choice of, 31–32
  grouping, 121
  guns, movement to control, 75–76
  television advertising for, 131
Toy stores:
  children's participation in shopping at,
    119
  displays in, 120
  product arrangement in, 121
Toys R Us, 119
Trans World Airlines, 182
Trolls, 95
Tyco Toys, 95

U.S. Postal Service, 158, 180

V-Tech Electronic Learning Aids, 217–218
V.F. Corp., 78–79, 173, 177
Video games, 68, 86, 133, 167–168, 173,
  184–197, 213–214
  competition with television, 142–143

Wal-Mart, 191
Walkman, 82
Walt Disney Co., 85–86, 95, 129, 131, 133,
  158
Warner, 158
Where in the World is Carmen Sandiego?, 17,
  173, 218
Where's Waldo, 171
White Spot, 189
William & Clarissa, 90
William H. Wrigley Co., 180
Women, in work force, 8
Worlds of Wonder, 88, 90

Young Parents, 162
Your Big Backyard magazine, 150

Zillions magazine, 150

About the Author

A leading authority in her field, SELINA S. GUBER, Ph.D., is
president of the New York-based Children's Market Research,
Inc., and publisher of the *KIDTRENDS* newsletter, which has
more than 300 Fortune-corporate subscribers. She is currently
chairperson of Children's Marketing Leadership Council of
the American Marketing Association/New York, has been
widely published, and is frequently interviewed on TV.

JON BERRY is senior writer and demographics columnist for
BrandWeek magazine.